God's Country

"You can sense Brad Roth's love for rural people on every page in this book. . . . This is a book I will assign to divinity students and to a prominent position on my shelf."

—LEONARD SWEET, THEOLOGIAN AND FUTURIST, FROM THE FOREWORD

"Brad Roth has done a wonderful, unusual thing: he has thought about the rural church in a way that combines both honesty and hope. He is gentle with the flaws that often beset rural congregations while managing at the same time to see the small church as a unique servant of God."

—WILL WILLIMON, PROFESSOR OF THE PRACTICE OF CHRISTIAN MINISTRY, DUKE DIVINITY SCHOOL

"God's Country *is a must-read. It reminds us, wherever we live, of the deep connection we have with the land and the call of this present generation to reclaim the wisdom found in rural spaces. As a suburban gal who has spent most of her life in urban areas, I learned so much from Brad Roth's book. It is filled with wisdom and grace and a tenacious love for rural communities, which have much to teach us all. I recommend it highly!*"

—TRACEY BIANCHI, WORSHIP AND TEACHING PASTOR, CHRIST CHURCH OF OAK BROOK

"Drawing on his experience of serving the church in rural Washington, Kansas, and Peru, Brad Roth offers a vivid, uplifting, and informed vision for an 'ecclesioculture' that embraces the marginalized rural church. In a time where rural-urban polarization is increasing, Roth draws on the biblical image of Zion, imagined not as the privileged city, but as a place where 'holy city' and 'holy rural' coexist, equally valued and needed in the body of Christ. This is a book of inspiration for the whole church, in all *places."*

—JEANNE HOEFT, COAUTHOR OF *PRACTICING CARE IN RURAL CONGREGATIONS AND COMMUNITIES*

"Brad Roth really understands rural ministry—it's hard . . . it's beautiful . . . it's dangerous . . . it's worth it! He understands the challenges and yet still loves living and ministering in a rural town. As an author of a book on this same topic, I found God's Country *helpful and inspiring, and I think you will too."*

—DONNIE GRIGGS, AUTHOR OF *SMALL TOWN JESUS* AND PASTOR OF ONE HARBOR CHURCH, NORTH CAROLINA

"God's Country *is a beautiful book about a beautiful, vital part of Christianity: the rural church. Brad Roth helps us see the unique characteristics of the rural church without the typical, shallow stereotypes. He tackles our temptation to see only the surface, to either deplore the state of the rural church or romantically glorify it. And best of all, he calls us to love. We choose to tell a story of love, and that story shapes who we become. We love the rural church just as it is, and we love it enough to call it forth to new life."*

—MICHELE HERSHBERGER, BIBLE PROFESSOR, HESSTON COLLEGE

"Brad Roth deftly weaves his social and theological analysis of the rural church in America with his own challenging experiences in that context. As the writing shifts between a wide-angle analytical lens and a zoomed-in, standing-in-a-muddy-wheat-field anecdotal lens, readers will come to understand the problem and promise of the rural church in all its complexity."

—TOM MONTGOMERY FATE, AUTHOR OF *STEADY AND TREMBLING* AND *CABIN FEVER*

"God's Country *is a balm to the soul for all who seek the kingdom in rural communities. For anyone who fears that the sun has set on vibrant rural congregations, Brad Roth offers a sage call for hope and renewal. This renewal is not born of imported strategies for church growth. Everything need not change. It begins with 'loving rural' and making one's home among a people formed by ancient ways."*

—DAVID BOSHART, MODERATOR, MENNONITE CHURCH USA

God's Country

FAITH, HOPE, AND THE FUTURE OF THE RURAL CHURCH

Brad Roth

Foreword by LEONARD SWEET

Harrisonburg, Virginia

Library of Congress Cataloging-in-Publication Data
Names: Roth, Brad, author. | Sweet, Leonard I., writer of foreword.
Title: God's country : faith, hope, and the future of the Rural Church / Brad Roth.
Description: Harrisonburg, Virginia : Herald Press, 2017.
Identifiers: LCCN 2017011814| ISBN 9781513801612 (pbk. : alk. paper) | ISBN
9781513802398 (hardcover : alk. paper)
Subjects: LCSH: Rural churches.
Classification: LCC BV638 .R67 2017 | DDC 250.9173/4--dc23 LC record available at https://lccn.loc.gov/2017011814

Released by Herald Press, Harrisonburg, Virginia 22802. 800-245-7894.

Library of Congress Control Number: 2017011814
International Standard Book Number: 978-1-5138-0161-2 (paperback); 978-1-5138-0239-8 (hardcover); 978-1-5138-0240-4 (ebook)
Printed in United States of America
Cover and interior design by Reuben Graham
Cover photo by Stockbyte / Thinkstock

21 20 19 18 17 10 9 8 7 6 5 4 3 2 1

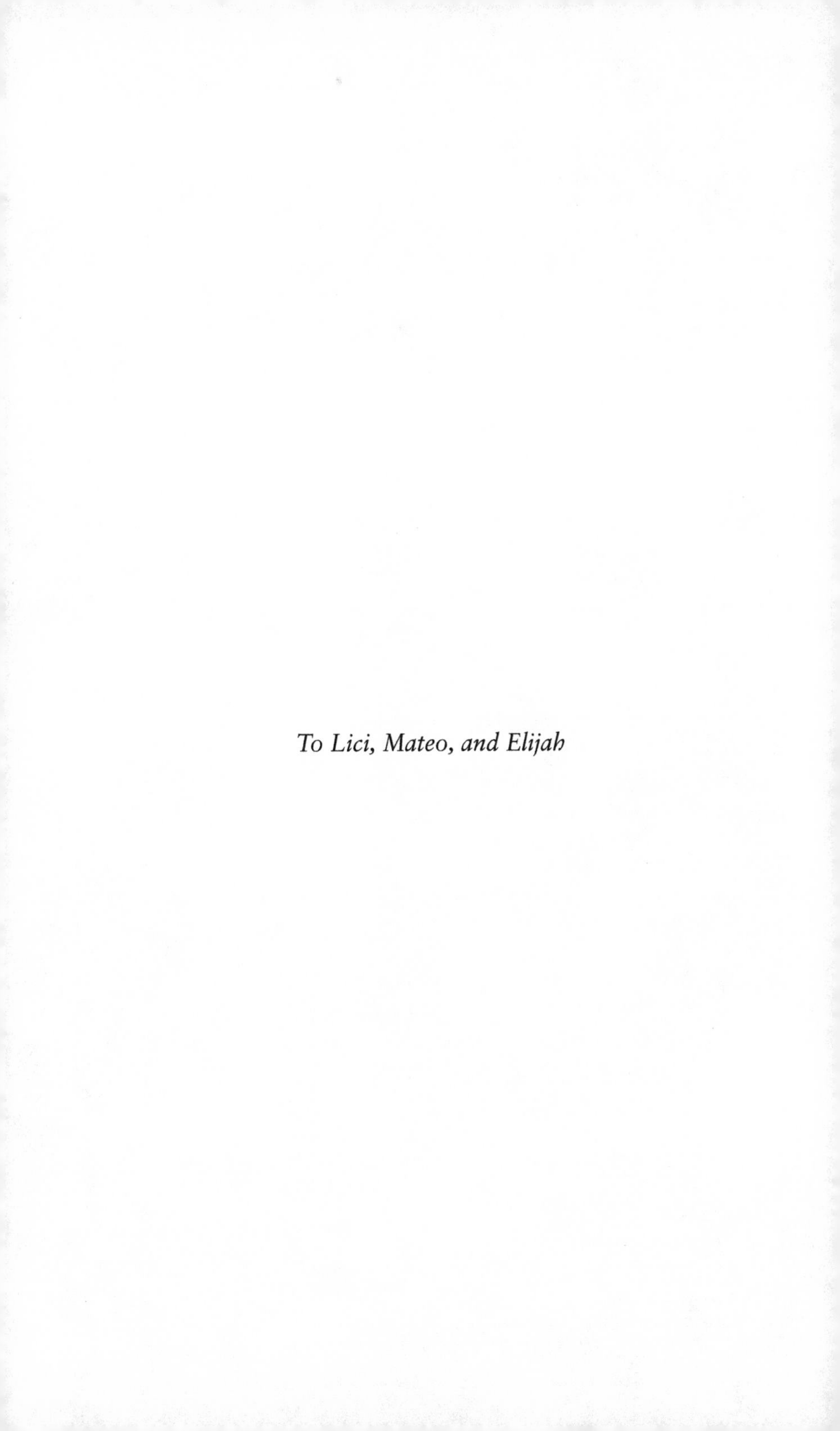

To Lici, Mateo, and Elijah

Contents

Foreword

I come from Appalachia, where if you didn't garden, you didn't eat. Vegetables were seasonal because vegetables came from a field and farmer, not a store or courtesy clerk. My Appalachian pedigree is further reinforced by being born one generation removed from the outhouse, in my case a two-holer that I visited regularly (after checking first for copperheads and black widows) when we stayed at Gramma's house in Alvon, West Virginia.

You can sense Brad Roth's love for rural people like my relatives who live in Appalachia, and not just in his opening words, "I love the rural church," but on every page in this book. This is good news for the reader. The truth about anything or anyone is only revealed when looked at in the light of love. This is also good news for the future of the church, since more and more people are looking to move to rural areas. Digital culture spells the death of distance, and any place can be every place.

Before I say any more about how much verve and velocity I found in the journey through *God's Country: Faith, Hope, and the Future of the Rural Church*, a full disclosure is required.

I live rural. For the past twenty-five years I have lived on a rural island filled with locals, urban runaways, and rural wannabes. My family physician is a specialist in rural medicine and runs a rural practice. Orcas Island is a place you go only if you're going there—especially to see orca whales. But my "insider" status also means I am not nostalgic about rurality. There are as many rural myths as there are urban ones, and I know firsthand the underside of rural living, a shadow side the author of this book does not seek to hide.

What comes shining through in Brad Roth's beautiful book is the need to rediscover two words we have lost, or at least the concepts behind the two words: *topophilia* and *totus*. Topophilia means the love of place. Totus is the Latin root of the word *total*, meaning whole or entire.

Every generation looks back in horror at its ancestors' blindness to great evils. What will our descendants say are the great evils we missed? Among many candidates, I name three: our prison system and its incarceration rates caused by the criminalization of poverty; our insouciance about the environment; and our disconnect between the earth and the table, which is part of the larger problem of our "out-of-placeness." This third calamity—the failure of the church to incarnate a sense of place and to see our "placement" as a divine appointment—is one of the subjects of this book. Topophilia is the overarching concept; *ecclesioculture* is Roth's word for incarnating the gospel in your zip code. We live displaced lives with packaged faith and franchised churches. Roth shows how our theology will be out of place and out of kilter until we discover that incarnation means a GOOD (Get-Out-Of-Doors) church with a down-to-earth faith where the table is connected to the earth.

In fact, the author suggests that agriculture is not necessarily the main feature of rural communities. I learned that only around 6 percent of the rural population is employed in agriculture, as opposed to 1 percent in the city. The defining difference between urban and rural may be less geographic and demographic than relational: Roth writes that "rural communities are marked by knowing and being known."

Wholeness, in the sense of total and its root, *totus*, relates both to being restored, or cured, and to being measured. Every living thing to be "well" and "whole" has a right "inward measure" that is according to scale. When an organism is in harmony and there is an economy of scale in place, there is wellness and wholeness, no matter what the size. In other words, a stable rural church of fifty may be more "well" and "whole" and "perfect" than a growing church of five thousand.

This is a book I will assign to divinity students and to a prominent position on my shelf. But most of all, Brad Roth tells stories that will linger in my mind and imagination and shape how I think about the future of all churches.

My deepest thanks to Brad Roth for writing such a multi-layered, many-sided book.

—Leonard Sweet
Drew University, George Fox University, Tabor College

CHAPTER 1

Gather Up the Fragments: Reclaiming a Kingdom Vision for the Rural Church

[Jesus] said unto his disciples, "Gather up the fragments that remain, that nothing be lost."
—John 6:12 (KJV)

I love the rural church.

But it wouldn't have had to be that way. Although I grew up on a farm in central Illinois, I was the bookish farm kid, the one who never really learned how to back up a trailer. My summers were spent baling hay and walking beans, but I was always longing to steal away to read and write. I envied town kids with their copious free time.

College could have been my escape, my clean break with cornfields and one-stoplight towns. After college in a midsized city in Illinois, I took off for Boston, diving in way over my head at Harvard Divinity School and immersing myself in the New Testament. Early on, a prospective landlord in Boston asked me in concerned tones if I would be able to hack it at Harvard, seeing as how I was from that vast prairie state of Illinois. While they did use big words at the university, I found my way somehow. And I rented from someone else.

I studied hard out east, stumbling my way through that first winter at Harvard, through constant bloody noses from too little sleep and too much snow, caffeine, and Latin. I was an Illinois farm boy trying my best to look the Harvard part, storming the gates of the Ivy League.

"Where are you from?" asked a classmate one time in the usual trading of stories and study interests.

"Illinois," I said.

"You know," he responded, "that's flyover country."

"Oh, really? Where are you from?"

"New York City," he said.

"New York City?" I scolded. "Don't you know where your food comes from?"

I caught my stride after a couple of semesters, and I eventually got married and graduated. After a few frustrating and glorious years working in the theological library, I shimmied a moving truck out of our alley, bound for ministry studies at the Mennonite seminary and the birth of our first son. I eased my urban wife into rural, working our way along I-90 from Boston to Elkhart, Indiana, a city of some fifty thousand in Chicago's orbit, for seminary. Only after seminary did we move on to our first church in little Warden, a multiethnic community in eastern Washington State. I had no idea what I was getting into, but a congregation took a chance on me and invited me to be their pastor. Come out west! So we did, buckling our toddler son into the back seat and hitting the road for parts unknown in Washington. I came to love that little rural church. They had me at *hola*.

After that, it was south to the mountains of Peru, where we would slip out over the gravel roads leading from the city of Cuzco, the Incas' "Navel of the World," and up into tiny communities perched along breathless mountain landscapes gouged from some condor's dream.

And now to Moundridge, Kansas, a community that has, as our littlest son sagely declared early on, everything we need: a church, friends, and a lumberyard. I've found my way to the Sunflower State, just up the road from Newton, that other Navel of the World. I get to walk with God's people on these Great Plains. My wife and I raise veggies, chickens, blackberries, strawberries, apples, and two sons.

I stumbled into my love affair with rural communities and congregations, and they've continued to grow on me. It's a love that developed as I came to see the beauty and share the struggles of places and people far from the city centers. I was drawn back to rural.

I got called.

Rural's double ring

Christ loves the rural church. In fact, I'm convinced that there is no church without the rural church. We might be tempted to think otherwise. After all, the Bible ends in a city—cubically shaped with twelve doors and twelve glittering foundations (Revelation 21–22). But we would lose something—many things, actually—without the rural church, for it represents the church's commitment to the margins, to those who fall outside our globalizing era's citified vision of the good life. The rural church is a sign of Christ's commitment to being present with people in all places. The church is ever and always called to think outside the cube. God does. There's more to that vision in Revelation than city streets paved with gold. There's also the garden, right in the heart of the city.

Rural is a word that's long had a double ring to it. The term comes from *rus/ruris*, Latin for "country" or "farm." For many, *rural* brings a positive, sentimental vision of the untouched countryside populated by good-hearted people with a little dirt under their fingernails. Or maybe, in the other vision of *rural*, they're local yokels who say *crick* when they mean *creek* and have a strange fondness for old pickup trucks and chewing tobacco. This all adds up to an easy dismissiveness of rural people and places.

What I've learned along the way is that all too often, rural is either idealized or disparaged. This double vision of rural goes way back. The ancient Romans saw rural life as the source of authentic

Roman farmer-citizen-soldier values. The famous Roman poet Virgil idealized the agrarian countryside, waxing lyrical about life in a cottage by a stream at the edge of the woods. It sounds all Tuscan and lovely, but Virgil forgot to mention that most ancient Romans didn't actually want to live in the country—unless, of course, they did so in an airy villa with marble columns, catered to by slaves. As far as Roman high society was concerned, the city of Rome was the real heart of the action.

Closer to our own day, Thomas Jefferson famously idealized the virtue of the "yeoman farmer" as the backbone of American democracy. Jefferson wrote in his *Notes on the State of Virginia* that "those who labour in the earth are the chosen people of God, if ever he had a chosen people."[1] That Jeffersonian agrarian ideal is still out there. As a farm kid, I was sometimes given a free pass because of my presumed rural virtue and work ethic. Someone once hired me to hang a cattle fence across a crick and to weed the flower bed. I did my best, though I had never hung a fence (and never did manage to get it hung), and I couldn't tell daisies from dead nettle.

All too often, rural people and places become objects of our cultural mythmaking, the focus of our fear or pity, meant to be saved or gawked at. We objectify rural by our gaze, converting the countryside into a projection—à la Jefferson and Virgil—of our own longings for wholesomeness and the rooted life and a vague nostalgia for a lost pioneer Eden.[2] In these scenarios, the city represents all that's wrong with the industrial world, and rural becomes a cipher for agrarian values of nurture, local community, and environmentalism.[3] Big Ag is the villain, and agribusiness is

---

1. Thomas Jefferson, *Notes on the State of Virginia* (New York: Penguin, 1999), 170.

2. Author Heidi Neumark similarly warns against this danger in her urban setting in New York City, referring to the tendency to objectify places, rather than relate to them in love, as "urban pornography." Heidi Neumark, *Breathing Space: A Spiritual Journey in the South Bronx* (Boston: Beacon, 2003), xiv.

3. Thus the tremendously influential writing of Wendell Berry, who articulately represents the agrarian philosophy of rural life and development over and against the Farm Bureau and university extension wing. See Berry's *The Unsettling of America: Culture and Agriculture*, 3rd ed. (San Francisco: Sierra Club Books, 1996).

seen as a projection of the city's mechanistic values and methods onto the pristine, agrarian countryside. It's a grudge match: *urbs* versus *rus*. If ministry in the city is gritty, then ministry in the country is earthy, a hotbed of agrarian values, one organic compost stir away from a revolution.

In both of these ways—idealizing and disparaging—we fail to meet rural communities and congregations on their own terms and to recognize the universality of human aspirations and fears. We need a new approach, one that sees rural communities not as places to pity or lionize but simply as *places*, places open to God's goodness and in need of God's grace.

A kingdom vision for the rural church: Developing a respectable ecclesioculture

We need a vision for the rural church that discovers its common vocation and destiny alongside the global church. The church is forever calling people to passionate worship of the God and Father of our Lord Jesus Christ. We're calling everyone to live as disciples of Jesus who challenge structures of sin in our lives, families, and communities. It's a life animated by the Holy Spirit.

The embodiment of this mission may vary from city to country—just as it varies from city to city or from neighborhood to block to backyard. We'll have to do our contextual theology. But the heart of the mission is the same. The church is doing battle with all the old gods. Perhaps we're tilted toward one end of the pantheon in the rural areas—Demeter over Zeus, or something like that. And mammon, mammon everywhere. But battle the old gods we must.

The identity of the rural church is found in being gathered up to Christ, not in any perceived rural distinctiveness or mission, however seemingly pressing. The rural church is nothing more—and certainly nothing less—than Christ's church, whole as it is gathered together with all the fragments. It's a vision that's bigger than urban or rural. It's a kingdom vision.

This book is about reclaiming God's kingdom vision for the rural church. It's about learning to praise, abide, watch, pray, grow, work the edges, die, befriend, and dream. Each of these disciplines is rooted in the biblical narrative and Christ's enduring commitment to the rural church. In each chapter, we'll explore one of these disciplines in depth. By drawing out the meaning of these disciplines, I'm making a case for what I'm calling *ecclesioculture*: authentically meeting congregations where they're at, while still dreaming of where God is calling them.

How we understand the church is our *ecclesiology*: our theology of the nature and mission of the church. Ecclesiology tells us something about how we live out God's calling. It tells us what it looks like to be the people of God. Ecclesiology is about doctrines and definitions, careful words and models for the church. In a lot of ways, this book is a practical rural ecclesiology.

But I'm actually striving for something slightly different.

Wendell Berry writes that developing a "respectable agriculture" means learning to think "competently and kindly of lands of all sorts."[4] I wonder if we could borrow a page from Berry's book, swapping out *lands* for *churches* in order to develop an ecclesioculture. If agriculture must learn to think competently and kindly of all sorts of *agros*—land—then ecclesioculture does the same for all sorts of *ecclesia*—churches.

The difference between ecclesiology and ecclesioculture is love. Ecclesiology begins in doctrine and aims to define the church. It points to ideal Zion. Ecclesioculture, on the other hand, begins in love. It aims to love the church as we discover it while still dreaming of where God is leading us. This is our respectable ecclesioculture—a vision for cultivating churches of all sorts in communities of all sorts.

In rural congregations, we practice ecclesioculture every time we come with curiosity rather than disdain for the established practices, structures, and traditions of the church. We practice ecclesioculture when we take time to cherish the church's story and dream with the church about its future. We practice ecclesioculture when we love.

---

4. Berry, *Unsettling of America*, 185.

The disciplines of ecclesioculture are ultimately acts of love, ways we tend the promise of the rural church. Love is at the heart of it all. As Paul told the Corinthians: without love, everything else we do is an empty gesture.

Church at a crossroads

In many ways, we've reached a critical juncture in the rural church.

At the turn of the twentieth century, mainline Protestant denominations in the United States awoke to the challenges rural congregations faced. Many of them founded "town and country" or "rural life" departments or joined forces with departments of agriculture and state universities to encourage the health of rural communities and churches.[5] Denominational offices were particularly concerned with the decline of rural congregations as population centers shifted to the cities. They implemented programs to address the economic and social challenges to family farms, as well as more ecological concerns like care for the soil.

In the Catholic Church, Bishop Edwin O'Hara founded the National Catholic Rural Life Conference (NCRLC) on the theory that the urban church was renewed by transfer growth from the rural church. Thus, if the rural church faltered, "the heavily urbanized Catholic Church was on the road to extinction in America."[6] The NCRLC focused on expanding Catholic education and religious communities to rural areas, promoting religious vacation schools, and developing correspondence courses, among other initiatives aimed at building up rural Catholic life. Earlier Catholic efforts had worked toward establishing impoverished immigrants, such as the Irish, in rural agricultural colonies.[7]

Likewise, in the Mennonite church, my own tradition, some leaders in the 1930s and 1940s specifically linked Christian community with rural life. Renowned leader Guy F. Hershberger

---

5. See Kevin Lowe, *Baptized with the Soil: Christian Agrarians and the Crusade for Rural America* (New York: Oxford University Press, 2016), esp. chaps. 1 and 2.

6. David S. Bovée, *The Church and the Land: The National Catholic Rural Life Conference and American Society, 1923–2007* (Washington, DC: Catholic University of America Press, 2010), 35.

7. Ibid., 11–12.

championed such an approach, arguing that "the Mennonite way of life can best be maintained in a rural environment."[8] Mennonite leadership advocated for the preservation of rural Mennonite communities in the face of emerging modernity, a transformation accelerated by the war footing of the U.S. government and its ravenous need for men, muscles, and machines. Mennonite programs and preaching came from a sense of being a "besieged Mennonite rural community" and emphasized "the farm as the foundation of their religious life."[9]

These impulses and organizations have largely faded from view, in part absorbed into the larger ecological and conservationist movements—although as Kevin Lowe notes, "In terms of simply stopping industrial agriculture or growing mainline denominations, Christian agrarians certainly failed."[10] Much of the reborn Christian ruralist-agrarian movement has taken on a decidedly nostalgic tone. Seemingly forgetting its own history and previous massive efforts at supporting small-scale agriculture and an overall agrarian vision for rural life, contemporary Christian agrarianism has gained little traction in the realities of rural people and farmers.

And while painting rural places in agrarian hues lends a bit of hardscrabble romance, *rural* and *agrarian* are hardly synonymous. Modern agrarianism is, among other things, a movement concerned with care for the earth and attentiveness to the ways that human communities live on the earth. Writer Norman Wirzba claims that "agrarianism is about learning to take up the responsibilities that protect, preserve, and celebrate life."[11] These responsibilities lead to certain postures in contemporary life: for instance, postures in favor of sustainable family farms, especially organic ones, and away from large-scale conventional agriculture. Rural people may share some of these commitments and skepticisms, but

---

8. Quoted in Perry Bush, *Two Kingdoms, Two Loyalties: Mennonite Pacifism in Modern America* (Baltimore: Johns Hopkins University Press, 1998), 132–33.

9. Ibid., 132.

10. Lowe, *Baptized with the Soil*, 174.

11. In Norman Wirzba, ed., *The Essential Agrarian Reader: The Future of Culture, Community, and the Land* (Washington, DC: Shoemaker and Hoard, 2004), 8.

only in an occasional, friendly overlapping of value systems. Rural and agrarian values sometimes conflict; we use Styrofoam plates at our rural church potlucks.

Indeed, for all the agrarian talk of rural people living closer to the land and serving as its stewards, urban people are often the most deeply committed to caring for the earth. Some older research showed rural people to be generally *less* concerned for the environment than urban people were, though recent analysis has demonstrated that environmental concern is more complicated than where a person lives. Farmers, in particular, tend to see environmental issues not in uncomplicated moral categories but as involving tradeoffs, such as between feeding people and protecting wildlife.[12]

At the same time, agriculture is not the exclusive province of rural people. Gardening among city dwellers has expanded substantially in recent years, and urban farming—in which farmers raise food using a variety of methods, such as hydroponics, and locations, such as rooftop gardens and rented or borrowed yards—has moved from a curiosity into the mainstream.[13] Norman Wirzba, in attending to this reality, speaks of an "urban agrarianism."[14]

Likewise, agriculture is not necessarily the main feature of rural communities. Only around 6 percent of the rural population is employed in agriculture, as opposed to 1 percent in the city.[15]

---

12. J. Allen Williams Jr. and Helen A. Moore, "The Rural-Urban Continuum and Environmental Concerns," *Great Plains Research: A Journal of Natural and Social Sciences* 1, no. 2 (1991): 211, http://digitalcommons.unl.edu/cgi/viewcontent.cgi?article=1022&context=greatplainsresearch.

13. See A. Cort Sinnes, "Food Gardening in the U.S. at the Highest Levels in More than a Decade according to New Report by the National Gardening Association," *National Gardening Association Learning Library*, April 2, 2014, http://garden.org/about/press/press.php?q=show&id=3819&pr=pr_nga; Elizabeth Royte, "Urban Farming Is Booming, but What Does It Really Yield?" *Ensia*, April 27, 2015, http://ensia.com/features/urban-agriculture-is-booming-but-what-does-it-really-yield/; and Curtis Stone's Urban Farmer website, theurbanfarmer.co/.

14. Wirzba, ed., *Essential Agrarian Reader*, 6.

15. "Rural Employment and Unemployment," United States Department of Agriculture Economic Research Service, last modified March 17, 2017, http://www.ers.usda.gov/topics/rural-economy-population/employment-education/rural-employment-and-unemployment.aspx#industry.

It's hard to pinpoint who the true agrarians might be—rural or urban. Is a wheat field more "natural" than a skyscraper? One is alive. But beyond that, both are products of human ingenuity and rely on human intervention on a vast scale. Furthermore, as author William Meyer has argued persuasively in his book *The Environmental Advantages of Cities*, cities often present a more ecological and sustainable lifestyle. Sure, cities consume more resources and have a greater gross environmental impact than rural areas, but when compared per capita, cities are ecologically superior to more dispersed ways of life. Among other things, cities limit the disruption of ecosystems to a more concentrated area and make more efficient use of resources by building up.[16]

What's the difference? The country soul is the city soul

So if agrarian values and agricultural production are not unique to or definitive of rural realities, then what exactly is *rural*?

Perhaps the most obvious and most significant difference between rural and urban is population. Although the long-term general trend has been for population to move from rural to urban—a trend that sparked Theodore Roosevelt to convene the National Country Life Commission and that preoccupied the field of rural sociology at the turn of the twentieth century—many rural areas have held their own or experienced slight population growth.[17] Yet this growth has been unevenly distributed. For instance, the Mountain West gained population in the 1990s, while the Great Plains, Appalachia, and the Corn Belt lost residents during that same period.[18]

A similar population shift toward the cities has taken place on the Canadian scene, though Canada has long been—and continues

---

16. William Meyer, *The Environmental Advantages of Cities: Countering Commonsense Antiurbanism* (Cambridge, MA: MIT Press, 2013); see especially chap. 2.

17. "Recent Population Change," U.S. Department of Agriculture Economic Research Service, last modified September 13, 2016, http://www.ers.usda.gov/topics/rural-economy-population/population-migration/recent-population-change.aspx.

18. Kenneth Johnson, "Unpredictable Directions of Rural Population Growth and Migration," in *Challenges for Rural America in the Twenty-First Century*, ed. David Brown and Louis Swanson (University Park, PA: Pennsylvania State University, 2003), 21.

to be—more highly urbanized than the United States (despite being the second largest country in the world by land mass). Likewise, most of Canada's rural population lives within commuting distance of a large metropolitan area.[19]

In the United States, growth has also been uneven over time—the population graphs sketch jagged mountains and troughs. During the farm crisis of the 1980s, the population of rural areas generally declined. In the 1990s, rural population growth picked up again—though it slackened between 2010 and 2015, when for the first time rural America as a whole had a net loss of population.[20]

I asked László Kulcsár, professor and head of the Department of Sociology, Anthropology, and Social Work at Kansas State University, to help me understand population trends in rural America. Kulcsár pointed toward a general rural population decline, which is "more pronounced in Kansas."[21] Rural places that lie near big cities and that have "significant natural amenities," however, have experienced growth. For small towns and rural counties far removed from hip cities and lovely mountains, population movement has mostly been one way: out.

Kansas exemplifies the long-term trend. The *Economist* reports that "more people left Kansas than moved there in 2013."[22] McPherson County, where I live and serve, is projected by the Wichita State University Center for Economic Development and Business Research to experience a population decline of 8 percent by 2040.[23]

---

19. Strengthening Rural Canada, "Fewer and Older: Population and Demographic Challenges across Rural Canada, 2015," accessed March 31, 2017, http://www.essentialskillsontario.ca/sites/www.essentialskillsontario.ca/files/Fewer%20%26%20Older%20-%20Population%20and%20Demographic%20Challenges%20Across%20Rural%20Canada.pdf.

20. "Overview," U.S. Department of Agriculture Economic Research Service, last modified September 13, 2016, http://www.ers.usda.gov/topics/rural-economy-population/population-migration.aspx.

21. László Kulcsár, email to author, May 20, 2016.

22. "Brownbackonomics on the Ballot," *Economist* 413, no. 8911 (2014): 29.

23. Hugo Wall School of Urban and Public Affairs, Wichita State University, *City of Moundridge Strategic Plan 2013*, 22, http://webs.wichita.edu/depttools/depttoolsmemberfiles/ppmc/Moundridge-Strategic-Plan.pdf.

This fits with anecdotal observations in our congregations that the kids have grown up and moved to the coastal metropolises. There are powerful, century-deep currents shaping rural communities and mind-sets. Communities that have experienced an extended period of net out-migration perceive life on different terms.

Urbanizing trends are global. The title of a two-decade-old United Nations brief published before the 1994 International Conference on Population and Development pointed to things to come: "The Future Is Urban."[24] As of 2014, the global urban population had tilted into the majority.[25] More people worldwide now live in cities than in the country and villages. Yet these dramatic statistics obscure the fact that in many developed countries, including the United States, urbanization trends have undergone periods of reversal where the rural population has grown along with the urban one—and sometimes even outpaced it.[26]

Indeed, if we look more closely, the much-touted population shift of the last decades has not been so much from rural to urban, but from both rural and urban to suburban.[27] City and country have met in the middle. Perhaps the UN report should have read "The Future Is Suburban." Maybe we're all living in one big suburb; it's just spread out a little more in places. In the United States, this may be more culturally true than we care to admit. It's certainly true by some statistical measures, which show the U.S. scene being far less urbanized when measured by density.[28] Canada's

---

24. "The Future Is Urban," United Nations Population Network, accessed March 31, 2017, http://www.un.org/popin/icpd/newslett/92_09/The+Future+is+Urban.html.

25. "Urban Population Growth," World Health Organization, accessed March 31, 2017, http://www.who.int/gho/urban_health/situation_trends/urban_population_growth_text/en/.

26. David Brown and Kai Schafft, *Rural People and Communities in the 21st Century: Resilience and Change* (Malden, MA: Polity Press, 2011), 25–26.

27. Jed Kolko, "How Suburban Are Big American Cities?" FiveThirtyEight, May 21, 2015, http://fivethirtyeight.com/features/how-suburban-are-big-american-cities/; Theodore Caplow, Louis Hicks, and Ben J. Wattenberg, "Population," chap. 1 in *The First Measured Century: An Illustrated Guide to Trends in America, 1900–2000* (Washington, DC: American Enterprise Institute, 2001), http://www.pbs.org/fmc/book/1population6.htm.

28. Chandan Deuskar and Benjamin Stewart, "Measuring Global Urbanization Using a Standard Definition of Urban Areas: Analysis of Preliminary Results" (World Bank

population has taken a similar trajectory. For instance, in the ten years between 2001 and 2011, some 80 percent of the growth of the Toronto, Montreal, and Vancouver metro areas occurred in the suburbs.[29] Much of the urbanization that makes for the UN's dramatic statistic has taken place in China and India.

At the same time, some previously rural areas have suburbanized rapidly in the last decades, for example in southern New Hampshire, which was encompassed by "Greater Greater Boston" as small towns became bedroom communities feeding into the city.[30] No doubt many congregations in these communities maintain a rural feel, even as populations have ballooned.

Apart from columns on census charts, the differences between rural and urban are hard to track. Are there qualitative differences, some sort of cultural markers that distinguish rural and urban areas, or are we merely dealing in trivialities?

Let's state the obvious: rural places are not cities. In fact, the U.S. Census Bureau defines "rural" in exactly this way: "All territory, persons, and housing units not defined as urban."[31] The exact population needed to count as "urban" (or for the Census Bureau's further classifications, "urbanized areas" or "urban clusters") has shifted over the decades, but since 1910, the threshold was set at a population of 2,500 people with a density of 1,000 people per square mile.[32] Alternatively, the U.S. Department of Agriculture categorizes "metro" and "nonmetro" along a continuum that measures "degree of urbanization and adjacency to

---

Land and Poverty Conference 2016, accessed online April 14, 2017), see table 5, p. 18.

29. Wendell Cox, "2011 Canada Census: Strong Growth and Suburbanization Continues," *New Geography,* February 9, 2012, http://www.newgeography.com/content/002668-2011-canada-census-strong-growth-suburbanization-continues.

30. Wendell Cox, "The Evolving Urban Form: Sprawling Boston," *New Geography,* July 16, 2015, http://www.newgeography.com/content/004987-the-evolving-urban-form-sprawling-boston.

31. "Urban and Rural Areas," U.S. Census Bureau, last modified December 7, 2016, https://www.census.gov/history/www/programs/geography/urban_and_rural_areas.html.

32. Ibid.

a metro area."[33] This aligns with current thinking in the field of geography that speaks of a range of "urbanness" and "rurality" and resists an urban-rural binary.[34]

The difference between urban and rural can be hard to define, which is why some sociologists claim the concepts are no longer useful. In the United States and Canada, in our age of mass communication, high-speed Internet, and reliable transportation, the categories don't matter as much.

A century ago, some sociologists argued that rural was an outmoded category shed by the advance of history. According to this school of thought, urban life was the result of an evolutionary process whereby people left their primitive rural backgrounds behind and developed advanced urban societies.[35] Rather than a distinct and valid way of life, rural was a vestige of the past. Modern people were urban people.

But beyond this cartoon vision of human society, there is something to the question of whether *rural* and *urban* are still valuable explanatory categories in the United States and Canada. If the differences between rural and urban people are hard to pin down, perhaps it's because they have more in common than not. Does someone working in a factory and living in an apartment in a small town really experience the world so differently from someone working in a factory and living in an apartment in a big city?

In the end, rural and urban are *human* realities, and any distinctives of rural or urban mind-sets and lifestyle will always be limited by that fact. Regardless of what the country mouse and the city mouse might think of each other, in fundamental ways, the country soul is the city soul. We're talking about people, and people have the same hurts and hungers wherever they happen to live.

---

33. "Rural-Urban Continuum Codes," U.S. Department of Agriculture Economic Research Service, last modified October 12, 2016, http://www.ers.usda.gov/data-products/rural-urban-continuum-codes.aspx.

34. See Tony Champion and Graeme Hugo, eds., *New Forms of Urbanization: Beyond the Urban-Rural Dichotomy* (Burlington, VT: Ashgate, 2004).

35. Suzanne Smith, "The Institutional and Intellectual Origins of Rural Sociology," (paper, Rural Sociological Society 74th Annual Meeting, July 28–31, 2011), 16–17, http://www.ag.auburn.edu/~bailelc/Smith.2011.pdf.

Rural route to rural culture: Perceiving the rural

We didn't get an address until I was in high school. In the age of GPS precision, this may be hard to believe, but our mail went simply to the Roth family at Rural Route 2. It wasn't until much later that we were assigned a numerical address and our little country road was given a name: Roth Road.

But it turns out that rural identity can't be chalked up to addresses. It can't be measured solely by statistics. Rural identity has more to do with how rural people experience the world. Social scientists David Brown and Kai Schafft speak of the "social constructivist approach to defining rural."[36] What this means is that rural identity is more of a worldview, more like a culture—a distinct way of framing and knowing the world.

For instance, rural people often place a high value on close community, trust, and nonmonetary work exchange. Much of this comes from the capacity to relate to and know neighbors in rural areas.

We can watch this play out in the way people think of their communities. It turns out that people are more apt to identify where they live as rural, suburban, or urban based on the *feel* of the place—a kind of preconceived schema for what makes rural *rural* or city *city*. For example, in one survey, individuals were more likely to self-identify their community as "urban" if the community was business-dense or had older houses or lower incomes. Their choice of identification did not necessarily correspond to the census designation for where they lived.[37]

The difference is one of perception.

Think about it. The defining difference may be that rural communities are marked by knowing and being known. We know our neighbors and they know us. We greet them on the street. We give them the wave from our pickup trucks. *Hidy ho, neighbor!*

And while people may know their neighbors and form deep bonds within their neighborhoods, much of city life is marked by the anonymity that comes with sheer numbers and cultural

36. Brown and Schafft, *Rural People and Communities*, 4.

37. Kolko, "How Suburban Are Big American Cities?" FiveThirtyEight.

diversity.[38] One urban pastor colleague of mine speaks of the "strangerness" of the city—we're strangers to each other on those crowded streets.

Even the spaces of our rural towns are known. Our communities are small enough that we can walk them. We've been to all the restaurants. (There are only two.) We've played in all the parks, passed by all the industry.

This sort of knowing shapes our view of the world. In rural areas, we can come to expect that people are connected. In a positive sense, it means knowing our neighbors and having a sense of close community. But it can also lead to fear of outsiders and a kind of boundary rigidity in communities and congregations. We like the size we are now. We all know each other.

A common reaction to threats to our known and knowable community is the one voiced by residents in one Nebraska town when a large poultry processor explored setting up its operation there. Some feared for the character of their community. One individual mused, "I'm worried about the type of people this is going to attract."[39]

Such responses may be born out of xenophobia or a bourgeois disdain for the rabble. Then again, they may also be profound expressions of human anxiety about perceived threats to the good of community: that slow-growing fiber of relationships and knowing that develops over generations.

There's something universal to these concerns. Our family served as missionaries in the rural Andes of Peru. When the Peruvian government laid plans to build a paved road past an isolated community that we related to, church members expressed their fear of the type of people who might show up. Will adultery increase? Will our young people leave? Might our children exchange their native Quechua for Spanish? I wonder if the fears of rural Nebraska are so different from rural Apurimac.

---

38. Famously described by Harvey Cox in *The Secular City: Secularization and Urbanization in Theological Perspective* (1965; repr., New York: Macmillan, 1971).

39. Scott McFetridge, "Tiny Nebraska Town Says No to 1,100 Jobs, Citing Way of Life," Associated Press, May 2, 2016, http://bigstory.ap.org/article/dd5cc190b42b4375830a97d163dbb5fd/tiny-nebraska-town-says-no-1100-jobs-citing-way-life.

At the risk of propping up shabby stereotypes, we can say that a rural mentality is marked by familiarity, while an urban frame of mind generally experiences much more anonymity in day-to-day encounters. Undoubtedly, this affects how rural people view their communities and understand their faith.

What's more, the country brain is different from the city brain. Some studies have shown that people living in high-density urban areas are at significantly greater risk for anxiety and mood disorders. The risk of schizophrenia is twice as high for those born and raised in cities—a fact researchers attribute to the mental impact of complicated urban social environments.[40]

On the other hand, mortality and morbidity rates for rural people have increased dramatically since 1990. Mortality has risen almost 48 percent for rural white women between the ages of 35 and 39.[41] The difference is particularly striking when compared to urban white women in the same age range, for whom the mortality rate has risen a mere 1 percent. Being diagnosed *rural* is a dangerous thing. For instance, people inhabiting extremely rural counties (counties that do not contain a city of ten thousand or more) are 6 percent more likely to die from heart disease and 3 percent more likely to die as infants as compared to those living in metro counties with a large central city.[42]

So urban might make you crazy, but rural might kill you. No wonder everyone's moving to the suburbs.

In any case, people and communities are complex. Rural is only one frame of reference. Just as in urban areas, race, educational attainment, income, and age also shape attitudes. Yet the enduring value of *rural* as a way to understand people, communities, and

---

40. Alok Jha, "City Living Affects Your Brain, Researchers Find," *Guardian*, June 22, 2011, https://www.theguardian.com/science/2011/jun/22/city-living-afffects-brain.

41. Joel Achenbach and Dan Keating, "A New Divide in American Death," *Washington Post*, April 10, 2016, http://www.washingtonpost.com/sf/national/2016/04/10/a-new-divide-in-american-death/?hpid=hp_no-name_whitedeath-underdisplay_1%3A-homepage%2Fstory&tid=a_inl.

42. According to statistics listed at "Rural Health Disparities," Rural Health Information Hub, last modified October 31, 2014, https://www.ruralhealthinfo.org/topics/rural-health-disparities#mortality-rates.

congregations lies in its predictive power. For instance, a recent Pew study shows that folks who value open space, like-minded neighbors, and conservative political views tend to favor living in rural communities.[43]

Yet we must also keep in mind that there is not one "rural," but rather multiple ruralities, both in terms of the kinds of rural spaces people inhabit and in the ways that people understand themselves to be rural. The rural Great Plains are far different from rural Appalachia, just as rural Saskatchewan only distantly resembles rural Quebec.

The way race factors into rural identity is also widely divergent across the United States and Canada. While some parts of rural America have grown in diversity in recent years, it's true that many rural communities are largely white. In small communities held together by generations of relationship, coming in as a racial minority can be challenging. One African American pastor I interviewed described how he discovered that his congregation had discerned whether they wanted to call a black pastor. Of course, they were circumspect in describing their motives, following the age-old rule of their southern small town to never say anything overtly negative, preferring instead to focus on the pastor's "tone" or "vision" or the fact that he had once preached from his open laptop in the pulpit. "It can be difficult to be a person of color in a rural community," he said.

Nevertheless, race can play out in surprising ways in rural communities. The legendary and beloved pastor of one white, rural congregation we know was a man originally from Sri Lanka. Some parts of the United States—particularly Louisiana, Mississippi, and South Carolina—boast substantial African American populations in rural communities. Various Native American groups make up the majority, or a large minority, in many small towns in Alaska. And some rural communities in the United States are ahead of national trends, transitioning to majority Hispanic, minority

43. Drew Desilver, "How the Most Ideologically Polarized Americans Live Different Lives," Pew Research Center, June 13, 2014, http://www.pewresearch.org/fact-tank/2014/06/13/big-houses-art-museums-and-in-laws-how-the-most-ideologically-polarized-americans-live-different-lives/.

white. This includes communities along the border, but also places like North Carolina and Washington State.[44] This was the case in Warden, the community we served in eastern Washington. The town, like others in the area, was around 75 percent Hispanic; most of those folks were from Mexico.

All of this is to say that rural identity is complex and diverse. Rural is a kind of spiritual and psychological landscape populated by a relationship to the city, nearness of neighbors, agriculture, and a history of marginality and loss. Rural is the kind of internal landscape sociologists call "social space."[45] In this way, rural is not just a population designation. It's a way of seeing the world.

Twelve baskets full: The church gathered into one by the Holy Spirit

The global church would be incomplete without the rural church. In our ever more urbanizing age, rural has become marginal, and it is at the margins that the church discovers its identity and calling. The church identifies with the margins and commits to being present among "every nation and tribe and language and people" (Revelation 14:6).

Of course, rural isn't the only margin. Cities have margins as well. The seams of poverty, racism, and abuse run right through the city. Suburbs have fescue-lined margins. And in the American context, outsized power is sometimes wielded by rural states. Wyoming, with half a million people, gets two U.S. senators, just as California, with 39 million, does. As became clear in the 2016 presidential election, the U.S. Electoral College assigns disproportionate clout to low-population rural states.[46]

---

44. Housing Assistance Council, "Race and Ethnicity in Rural America," *Rural Research Brief*, April 2012, http://www.ruralhome.org/storage/research_notes/rrn-race-and-ethnicity-web.pdf.

45. Douglas Porpora, *Landscapes of the Soul: The Loss of Moral Meaning in American Life* (New York: Oxford University Press, 2001), 25.

46. Emily Badger, "As American as Apple Pie? The Rural Vote's Disproportionate Slice of Power," *New York Times*, November 20, 2016, https://www.nytimes.com/2016/11/21/upshot/as-american-as-apple-pie-the-rural-votes-disproportionate-slice-of-power.html?_r=0.

But marginal isn't just a measure of brute political clout. As in the ancient world, cities are condensations of power and wealth. Cities are capitals. Cities are centers. All roads lead to Rome.

The centers of cultural gravity and attraction are urban. The framework for our thinking and the universities that foster it are urban. In this long-running narrative of the West, civilization is urbanization. Cities are like nirvana: the enlightened go there. The allure of the city remains potent, and it's growing more so with each generation. There's energy and innovation and that magic elixir: youth. There's the viscous swirl of cultures and a thumping bigness that reminds us that while we may be individually so small, in the city we can become a part of something grand. The horizons of the city go *up*. It's Carl Sandburg's poem "Chicago":

> Come and show me another city with lifted head singing
> so proud to be alive and coarse and strong and cunning.
> Flinging magnetic curses amid the toil of piling job on
> job, here is a tall bold slugger set vivid against the
> little soft cities . . .[47]

To many, our rural communities are Sandburg's "little soft cities" murmuring along in quiet and quaintness. As a friend who settled in New York City once put it, "Once you've lived here, you wonder why people would want to live anywhere else." Johnny's seen Paris and won't go back to the farm.

The rural church is a sign of the universal church's identity, for the rural church reminds us that Christ's body is always off-center, always called toward the margins, always skeptical of the claims of the dominant culture. The rural church represents Christ's commitment to be among all people everywhere, regardless of the value attributed to them by global centers of power. Christ orients the church toward the edges of society.

The church takes after its self-emptying Savior (Philippians 2:7) and stands in contrast to the logic of the world. The church follows the logic of the cross, and thus the church insists on ministering in the most out-of-the-way places, including the villages and

47. Carl Sandburg, "Chicago," in *Chicago Poems: Unabridged* (Mineola, NY: Dover, 1994), 1.

open country that make up the anonymous stretches of cornfields between the heaving cities.

The importance of the rural church isn't always obvious, even to rural congregations themselves. I once took an informal poll of the small-town congregation we served. I asked, "Why is the church here?" Folks gave me answers that were sincere, yet unreflective—along the lines of "Well, there were a bunch of us living here, so we decided to form a congregation." True enough. But in my fresh-out-of-seminary earnestness, I was hoping for something more substantial—something theological, even. I wanted an essay-form response, five hundred words or less: *Using the terms* vocation *and* destiny, *describe why your rural congregation is here.* Alas.

This is the thing: rural congregations testify to the church's eternally off-center vocation and point forward to the church's destiny in the kingdom. Pastors and rural church leaders need to gird themselves with these convictions.

There's more. The rural church is a sign of the *wholeness* of the global church. This is part of what Jesus was getting at when he fed the five thousand. His miracle was not only about sustenance, about his role as the "bread that came down from heaven" (John 6:41). It was also a sign of the complete people of God. The crowd declared that Jesus was "the prophet who is to come into the world" after the twelve baskets were gathered together (John 6:14). The "sign" he performed was multiplication *and* gathering.

The key is the number of baskets: twelve, a number signaling that we're talking about God's whole people. There are twelve tribes and twelve apostles. The book of Revelation is filled with twelves.[48]

In the New Testament, bread is a sign of both the sacramental body of Christ offered at the communion table and the gathered body of Christ, the church. The one bread points to the one church (1 Corinthians 10:16).

48. Twelve gates and twelve angels (Revelation 21:12); twelve foundations and twelve apostles (Revelation 21:14); number of people of God (Revelation 7 and 14); twelve thousand from each tribe (Revelation 7); twelve stars (Revelation 12); twelve kinds of fruit (Revelation 22:2).

One first-century text called the Didache describes the teaching of the early church. The Didache picks up the theme of the unity represented by the one loaf of communion bread: "As this piece of [bread] was scattered over the hills and then was brought together and made one, so let your church be brought together from the ends of the earth into your Kingdom."[49]

Thus, when Jesus called the disciples to "gather up the fragments that remain, that nothing may be lost" (John 6:12 KJV), he was pointing beyond bread and baskets to the whole people of God.[50] It was a sign. Jesus was talking about the church. Let none be left behind or ignored or disparaged. Let none be lost. Gather up all the fragments into the kingdom.

Without the rural church, some fragment would be lost. The rural church represents God's commitment to be with all people, everywhere, through the church, which is Christ's "body, the fullness of him who fills all in all" (Ephesians 1:23). This includes all peoples and all places, big and small. The church cannot remain in the city or suburbs and be the church.

It's the nature of the church to cultivate a presence in the country. Not every organization is like this. Take shopping malls. No one is surprised that shopping malls are only found in cities and suburbs. Their aim is commercial, and commerce requires people interested in purchasing products. Miles of wheat fields just don't have the critical mass of ennui-struck teens.

The church, however, is called to be with people in all places, however small. Jesus sent the Holy Spirit upon the apostles so that they might carry the gospel "to the ends of the earth" (Acts 1:8), and rural places are often the consummate *ends*. There's a way in which the unity of the whole church spread throughout the world must come together to fully embody the life of Christ.[51]

---

49. In Cyril Richardson, ed. and trans., *Early Christian Fathers* (New York: Touchstone, 1996), 175.

50. Likewise, in the feeding of the four thousand, seven baskets were gathered up (see Mark 8:8), possibly pointing to inclusion of the Gentiles and their representation in the seven deacons of Acts 6.

51. This is known as the church's *catholicity* in the classical formulations, one of the four marks of the church, along with the church being *one*, *holy*, and *apostolic*.

All the fragments must be gathered into the twelve baskets. That's what makes the church whole, and it's why there can be no church without the rural church.

But so too there can be no church without the urban church. We need each other. *Urbs cum rus.* This is why any vision that disparages country or city—or anywhere in between—proves inadequate. We need a kingdom vision, a vision of the church gathered into one by the Holy Spirit.

When Augustine of Hippo wrote about God's kingdom breaking into the world across history, he spoke of the "city of God": a nod to the cubed city of Revelation and an ode to Augustine's own beloved Rome. His famous book begins, "The glorious city of God is my theme in this work."[52]

Maybe we can give Augustine's kingdom vision a rural spin: God's glorious *country* is our theme in this work.

52. Augustine, *The City of God*, trans. Marcus Dods (Peabody, MA: Hendrickson Publishers, 2009), 3.

CHAPTER 2

Praise in Place: God Is Somewhere

"After all," said Shasta, "this road is bound to get somewhere." But that all depends on what you mean by somewhere.
—C. S. Lewis, *The Horse and His Boy*[1]

I live and minister somewhere.

That may not sound like much, but there's a segment of my generation that considers vast swaths of middle America *nowhere*. Flyover territory. You don't go there on purpose; layovers in Chicago are painful enough.

Not long ago, my second-grade son had to match opposite words on a classroom worksheet. He matched earth to sky. Black to white. City to . . . what, exactly? Country? Town? Field?

My son chose "somewhere" as the opposite of "city."

Somewhere is where we live: not a city, but the big-sky Great Plains of Kansas.

What makes a place *somewhere*? Too often, we've been taken in by the narrative that the *somewheres* of the world are all urban, all coastal (or at least mountainous), all busy-busy. The countryside is a nice place to visit Grandma and Grandpa, but it's not where we'd ever choose to live. We want to be at the heart of

1. C. S. Lewis, *The Horse and His Boy* (New York: HarperCollins, 2000), 161.

the action, and whatever that action is, it's clearly happening in the big urban centers of the world. The rural communities and hamlets that dot plains, woods, and wide-open spaces are slow, sleepy, and spent. Hit the interstate and punch it up to eighty. Get me to the nearest city.

We define our geography by cities. We live two hours outside Chicago. We're about an hour north of Wichita. Some of it's a convenient triangulation, a shorthand for our personal elevator speech. But there's also a kind of valuation going on, a way in which rural communities exist only in relation to the city they're closest to. In this topographical constellation, we're the unmarked speck along the dotted lines between cities. Being *somewhere* is contingent on how many hours' drive we live from New York, or Philadelphia, or Toronto. As geographer Tim Cresswell makes clear: "Place, at a basic level, is space invested with meaning in the context of power."[2]

But mine is no anti-city rant. I love cities for what they are: among other things, diverse mosaics of humanity. Where else can you get *palak paneer* for lunch and falafel for dinner? We have no such luck in our small towns (unless we make it ourselves!). Rather, I'm challenging the devaluation of place that haunts rural communities and congregations. We're somewhere!

Here's the problem: as rural places are devalued or even despised, rural pastors and lay leaders can experience burnout and despair, and rural congregations can become overshadowed by a diminished sense of significance and self-worth. I'm convinced that one way we discover a cure is by coming to recognize that God delights in and is present in rural places, and that all places can offer authentic praise to God. We are somewhere because God is somewhere. Rural pastors and congregations are called to live and minister as if this were true. Because it is.

Of course, though the problem is particularly pernicious for rural areas, it's bigger than how we treat rural areas. It's something that concerns all of us who inhabit the modern/postmodern world, no matter where we make our homes. This is because the loss of

---

2. Tim Cresswell, *Place: A Short Introduction* (Malden, MA: Blackwell, 2004), 12.

place is ultimately the loss of the sacred. Rowan Williams puts it this way: "The world without the sacred is not just disenchanted but deprived of some kind of depth."[3] It is not just the sacred as such that has been lost, however, but also the doxological imagination. The doxological imagination is our ability to perceive all places as praise-able: fitting spaces for praising God, places that offer praise to God. Instead, rural places frequently become what anthropologist Marc Augé speaks of as "non-places."[4] They become indistinct places, impersonal places. "The end result," writes Norman Wirzba, "is that our senses become deadened. Our affections wither in the face of so much anonymity."[5]

The Holy One in the land: Sacred place in the Scriptures and beyond

Contrast this with the vision of the Scriptures, in which the world is the place where God meets his people. God "chose us in Christ before the foundation of the world" (Ephesians 1:4), which is to say that the world finds its meaning and value as the place where God calls and relates to God's people.[6] The Promised Land is the summit of this vision of place, but the vision is about more than just some lines on the sacred map. Even within the Promised Land the people of God are called to worship God in the "place that the Lord your God will choose . . . to put his name" (Deuteronomy 12:5). The landscape is pinned with sacred markers: pillars, altars, springs, mountains, and shrines.[7]

Sometimes, God's holy presence in a place takes his people by surprise.

---

3. Rowan Williams, *Dostoevsky: Language, Faith, and Fiction* (Waco, TX: Baylor University Press, 2008), 229, quoted in Norman Wirzba, *Food and Faith: A Theology of Eating* (Cambridge: Cambridge University Press, 2011), 31.

4. Cited in Wirzba, *Food and Faith*, 40.

5. Ibid., 41.

6. Simon Chan, *Liturgical Theology: The Church as Worshiping Community* (Downers Grove, IL: InterVarsity Press, 2006), 23.

7. Pillars/stones (Joshua 4:20-21); altars (Judges 6:24); springs/water (Numbers 21:16-18); mountains (e.g., Sinai—Deuteronomy 33:2); and shrines (e.g., Shiloh —1 Samuel 1).

Think of Jacob, fleeing his brother Esau's wrath and searching for a bride (Genesis 28). He camps at a "certain place" along the dotted line between the cities of Beersheba and Haran (vv. 10-11). The place has no name. It's rural, trod-over territory that you only get caught visiting on layover when the sun goes down. Thankfully, its stones make good pillows.

Then, as Jacob sleeps, he sees a ladder, or stairway, reaching up to heaven with angels ascending and descending upon the place. Jacob is about to learn that this is more than just empty country. The Lord stands "beside him" (v. 13) and pronounces a blessing—the same blessing the Lord earlier gave to Abraham—*I will bless you by giving you this land, and I will bless all the families of the earth through you. I am with you wherever you go. I will bring you back to this land and fulfill my promise to you* (vv. 13-15).

Jacob gets it. When he awakens, he declares, "Surely the Lord is in this place—and I did not know it!" (v. 16). The fear of the Lord comes upon him. Jacob has just encountered God in the most unsuspected place. He has discovered, "How awesome is this place! This is none other than the house of God, and this is the gate of heaven" (v. 17). Jacob goes on to transform his stony pillow into an altar to the Lord, resting his hope where he had rested his head, and to make promises in response to God's promise to him.

Jacob's story is a fitting parable for rural ministry. Following Jesus' lead, the church finds itself ministering in places far from the geographical centers of importance: rural communities on the prairie of Saskatchewan, in Appalachian valleys, along broad rivers or deltas. To many, they are non-places. You haven't heard of them. Once, a family friend from the heartland, speaking about the area of eastern Washington where we lived and ministered, remarked that he had driven through our area once. He went on to declare that it was "the most godforsaken place" he had ever visited. If you hadn't lived there, you might have agreed. Miles of rolling sagebrush aren't the stuff of postcards. It's the same stretch of inland territory sometimes called the Big Empty.

Yet the Lord is in these "empty" places, though we do not know it. The Holy One is in the land. We all too often fail to see God's presence, and our failure is in fact a failure to value rural places. It's a failure to love.

Country despair: Suffocating in acedia's coils

In pastoral ministry, the inability to love rural, sparsely populated places leads to several dead ends. An especially dangerous dead end for rural pastors is the sin of *acedia*. Acedia is a kind of spiritual despair—a lack of care for life, others, God, or even ourselves. In the ancient catalogues, acedia was listed among the seven deadly sins: a soul-killing attitude that damages a person's capacity for love of God and neighbor. Acedia is indeed deadly. It erodes our sense of worth, our sense of self, and it drives us into the arms of escapism and apathy. In my mind, acedia is the great scourge of our age, the especially deadly sin of rural communities. In our rural communities, we can sometimes feel as if everything we do is so small, as if it doesn't matter. We suffocate in acedia's coils.

The word *acedia* in Greek literally means "without care." *Cedia* are the ties of love that bind us together.[8] So when we are caught up in *a*cedia, those ties come undone. We experience the unraveling of love. We are *without care* for the things that matter most. And when those ties go, even our own sense of self can come unraveled.

Author Kathleen Norris writes: "Much of the restless boredom, frantic escapism, commitment phobia, and enervating despair that plagues us today is the ancient demon of acedia in modern dress."[9]

Acedia manifests itself as a boredom that anchors its gangly roots in the belief that God is not present or at work in the places or life situations where we find ourselves. Acedia is the humid

8. The *kedos* or *kedeian* family of words include marriage ties, care for another, and funeral rites. See *An Intermediate Greek-English Lexicon Founded upon the Seventh Edition of Lidell and Scott's Greek-English Lexicon* (Oxford: Oxford University Press, 1997), 431. Cf. the use of *kedeia* in 2 Maccabees 4:49, where it means "funeral."

9. Kathleen Norris, *Acedia and Me: A Marriage, Monks, and a Writer's Life* (New York: Riverhead Books, 2008), 3.

little whisper telling us that we were made for bigger and better things, that in the "real world" our skills and heaps of degrees would be appreciated. We would really make a difference if we were ministering *somewhere else*. This place, these people—they aren't completely worthy of us.

Author and pastor Richard Lischer recalls a conversation he had with his father as he considered an invitation to minister in a rural Lutheran congregation while holding out for a call from a "significant" urban church. Lischer's father cornered him: "These people are saying, 'Come, we've been waiting for you. You can be our pastor,' which is what you said you wanted all along. And now it has to be *significant*? Isn't the ministry significant? I thought it was. All of it. Everywhere."[10]

Lischer was staring into the toothy face of acedia, the "noonday demon" that so plagued ancient monastics.[11] Their demon came to them as the recurring, clinging thought that a life of prayer spent in the desert—the life they had committed themselves to—was not all it was cracked up to be. The monks' fantasy was a return to the city.[12]

The scale of rural ministry can also lead to a biting acedia. So much about our ministries matches the scale of the places we serve. They're small ministries. Our food bank in rural Washington gave out in one month what a Seattle food bank sent through its doors in an hour. Our entire community was the size of some city churches' membership rosters.

But it's more than just who has the biggest congregation. There are small urban churches and large country churches. The real issue is a nagging feeling that congregations and pastors are doing Very Important Things—things that matter—in the city.

So many pastors, reared on a diet of *promise* and *potential*, digesting books hot off the church-turnaround press, find

10. Richard Lischer, *Open Secrets: A Memoir of Faith and Discovery* (New York: Broadway Books, 2001), 45.

11. Norris, *Acedia and Me*, 5.

12. Rebecca Konyndyk DeYoung, "*Acedia*'s Resistance to the Demands of Love: Aquinas on the Vice of Sloth," *Thomist* 68, no. 2 (April 2004), 3, https://www.calvin.edu/academic/philosophy/virtual_library/articles/deyoung_rebecca_k/acedia.pdf.

themselves preaching to a tiny gathering of graying saints. Hadn't their seminary professors hinted that they were destined for *significant ministry*?

You see, somewhere along the line it was communicated to my generation of leaders that we had to save the church. (And while we're at it, we might as well save the polar ice caps, the whales, and the world.) If you're anything like me, when you graduated from some place, at some time (it doesn't matter where or when), they told you to go out and make a difference. Change the world. You might have thought that what they were talking about is life *out there*, moving fast, shaking things up—probably off in the city. You might have imagined a sort of jet-setting life where you would make peace in Timbuktu but wouldn't have to make your bed. It was life lean and gleaming like a rocket, fueled by potential.

Some folks live that sort of life. I've met them, mostly by accident. I once shook hands with someone in a lunch line at an event and later realized he was Really Someone, the guy who writes books and endorses candidates and holds rallies for environmental justice. But when we met, we were just two guys holding compostable plates and eyeing the kale salad.

Most of us don't live Great Big Lives, and even when we do, we still have to wait in line for the salad bar and make our beds. Does this mean that we've failed?

Certainly some rural pastors draw that conclusion. In a study of rural Anglican clergy published in 2006, Christopher J. F. Rutledge discovered that about one out of eight rural pastors "feels that he has accomplished little of worth in his ministry."[13]

No doubt there are special factors that contribute to this sense of malaise among rural Anglican leaders, factors that might not describe the situation of pastors serving other denominations in the United States. Yet the teeth marks of the desert monks' old enemy acedia are clear. The struggle with acedia arises from a fundamental question: Am I making a difference? And a difference is a very challenging thing to measure.

13. Christopher J. F. Rutledge, "Burnout and the Practice of Ministry among Rural Clergy: Looking for the Hidden Signs," *Rural Theology* 4, no. 1 (2006): 62.

The real problem is not that rural life and ministry play out on a smaller scale than they do in the city. What really enervates pastors and leaders is the enormity of the church's challenges compared to the seeming smallness of our work and gifts. It can feel as if there's nothing we can do that will change the course of our church. And perhaps there isn't.

It could be that life in the city obfuscates this dynamic. There's always something going on, something big happening. In the city, we're carried along in the flow of discovery and innovation, and it can make our lives and work feel big and innovative too—whatever it is we're doing. Sipping a mocha in Harvard Square somehow seems more consequential than having coffee at the small-town gas station. But it's not.

Life and ministry in the rural church lays bare our smallness. Preparing the Sunday bulletin doesn't feel like world-changing work. Then again, a lot of times neither does prayer.

Kathleen Norris writes, "Acedia is a danger to anyone whose work requires great concentration and discipline yet is considered by many to be of little practical value."[14] Whatever doubts leaders in the church may feel about the value of their own work, our de-Christianizing communities are even less indulgent of the pastoral vocation, and increasingly so.

I once hired a man to do some home renovation for me. In the midst of explaining his progress and pointing out his next steps, he suddenly turned and sized me up, head to toe. "I know what you pastors do all day," he announced. The unspoken message was clear: *Nothing much*. And then, to lend his assessment some authority, he revealed, "My mother was a church secretary."

I imagined him peering at the pastor from behind his mother's desk as she pecked out the church bulletin on the typewriter. There you have it: he had learned everything he needed to know about ministry by age twelve.

What do you do all day? he wondered.

I had my own secret and unspoken answer: *I pray for guys like you.*

---

14. Norris, *Acedia and Me*, 43.

But it's true: we have no neat stack of product to show off at the close of the working day. Perhaps, like the ancient desert monks of Egypt, pastors should weave a few baskets in between writing sermons and chairing planning committees. At least then we could point to some tangible work to satisfy naysaying curiosity. *What do I do all day? I make baskets. Need one? And I pray a little.*

Acedia's languorous fruits: Flight and boredom

There are two common responses to acedia. The first is a longing to leave. We flee. A pastor in a community I served was infamous for enumerating the days he had spent in our rural town. He tallied time as if it were a sentence, hash marks chalked on a prison cell: *I've been here eight years, seven months, and twenty-two days.* And he did this publicly, before funerals. It did not exactly endear him to the community.

The devil monogrammed the sin of acedia special for rural pastors—it has our names written all over it. And it's uniquely dangerous. Pastors are called to rural places, often after spending considerable semesters and sums in urban centers of education. We often lack the familial geography that gives meaning to a place. As one character puts it in Gabriel García Márquez's *One Hundred Years of Solitude*, "A person does not belong to a place until there is someone dead under the ground."[15] Pastors are many times outsiders with no ties to the land. We can marry into or bury into the places we serve, but since most pastors do neither, we rely on a sense of calling, which can be lost or dented by conflict or rejection. Thus either we meet and defeat acedia and become wise or we get jaded, burn out, and pack up our stuff. We move *somewhere else.*

What this means is that rural pastors' sense of place cannot and will not come by the usual channels. They'll need other attachments, other ways of loving the places and people they minister to. It also means they'll face the special risk of acedia.

---

15. Gabriel García Márquez, *One Hundred Years of Solitude*, trans. Gregory Rabassa (New York: HarperCollins, 2006), 13.

I've experienced this. In my first calling, the small, rural congregation in eastern Washington State—that family friend's "godforsaken place"—I found myself deeply frustrated by the slow process of being accepted into the community. This led to a resentful streak in my ministry. Why were we even there? It wasn't that people were unfriendly or uncaring. They liked us well enough, both within the congregation and without. But we were only slowly allowed into the neighborhood culture of birthday parties and *quinceañeras*, baptisms and funerals and dinner invitations.

I have no doubt that some of my struggle was racial and cultural. As a white man, I was not always extended trust. But why should they have trusted me? A whole history of institutional racism and encounters with some exploitative white bosses lay between us. True, I speak Spanish, and that earned me a point or two on the scale of trust, but my Hispanic wife often had to play the role of cultural ambassador. Even then, relationships took time to develop. My wife is Peruvian, which placed her a degree closer to the majority Mexican culture of our community, but nevertheless marked her as an outsider.

It was not until at least the third year—or probably the fourth—that we began to tease out the deep histories of family feuds and alliances. Were you from Los Ramones, Mexico? Had your family homesteaded when the Grand Coulee Dam blocked up the Columbia and brought water to the Basin? No? Then you have to earn your place. Trust was something we had to grow into. It wasn't a given.

Another risk is that we come to disparage our rural communities as dull and unbeautiful. But this is really just a flight of a different kind—a mental flight where we imagine that we were made for more attractive places. By turning up our noses at our rural surroundings, we stretch a space between ourselves and them. Our eyes, glazed to the beauty before us, gaze into the distance at a more promising horizon. Our minds move on, even if our feet haven't.

Strange forces conspire to solidify prejudices against certain rural landscapes. In the 1990s, the USDA developed a "natural amenities index" that sought to measure, and thereby privilege, "environmental qualities most people prefer."[16] Writer Christopher Ingraham, reporting on the scale for the *Washington Post*, found himself on the wrong side of Red Lake County, Minnesota, which landed at the bottom of the scale. His tongue-in-cheek report incited residents of the rural county to action.[17] Folks sent him pictures of Red Lake County's lovely landscape and people. They invited him to visit. Surprisingly, he did. In fact, Ingraham went even further, becoming so enchanted by Red Lake County that he decided to move there with his family. He writes, "The visit was a shot of pure country. A newborn calf suckled my thumb as the [Schindler] brothers told me about life on the farm. The earthy smells of a dairy operation—manure and hay and sawdust and dirt—hung thick in the air. It sure didn't seem like the worst place in America—or one particularly lacking in natural amenities, or natural beauty, either."

Ingraham goes on to write that after his initial visit, he left feeling like he'd "barely scratched the surface of all there is to see and know about the county and the people who call it home."[18] His journey would become a movement more deeply *into* place, rather than a succumbing to acedia's longing to flee to someplace else.

A second, wicked manifestation of acedia is a kind of generalized boredom that can envelope rural people. Culture writer Casey Quinlan, plumbing the lyrics of country music, puts it this way: "Like all real cultures, rural life has its shortcomings. People become bored in a way that is distinct to an isolation of place. Rural boredom is different from urban boredom: Much of the appeal of cities is rooted in the excitement of newness, of novelty, so urban boredom is a result of being surrounded by stimulation

---

16. "Natural Amenities Scale," U.S. Department of Agriculture Economic Research Service, last modified October 3, 2016, http://www.ers.usda.gov/data-products/natural-amenities-scale.aspx.

17. Christopher Ingraham, "Every County in America, Ranked by Scenery and Climate," *Washington Post*, August 17, 2015, https://www.washingtonpost.com/news/wonk/wp/2015/08/17/every-county-in-america-ranked-by-natural-beauty/.

18. Ibid.

yet still feeling alone. Rural boredom, by contrast, is often exacerbated by the tendency to wonder what you're missing out on."[19]

For pastors, this is more than just not having the same entertainment, dining, and cultural possibilities as hip urban areas. It's not just that we would like the occasional dinner and a show. It's that urban areas feel like the true centers of cultural production. The writing and painting and music making happen on the city scene. Meanwhile, we deal with the smell of the mass confinement hog lot.

You see, there's a way in which ministry is about culture making: the church culture, the Jesus culture, the kingdom culture. We're idea people. We're in the thick of it, hammering away at distinctive Christian community, stretching the wiring for the kingdom of God. We're using word and rite and song and sermon to craft a new sort of culture into being. And in the face of the massive culture production of the cities, our efforts are dwarfed and swamped simultaneously. Maybe we're not producing much of anything. Stories and gadgets flow out of the cities on airwaves and trucks, and our work in rural congregations seems dittoed, superfluous, and hackneyed. Maybe we should go somewhere else.

Author and farmer Wendell Berry writes in his essay "The Work of Local Culture": "A human community too must collect leaves and stories, and turn them into an account. It must build soil, and build that memory of itself—in lore and story and song—which will be its culture. And these two kinds of accumulation, of local soil and local culture, are intimately related."[20]

In rural areas, we are so often living on depleted cultural soil. Our stories and ideas feel as if they are not our own, as if we were not involved in their production. We struggle to do something that will put us on the map.

Eugene Peterson writes about how pastors typically engage this struggle: "We start dreaming of greener pastures. We preach BIG

19. Casey Quinlin, "When Country Music Goes to the Dark Side of Small-Town Life," *Atlantic*, November 19, 2013, http://www.theatlantic.com/entertainment/archive/2013/11/when-country-music-goes-to-the-dark-side-of-small-town-life/281544/.

20. Wendell Berry, "The Work of Local Culture" in *What Are People For? Essays* (Berkeley, CA: Counterpoint, 1990, 2010), 154.

IDEA sermons. Our voices take on a certain stridency as our anger and disappointment at being stuck in this place begin to leak into our discourse."[21]

We get stuck in the fundamental doubt that God is doing something that matters in rural contexts, in rural ministries. There's nothing Big going on. We spin our wheels in the niggling sense that maybe we really are living in a godforsaken place out in the middle of nowhere. God is somewhere, but that somewhere is not here. I'm convinced that this feeling of *stuckness* is a uniquely rural manifestation of acedia leading to rural pastor burnout.

Just as with pastors, a similar malaise can overshadow rural congregations, diminishing their sense of significance and self-worth. Rural churches look to the "tall steeples" in the cities to spark theological conversations and convene conferences. They import ideas.

Sara Miles, a writer and food-security activist from Southern California, notes how folks visiting her ministry often write themselves off. They feel that they couldn't possibly do the kind of creative work Miles's urban congregation takes on. They seem to believe her church has "some mysterious kind of permission that allows [them] to be so cool and daring." Miles isn't buying it. "What more permission do they need?" she asks. "'Receive the Holy Spirit' isn't enough?"[22]

It doesn't have to be this way.

In 2010, our small-town congregation wrote our own vacation Bible school curriculum based on the book of Revelation, foregoing the usual (and expensive) big box sets. The question was, *Can we really do such a thing?* It turned out that we could. There was a tremendous local originality and creativity that we tapped to write skits, songs, and curriculum. And it was probably the first time we had a rowboat in our church basement.[23]

21. Eugene Peterson, *Under the Unpredictable Plant: An Exploration in Vocational Holiness* (Grand Rapids: Eerdmans, 1992), 129.

22. Sara Miles, "Kitchen Communion: From the Food Pantry to the Table," *Christian Century* 127, no. 3 (2010): 24.

23. "Washington Churches Create VBS Lessons on Revelation," *Mennonite World Review*, September 6, 2010, http://www.mennoworld.org/archived/2010/9/6/washington-churches-create-vbs-lessons-revelation/.

These acts of creative derring-do are not unique to our congregation. Rural churches are preparing community meals and founding daycares and calling neighborhood hog roasts. But there's something that has to happen to hit that switch, to empower small-town and country churches to make and export rather than merely consume and import.

Pulling acedia up by its crooked root: Praise in place

We've got to be honest about the real root of rural acedia. While some might be inclined to see acedia as a natural result of the shortcomings of rural life, in fact the taproot of acedia goes much deeper. So too do pastors tend to overestimate the challenges of rural ministry over and against service in suburban and urban congregations. Researchers Andrews Miles and Rae Jean Proeschold-Bell, affiliated with Duke University, repudiated the notion that rural ministry is uniquely stressful compared to the urban variety. In a sociological analysis of United Methodist ministers in North Carolina, Miles and Proeschold-Bell found that city and country pastors face stress, criticism, financial difficulties, and burnout at comparable rates. Miles and Proeschold-Bell conclude that rural ministry is not "unusually stressful," and furthermore: "We see no indication that pastors, male or female, have any reason to fear working in a rural church."[24]

No doubt they're right. Yet the issue is not so much whether rural ministry is *more* stressful than urban ministry. Serving the church is hard, period. Rather, the issue is the spiritual challenges associated with rural ministry, and I'm convinced that acedia plays a unique and outsized role.

The great medieval theologian Thomas Aquinas opposed acedia to the "spiritual joy whereby one rejoices in the Divine good."[25]

---

24. Andrews Miles and Rae Jean Proeschold-Bell, "Are Rural Clergy Worse Off? An Examination of Occupational Conditions and Pastoral Experiences in a Sample of United Methodist Clergy," *Sociology of Religion* 73, no. 1 (2012): 13, https://divinity.duke.edu/sites/divinity.duke.edu/files/documents/chi/Pastoral%20experiences%20for%20rural%20and%20non-rural%20pastors%20accepted%20Sociology%20of%20Religion_formatted.pdf.

25. Saint Thomas Aquinas, "Second Article, Objection 3" in *Summa Theologiae*, trans. Fathers of the English Dominican Province, vol. 3, *Part 2, Second Section* (1911; New York, Cosimo, 2007), 1340.

Rural acedia ultimately flows from a restless failure to take joy in the God who is present in rural congregations and communities. It's failing to delight in the presence of God in rural people and locales, and in response to offer praise. Seeing God is a grace. But seeing God is also an act of will, an intentionality whereby we consent to recognize and rejoice in God. It's obeying the command to love (John 13:34; 1 John 4:7-8) by coming to deeply, continuously, and faithfully love a place and a people. Joy follows.

I'm convinced that if we're going to pull acedia up by its crooked root, we'll have to learn to praise in place. The trouble is that we've lost our doxological vision. We've failed to imagine that God values and is present in rural places, and thus we've failed to imagine that all places can offer authentic praise to God.

Doxology is an ancient Greek word meaning "praise." Doxologies are sprinkled throughout the New Testament. They are short, sparkling snippets of praise to God (see, for example, Romans 11:36; Ephesians 3:20-21; Jude 24-25). A version of the Romans 11:36 doxology is sung at the high point of the Catholic Mass, when the bread and cup are raised in consecration. In Mennonite circles, the doxology is the harmoniously complex "Praise God from Whom All Blessings Flow," an anthem version sung at national church gatherings, worship celebrations, and college soccer games.

Can we learn to see rural places doxologically, as places in which God is praisable and praised?

We'll need to start by rediscovering and naming the surprising, beautiful, and creative ways that God is present in our rural communities. We'll need to recall that our human vocation is found in praising God where we live and move and have our being—which, incidentally, is the only place that anyone has ever praised God.

In other words, it's not going to be possible for us to offer our praise vicariously through the high altars of the Big City. We've got to live and love and do right here and now, in our places, as small and unassuming as they may seem.

And let's be honest, many of our rural communities are rather small and unassuming. They're places like Toronto, Kansas (population 273), which has a liquor store and a gas station *that does not sell gas*—though they do carry energy drinks and processed meat sticks. Yet I submit that these places are just as worthy as Kansas City or New York or Jerusalem, even though they're mere smudges on the topographies of importance.

Our first step then, is to see, as Jacob did, that the Lord is in these places and we did not know it. We begin to plot out the world on God's geography, not the geography of proximity to the city.

New glasses: The disciplines of noticing and naming

Noticing and naming are key disciplines in learning to praise God in place. In noticing, we pay attention to the ways that God is, in fact, present. We practice attention to place.[26] This means noticing not all that *is not*, but rather all that which, by God's grace, *is*. And then we name these things, these ways that God is present in our rural communities and churches. Jacob gave the wilderness a God-infused name: Bethel, which means "house of God." Naming the place transformed it from a non-place to a God-place. Jacob *placed* it. It became *somewhere*.

We notice and name how God is present in the landscape. This means seeing the beauty of the place: the glorious, heavy heads of wheat, the storm clouds, an old gnarled tree. We give our rural communities the *National Geographic* treatment, paying attention to their special poetry of earth, sky, and water. Annie Dillard writes that the very "soil is an intricate throng of praise. Make connections; let rip; and dance where you can."[27]

Yet beauty does not bound God's presence. Indeed, "beauty" can all too easily become a cipher for whatever happens to please us. Note that Jesus did not go out into "deserted places" (Luke 5:16) because they were beautiful. He went because, although they were deserted of human life, they were present to God. In this way, the Lord lent a special preciousness to empty spaces, a fact we do

26. More on noticing in chapter 4.

27. Annie Dillard, *Pilgrim at Tinker Creek* in *The Annie Dillard Reader* (New York: HarperCollins, 2004), 340.

well to remember whenever we look out over sparse prairie or scrubby woods.

Our family has a short bike loop that we like to make around the edge of town. We always pause at a bridge over the thin trickle of Black Kettle Creek. It's not exactly a scenic overlook; there's an algae-smeared kitchen sink half submerged in the water. But when our oldest son got glasses and peered into the woods for the first time sans myopia, he spoke as admiringly as if he were looking over the Grand Canyon. It was lush and chirping, and a tawny owl took off from a rough, brown branch. Did you see it? Do we notice such things? Something is going on here. As poet Richard Wilbur puts it, "Any greenness is deeper than anyone knows."[28]

Marci Penner and WenDee LaPlant of the Kansas Sampler Foundation put the disciplines of noticing and naming into practice by visiting every community in Kansas over a period of four years. Their work was undertaken as research for their *Kansas Guidebook for Explorers*.[29] Theirs is a profound commitment to discovering the enchantment of rural communities—and a profound conviction that there is enchantment to discover.

Our rural communities are also often places of moral beauty. A web of reciprocal relationships knits many rural communities together. People exchange work, clean up their neighbors' yards after storms, and bake casseroles for new mothers. Our family, new to the area, is continually delighted by signs of neighborliness and care. Our mechanic picks up our car from our driveway. I leave it out, the keys in the ignition, and when he's done changing the oil, he returns it with the bill on the seat. Once, I accidentally left a gallon of milk in the back seat of the car. In our absence, the mechanic let himself into our house and stashed the milk in the fridge. There's a precious moral beauty in acts like that, and I'm tempted to think it's unique to our rural communities.

---

28. Richard Wilbur, "The Beautiful Changes," in *The Sacred Place: Witnessing the Holy in the Physical World*, ed. W. Scott Olsen and Scott Cairns (Salt Lake City: University of Utah Press, 1996), 3.

29. "Research Duo Completes Statewide Tour," Kansas Sampler Foundation, November 30, 2015, http://www.kansassampler.org/newsview.php?id=211.

Again, "beauty" gets us into slippery territory. There are also moral shadows: exclusivity, suspicion of outsiders, resistance to diversity. There are family systems that sweep abuse and hurt under the rug in order to keep the peace and seamlessly pass farmland to the next generation. But neither is it Pollyannaish nostalgia to name and value the special moral beauty that can inhere in rural communities. It's a way that God is present.

It's precisely God's presence that gives rural communities the capacity for authentic praise. The rock pillow can become the cornerstone of the altar. Because God is authentically present in rural places, we can authentically worship him in those places. Our worship hallows our place. Worship recognizes the sacredness of place. It validates and values. It delights. The fact that we can pray and bless and praise in rural places means that they are "understood and received in terms of [their] life in God."[30] Our doxological vision means that we praise God *in* these places.

This is a subversive geography, because we're turning the world's usual value system on its head. From our doxological perspective, it doesn't matter how big a place is, how close it is to the city, or how many World Series pennants it boasts. The value of a place arises from the fact that it is cherished by the God who created and sustains it. The value of a place is rooted in its nearness to God.

I also have in mind a second meaning for the doxological vision I'm describing. In the Scriptures, it is not just human beings who praise God, but all creation. Psalm 150 sings, "Let everything that breathes praise the Lord!" (v. 6). And even those things that do not breathe—those aspects of creation that are not alive to us—are alive to God in praise. Psalm 148 speaks of "sun and moon" and "shining stars" praising the Lord (v. 3). The "fire and hail, snow and frost, stormy wind fulfilling his command" all praise God (v. 8). In Isaiah 41, it is the personified coastlands (or islands, NIV, KJV) that praise God. Our doxological vision claims that places themselves praise God, that rural places are worthy of being inhabited by the living God, and that their existence is itself an

30. Wirzba, *Food and Faith*, 33.

ongoing form of praise. Thus, let us not despise what God has inhabited and imbued with the powers of praise. Rural places can never be *nowhere*, because God is in them. They praise God in their own unique way.

The work I'm describing is the work of re-enchantment of place. Pastorally, it means being willing to dwell in a place long enough to know the distinct ways that it gives praise to God. We build altars of praise in unlikely places. William Cavanaugh evokes the biblical idiom when he writes, "In an economy of hypermobility, we resist not by fleeing, but by *abiding*."[31] We abide in rural places because God abides in them, and our abiding resists the powers and trends that fray the value of rural life and ministry.

Abiding is to take seriously Eugene Peterson's observation that "pastoral work is geographical as much as theological."[32] It's learning to pastor rural churches as rural churches, to love them as rural churches. It's learning to honor the unique dynamics of rural congregations. It's giving thanks for what is good and beautiful and abundant in our congregations, because to do so is to name that-of-God in them.

Of course, the ultimate source and shape of this work of re-enchantment is love. We're simply seeking to love rural peoples and places as God loves them. God's love permeates and upholds and gives value to all places, and it is God's love that animates our lives and ministries in those places as we accompany rural congregations and communities in neighborliness.

Ultimately, the goal of a doxological vision is to point us toward and ground us in God's love.

In the depth of God's love, rural communities and congregations are *somewhere*.

And that is enough.

---

31. William Cavanaugh, "The World in a Wafer: A Geography of the Eucharist as Resistance to Globalization," *Modern Theology* 15 (1999): 192 (my italics).

32. Peterson, *Under the Unpredictable Plant*, 123.

CHAPTER 3

Abide: Becoming the Dust of the Earth

The Word became flesh and lived among us.
—John 1:14

We must be made from the dust of a place.

Over the course of seven years (or maybe it's ten), all the cells in our bodies replace themselves. A new *us* is progressively rolled out, made from all that we've eaten, drunk, and breathed—the tomatoes from the soil of our garden, the beef from the farm down the road, and the occasional bug that we swallow on our bike rides. Thus is the stuff of our new body.

Of course, this isn't exactly true. The idea that our bodies are remade every seven or ten years is a myth, though a nifty one. Many of our cells regenerate constantly—skin cells and intestinal lining cells and those little donut red blood cells are continually being replaced. But other cells take much, much longer and may never regenerate in a person's lifetime. You only get one pancreas. Treasure it.

While the idea is questionable biology, it's lovely theology. We are made from the dust of the earth. God formed the *adam*—human—from the dust of the *adamah*—earth (Genesis 2:7). To be cast out of lush Eden was to be destined to return to dust (Genesis

3:19). When Abraham got into a moral haggle with God at the gates of Sodom, he demurred, "I . . . am but dust and ashes" (Genesis 18:27). "How can dust and ashes be proud?" asks the sage Sirach in the Apocrypha, for "even in life the human body decays" (Sirach 10:9). We all bear the image of the "man of dust," but "we will also bear the image of the man of heaven" (1 Corinthians 15:49). We're made of dust all right, but precious dust: dust glittering with the grace of God, dust sprinkled with the blood of Jesus' cross. We're dust to die for.

The rural places where I've lived know something about this, both literally and figuratively. Eastern Washington is notoriously dusty—nothing like the clouds and rain of Seattle. People speak of the days before center-pivot irrigation was widely adopted. The fine, ashy soil of the Columbia Basin was turned by plows and lifted by exuberant winds coming down out of the Cascades. The sky became a prickly brown, and you had to stuff wet rags under your windows and doors.

We experienced this pulverous mix once when we drove into a gully during a windstorm. It was Sunday morning, and we were hurrying on our way to a joint worship service at another church. Is there anyone more foolhardy than a pastor late for worship? We found ourselves enveloped in dust, shrouded in a total brownout, sudden unhappy neighbors to several other folks who had also driven their vehicles down into the dirty gully and gotten trapped. There we waited until rescue officials could come and direct us out. Slowly goes it. Slink back up out of the dust.

Now we live in Kansas, on the margins of the Dust Bowl. It's not bad now, but poet Kathleen Johnson describes the scene in her poem "Dust Bowl Diary, 1935." She calls the sun "a dim smear" and writes, "No stars, no moon for weeks."[1] And whether or not we're aware of it, we're surrounded by mites and motes. We breathe dust from the air. Author Hannah Holmes, in her book *The Secret Life of Dust*, writes:

---

1. Kathleen Johnson, "Dust Bowl Diary, 1935" in *Begin Again: 150 Kansas Poems*, ed. Caryn Mirriam-Goldberg (Topeka, KS: Woodley Press, 2011), 130.

> Every time you inhale, thousands upon thousands of motes swirl into your body. Some lodge in the maze of your nose. Some stick in your throat. Others find sanctuary deep in your lungs. By the time you have read this far, you may have inhaled 150,000 of these worldly specks—if you live in the cleanest corners of the planet. If you live in the grubbier regions, you've probably just inhaled more than a million.[2]

A lot of the same elements that are in dust are in us—carbon and phosphorus and potassium—because plants grow in the dust of the earth, and we eat those plants, or we eat things that eat those plants. To be made of flesh and bone is to be made of dust.

Sometimes, pregnant women even develop a craving—called "pica"—for dirt. A friend of ours told us that when she was a child, family trips to the beach involved her pregnant mother scooping surreptitious bites of sand.

We begin in dust—and to dust we shall return. Shakespeare got it right: "Golden lads and girls all must, / As chimney-sweepers, come to dust."[3] But in the meantime, we're also dust that lives and breathes, dust that dreams, dust that *moves*.

Thus it is in our rural communities. They're stirred-up places, places on the move. As we saw in chapter 1, much (though not all) of this movement has been *away* from the rural and *into* the cities. Some small towns have emptied out completely. They've become ghost towns, populated by tumbleweeds and silent but for creaking doors lolling in the wind. Or they're death's near neighbors, towns bypassed by the railroads. They didn't get the interstate exit. The grocery store closed. Last one to leave, please turn out the lights.

It's still happening—such as in Treece, Kansas, an abandoned, heavy-metal-saturated old mining town on the southeast Kansas border. In the 1920s, Treece was the top producer of zinc and lead used in war munitions. Combined with Picher, Oklahoma, just

---

2. Hannah Holmes, *The Secret Life of Dust: From the Cosmos to the Kitchen Counter, the Big Consequences of Little Things* (Hoboken, NJ: John Wiley and Sons, 2001), 5.

3. William Shakespeare, *Cymbeline*, in *The Oxford Shakespeare*, ed. W. J. Craig, (New York, Bartleby, 2000), 4.2.333–34 , quoted in Allen Verhey, *The Christian Art of Dying: Learning from Jesus* (Grand Rapids: Eerdmans, 2011), 1.

across the border, its population topped twenty thousand.[4] When mining companies abandoned the towns—along with the toxic wreckage of the mines—the population went into steep decline, and eventually the State of Kansas initiated a buyout.

It's a grim story, one repeated in many deeply rural communities in less dramatic—if just as devastating—ways. Perhaps nowhere do we see this more than in school consolidation. During the 1960s, Kansas underwent a period of legislated consolidation. Schools of less than four hundred students—many of them the one-room schoolhouses of Laura Ingalls Wilder fame—were shuttered or sold, the children bused to a central location. Consolidation never really ended. Since 2000, thirteen Kansas schools have consolidated, twelve of them in counties along the lightly populated Kansas-Nebraska border. Among those is Jewell County, which experienced a population decline of some 50 percent between 1970 and 2000.[5]

The challenge of keeping the local school open is mirrored in the difficulty of finding professionals—skilled doctors, teachers, pastors, and businesspeople—willing to make their lives and build their practices in rural areas. In their book, *Hollowing Out the Middle: The Rural Brain Drain and What It Means for America*, Patrick Carr and Maria Kefalas write of "communities left behind" as young, creative individuals abandon the country for urban opportunities.[6]

In the face of such change and loss, leaders in the church—and the church itself—are called to *abide*: to stay put long enough to be made from the dust of a place. Devoting ourselves to the discipline of abiding will mean caring for place, practicing the ministry of presence, living into an appropriate smallness, and practicing a spirituality of loose ends. Above all, abiding will mean learning to love.

---

4. "Treece, Kansas," *Wikipedia*, last modified February 25, 2017, https://en.wikipedia.org/wiki/Treece,_Kansas#cite_note-8.

5. Celia Llopis-Jepsen, "Rural Majority: School Consolidation Complex, Controversial," *Topeka (KS) Capital-Journal*, March 23, 2015, http://cjonline.com/news/2015-03-23/rural-majority-school-consolidation-complex-controversial#.

6. Patrick Carr and Maria Kefalas, *Hollowing Out the Middle: The Rural Brain Drain and What It Means for America* (Boston: Beacon Press, 2009), 2.

Abiding as spiritual discipline: Care for place

Abiding is not a new concept. Saint Antony, the revered pioneer of the third-century monastic movement, thought the best way to make the spiritual journey was not to journey at all, but rather to stay put. People sought out Antony in the desert for gritty advice on the spiritual life. Take this example: "Somebody asked Antony, 'What shall I do in order to please God?' He replied, 'Do what I tell you, which is this: wherever you go, keep God in mind; whatever you do, follow the example of holy Scripture; wherever you are, stay there and do not move away in a hurry. If you keep to these guidelines, you will be saved.'"[7]

When Benedict of Nursia gathered monks into communities in the sixth century, he laid down some rules now known as the Rule of Saint Benedict. Among helpful tips—such as that monks not "sleep with knives at their sides, lest they cut themselves" or that the abbot (the head of the monastery) assure that monks' clothing is "not too short for those who wear them, but fitted to the wearers"[8]—Benedict gives advice about the monks' spiritual lives. These men of constant prayer and fasting must commit themselves to "stability," to not being like some who play at the life of prayer but are "always on the move . . . [and] never settle down, and are slaves to their own wills and gross appetites."[9] They were not to monastery-hop, searching for the perfect community of prayer. Their task was to stay put.

Jonathan Wilson-Hartgrove has brought the concept of stability into our contemporary moment in his book *The Wisdom of Stability: Rooting Faith in a Mobile Culture*. He writes, "Like children stumbling off a merry-go-round, Americans are grasping for something to anchor our lives in a sea of constant change."[10] Or at least, some of us are. The merry-go-round will give you

---

7. Benedicta Ward, *The Desert Fathers: Sayings of the Early Christian Monks* (New York: Penguin Classics, 2003), 3.

8. Timothy Fry and Timothy Horner, trans., *The Rule of St. Benedict in English* (Collegeville, MN: Liturgical Press, 1981), 49, 76.

9. Ibid., 21.

10. Jonathan Wilson-Hartgrove, *The Wisdom of Stability: Rooting Faith in a Mobile Culture* (Brewster, MA: Paraclete, 2010), 10.

quite a rush. Not everybody is ready to get off. Those who dare sometimes discover "the stability we were made for as we come home to life with God in community with other people."[11]

But it's not easy.

Living into the kind of stability that Antony, Benedict, and Wilson-Hartgrove sketch out will require us to question some of our assumptions about what progress looks like. We'll need to confess that for a lot of us, life has developed a wobble, and we need to recenter ourselves in Jesus. We'll have to learn to abide.

Part of the reason we find this life of abiding difficult is that we're not sure we really want it. Just as the dominant cultural motif of the moment points toward urban life as the truly human life, so too our society gives the impression that progress equals movement. The rolling stone gathers no moss. We move for school, move for work, move for hipper digs and mountain vistas. The satirical website *The Onion* pilloried our common addiction to speed and change with an article describing an "unambitious 29-year-old loser who leads an enjoyable and fulfilling life, [and] still lives in his hometown and has no desire to leave."[12]

Staying put has come to mean getting stuck, and nowhere is that more true than in our rural communities. Moving on is moving up. Perhaps even some of the church hopping so prevalent in our moment—our moving from place to place searching for the perfect community of faith—is fueled by the same ambition. Those who don't change towns can at least change churches. We're not unambitious losers, after all.

But what if all that movement has left us rootless, disconnected from the fundamental goods of community and identity—maybe even from God? We need to challenge our culture's narrative of movement. It's a distraction from what's really going on. We need to recognize that our restlessness is just that: rest-less-ness, a failure to "return, O my soul, to your rest" (Psalm 116:7). And once

11. Ibid., 19.

12. "Unambitious Loser with Happy, Fulfilling Life Still Lives in Hometown," *Onion*, January 23, 2013, http://www.theonion.com/article/unambitious-loser-with-happy-fulfilling-life-still-33233.

we've pulled the lid off our restlessness, we need to confront it. More often than not, it's not progress—it's rootlessness. Our boredom with place and failure to take joy in where we are and in the people who are around us lead us back to the deadly sin of acedia. We will not find God on that path.

Jesus knew we would end up here. It's human nature. He was trying to point us back home when he taught: "I am the vine, you are the branches. Those who abide in me and I in them bear much fruit, because apart from me you can do nothing" (John 15:5).

Jesus connects abiding with friendship, a theme we'll take up in chapter 5 when we talk about prayer, and will discuss more deeply in chapter 9. To abide in rural congregations and communities is to befriend them. But I think Jesus was getting at the discipline of being in a place as *he* was in a place: not by happenstance or with a longing to be somewhere else, but as an act of love. Jesus was made from the dust of the earth.

Think of Jesus' ministry. His work was both local and rural, thirtysomething years growing up in small-town Nazareth followed by three years ministering in its vicinity. Jesus was not a big traveler. His was a life rooted in place.

It wasn't because he didn't have any better options. Sure, travel wasn't as easy as it is (for some people) today. But people living under the Roman Empire could move about. Jesus' own family had traveled from Nazareth to Bethlehem to Egypt and back to Nazareth again. There were substantial Jewish populations in Alexandria and Rome—until they were expelled from the imperial city under Emperor Claudius (Acts 18:2). When some local leaders misunderstood Jesus' teaching, they wondered aloud: "Where is he planning to go? . . . Is he thinking of leaving the country and going to the Jews in other lands? Maybe he will even teach the Greeks!" (John 7:35 NLT).

Jesus *chose* to stay. He dedicated his life and ministry to a limited geography—mainly Galilee—and a particular people: the house of Israel. He resisted the illusion that effectiveness would come through garnering a broader audience (Matthew 10:5-6). He healed and taught and flicked the old demons away in a particular place. He trod down Death by death among a particular people. He came out of the same grave where they had laid him. Most of Jesus' resurrection appearances in the New Testament take place within twenty miles of each other—with his appearance to Paul near Damascus being the outlier, at a little over one hundred miles away from Nazareth. Yet Jesus' ministry to a particular people and place was in fact a ministry to the world. It was later, when he sent his disciples out to preach the gospel to the ends of the earth (Matthew 28:19-20), that he came to be fully present through them among every tribe and tongue.

Part of what I think this teaches us is that caring for the world means caring for a particular corner of it. This is abiding in place as a spiritual discipline, a practice that we take up with intentionality, regardless of how we feel about staying put at any given moment. It's staying put so that we can come to genuinely and deeply love a people and place, as Jesus did. We don't stay because we can't pull together bus fare to the city. We stay because we think it's the right thing to do—for our own soul and the soul of the community. This is to say that authentic abiding involves our choosing to be in a place. In this way, abiding is a healing act that counteracts the narrative of moving up and moving on. Abiding in our rural communities is an act of love. I choose this place, this community, these people. I choose you.

For leaders in the church, this means actually remaining in a place. One of the fundamental challenges of pastoral ministry is that our ministry is a reflection of our *selves*. If the ministry goes well, we take the puffed-up credit. But if things don't go as we might have hoped, our entire sense of self can start to unravel. *Who am I if I don't succeed here?* There aren't many variables in this equation, and pastors—faced with the rock and the hard place of seeing themselves as failures or seeing their congregations as failures—too often opt for the latter and move on. We would have succeeded but for that pesky congregation that was too old, too traditional, too stuck in their ways, too focused on themselves. Too human, really. Goodbye and good luck.

Many of us are addicted to the fresh start, to the new possibility of finally getting it right in a perfect location. We think that if we can get out of Dodge, we can get out of trouble, failure, and the knobby stubbornness of our neighbors. But so often, moving on is simply a flight from our own shortcomings. And our shortcomings have swift wings: they follow us. The truly countercultural move is to stay put. Staying is the first step in challenging our mistaken equating of movement with growth. "Staying is the new going," writes Jonathan Wilson-Hartgrove.[13]

The first step in learning to abide is to actually stay put. It's remaining in a place until we come to know its ins and outs, its saints and its rascals.

For many rural communities and congregations, abiding is a healing practice. True, many rural communities located near metro areas or picturesque natural panoramas are experiencing growth. But not so the one-traffic-light, God-bless-them little Podunk towns sprinkled across the continent. People, especially the young, are leaving those places, and each minivan that hits the road for State University is a dream realized—and lost. We watch our promising young people head off over the horizon.

This is one of those distinctly rural realities: a profound sense of loss haunts many rural communities. It doesn't help that the cultural narrative is often that of the triumphant city, the city as crème de la crème, the city as success. Rural places feel like jilted spouses. The best and the brightest left us for someone more urbane.

The ministry of presence

In situations of pastoral care, we speak of the "ministry of presence"—being lovingly present with a person in a tough situation. It's not about having some perfect words to speak into tragedy and loss. It's not about "fixing" the problem. It's about showing up—at the hospital bedside, in the living room after the death—and being present. This is the ministry of presence.

I'm convinced that one form abiding takes in rural congregations and communities is presence. We need our brightest, most

13. Wilson-Hartgrove, *The Wisdom of Stability*, 11.

promising young people, including pastors, to commit to being present in our most out-of-the-way places.

That rural places might truly be on the table as an option for young professionals will take some getting used to. At a recent conference, a sincere young woman stood and bared her heart to the speaker and large crowd of attendees. She asked, "With all the places that we can go after graduation, how do we choose?" I was more impressed that she asked the question at all than by the answer the speaker gave (which I frankly don't remember). How do we choose?

In a recent interview, author and pastor Eugene Peterson, now in his eighties, made this recommendation to "younger Christians who are itchy for a deeper and more authentic discipleship": "Go to the nearest smallest church and commit yourself to being there for 6 months. . . . Sometimes it doesn't work. Some pastors are just incompetent. And some are flat-out bad. So I don't think that's the answer to everything, but it's a better place to start than going to the one with all the programs, the glitz, all that stuff."[14]

Peterson was speaking of churches, but his advice could just as easily apply to communities. Pick a small town and stick with it. Abide. Perhaps our rule of thumb for abiding should be seven years, a lovely, biblical number. Stay in a church and community at least seven years: long enough for your body to be made from the dust of the place. That's what I mean by abiding.

Learning appropriate smallness: We're not too good for rural places

To abide is not just to stay put, but to become incarnate in a place, to be made and remade from the dust of that particular spot of earth. It's what Jesus did in his ministry. Peterson, riffing on John 1:14, wryly points out, "The Word did not become a good idea, or a numinous feeling, or a moral aspiration; the Word became

---

14. Jonathan Merritt, "Faithful to the End: An Interview with Eugene Peterson," *Religion News Service*, September 27, 2013, http://religionnews.com/2013/09/27/faithful-end-interview-eugene-peterson/.

flesh."[15] And Jesus' flesh, as ours, was made from the dust of our earth. The Word put on dust.

It's the same ministry Jesus asked his disciples to perform for him in the garden of Gethsemane. Near death, his heart "deeply grieved," he said, "Remain here . . . with me" (Matthew 26:38). The word for "remain" is the same word in Greek that Jesus used in John 15:5 for "those who *abide* in me" (my italics). Significantly, in Matthew 26 he bundled the ministry of remaining with the ministries of watching (v. 38 again) and praying (v. 41)—the next two key postures of the rural church that we will take up in the following chapters.

But we have to be careful when we talk like this that we don't come to think that it's all about the benefit to rural congregations and communities. This isn't the usual boosterism, the stuff of rural highway signs ("It's small but it's home" or "If you lived here, you'd be home by now"), in which we try to coax the best and the brightest to deign to live in our humble rural communities. Some isolated school districts and rural states have labored mightily to draw in college graduates, to limited success.[16]

But as helpful as it is to have talented young professionals and entrepreneurs return to or discover our small rural communities, this isn't really the full extent of what I have in mind. I'm speaking more of a spiritual posture in the world, regardless of where we find ourselves. The discipline of abiding has an inward focus, a return to what pastor John Ortberg calls "appropriate smallness."[17]

---

15. Eugene Peterson, *The Contemplative Pastor: Returning to the Art of Spiritual Direction* (Grand Rapids: Eerdmans, 1989), 68.

16. See Celia Llopis-Jepsen, "Remote Schools Struggle to Fill Positions," *Topeka (KS) Capital-Journal*, March 22, 2015, http://cjonline.com/news/2015-03-22/remote-schools-struggle-fill-positions; Samuel Berbano, "Ads Hope to Get Young Families Moving to Iowa," *Iowa State Daily* (Iowa State University, Ames), April 11, 2005, http://www.iowastatedaily.com/news/article_58a773d4-a1c1-50a3-96ff-25ad356554c3.html.

17. John Ortberg, "'Appropriate Smallness': The Practice of Servanthood," chap. 7 in *The Life You've Always Wanted: Spiritual Disciplines for Ordinary People* (Grand Rapids: Zondervan, 1997, 2002).

You see, we turn to the city not just because there's opportunity and excitement but because we feel, deep down, that we're worth it. We're Big Time, and so we need a Big Time kind of place. We're fearful of being pegged as "those who fled back to the safety of the town after a try at college a few hundred miles from home."[18] We're fearful that others will think we haven't been able to graduate from rural. But as one rural pastor put it when told for the umpteenth time that he should really consider moving on to a larger, suburban church where he could make more money, "The church is not the corporate world. You need to get over that."

At the heart of this fear lies the deadly sin of vainglory. We think of ourselves more highly than we ought. We deserve more and bigger, better and shinier—more Shakespeare and less twang. We're worth it.

Abiding in rural places and communities reminds us how small we are. Cities can have this effect as well, because in the city, we're one-in-a-million. Literally. We're surrounded by action, and who are we in this great, big place? But in our rural communities and congregations, where claims to biggest and best are scarce on the ground, we're reminded of the limits of human life.

So sings the psalmist: "You have made my days a few handbreadths, and my lifetime is as nothing in your sight" (Psalm 39:5). Appropriate smallness is a nitty-gritty humility that comes upon us slowly. We're not too good for rural places.

Everything must change?

Abiding has a powerful impact on how we look at church leadership in rural communities. All too often, we envision leadership within a framework of change. Everything must change! It's the battle cry of our age, like "Remember the Alamo!"

The attitude usually plays out like this: A bright young pastor shows up, flexes her agenda, and sets about shaking things up. When the change causes friction, which all change does, the pastor shifts into a combative mode, and then finally a

18. Kathleen Norris, *Dakota: A Spiritual Geography* (New York: Houghton Mifflin, 1993), 50.

take-my-toys-and-go-home mode. And the pastor moves on from such a hopelessly retrograde, hidebound place.

Because everything must change.

And in the city, why not? In so many ways, the allure of the city is wrapped up in the potential for us to reinvent ourselves. There are cultures and subcultures and countercultures, and we can sip from them all, try everything. Despite all the concrete, the social contract of the city is premised on change.

But a different dynamic is in play in our rural churches and communities. Through the discipline of abiding, we come to recognize that change happens within the lived stories of people and communities, stories bigger than anything we're ever going to be able to wrap our heads around. We have to be committed to people before people will commit to change.

This means that while change happens, our first commitment in the rural church is not to shake everything up, but to be present to people and the church where they are. We're called to abide.

You see, sometimes the "everything must change" mentality gives pastors and lay leaders a martyr complex. Some leaders come in with a "burn the house down" mentality. They see tradition or smallness not as areas where they might deepen their relationship with people and place but as faults to remedy. They fling themselves at the church, change or bust—and most often bust. We justify any measure, any change, any half-baked new idea, because the church is falling apart (or so we think) and we've lost our young people, and it must be that all those who have come before us fiddled while Rome, Kansas, burned.

There's a white-knuckled, hang-on-for-dear-life kind of adrenaline rush that comes from this approach to ministry. It appeals to our insecurities and our grandiose need to be a hero. Isn't this what we went to seminary for: to save the church?

I confess that I've been there.

The first congregation I served was situated in a little town straddling multiple cultures in Washington's eastern sagebrush desert. I came in like a whirlwind, hot out of seminary, radical peacemaking up one sleeve, Christian community building up the other. I was ready to change the world, and our little church was ground zero. "They're lucky to have you," a denominational official confided. *Yes*, I thought. *I know*.

I launched a multipronged change effort, caffeinated by visions of success and egged on by a frantic desire to hold on to members of the small and imploding Spanish-speaking congregation that we hosted. This is going to be big, people. Just watch the new pastor work his golden boy magic!

But it didn't—*ahem*—work. At year three I found myself profoundly humbled and exquisitely aware of my own limitations, both spiritually and in terms of my leadership capacity. I had just enough sense not to try to scapegoat my way out of it, but I knew I was going to have to try a different approach.

I could tell my story in several ways. Like all our human stories, it's big and frayed. But the basic contour is this: I stopped trying to change everything and started abiding. I began practicing a ministry of presence in our community. I still dreamed big dreams for our congregation, but I held them more lightly. I came to learn that it wasn't all about me. I wasn't going to be able to make it all happen.

I had gone west with a vision for social justice. There was a neighborhood outside town populated by Mexican families and their goats and chickens. It was a dented-aluminum-trailer and shack affair slumping down into a grungy little gorge. In my mind, it was a slum, snaring its residents in ramshackle poverty while a wicked absentee landlord profited. Strangely, it was called Las Caserolas—"the Frying Pans." I didn't bother to find out why. I didn't bother to meet anyone who lived there. This wasn't a case for listening; this was a case for action. Sí, se puede! Cesar Chavez would be proud.

I talked to a city council member. Yes, there were some concerns. "But where would all those people live?" he said. "Are you ready to help them with finding new homes?" This was bigger than I thought.

I later came to meet folks who lived in Las Caserolas—and to learn the seedy reasons for its name. "Te gusta vivir allí?" I asked.

Do you like where you live? "Pues sí," they told me. "It's cheap, and it's just far enough out in the country that we can have goats and chickens like back in Mexico. It's a good place to live."

Oh.

And their neighborhood had a little local color. Sometime in the misty past, an argument between two ladies had escalated. It got so fierce that the women came out of their trailers brandishing frying pans. There you have it: Las Caserolas. The name stuck.

I had also gone to Washington to do Spanish-speaking ministry. That was my *thing*. I was Pastor Multicultural. When the Spanish-speaking church that our congregation hosted fell apart, I thought to launch a bilingual worship service. When that didn't stick, I tried a Spanish-speaking Bible study. When that ran its course, I gave up trying to force the community to conform to my identity and started just trying to make friends. After a couple of years of *quinceañeras* and birthday parties, I was invited to the home of a large Spanish-speaking family. Mom and dad and the kids were there. The uncle came over from next door. "Would you teach us about the Bible?"

I went once a week throughout the winter and into a chilly spring. When they weren't working late in the fields, I went in the summer too. In the colder months, they would have the heat cranked, and I would take my usual seat, stripping off a layer of clothing for every fifteen minutes of study. I did this nearly every week until we moved away.

They dropped by the house when we were in the midst of packing, cardboard boxes half-filled on the floor, tape in hand. "Pastor, you can't leave now! You're just getting started!" they told me.

Yes, I thought. *I know*.

I was just beginning to abide, and I was already contemplating my next move. I never made my seven years in the dust of Warden.

A spirituality of loose ends

We don't need change heroes in our rural congregations and communities. We need women and men committed to heroic abiding. Less heroic change and more heroic abiding. Jason McConnell, pastor of two small congregations in rural Vermont, noted that it takes time to build trust. "I keep telling them that I'm here for forty years," said McConnell. "They still don't believe me."

This is going to mean that we cultivate a spirituality of loose ends. Everything won't be wrapped up nicely. There are going to be a lot of things left hanging. I personally have long struggled with loose ends. They've kind of been my kryptonite. But what I've begun to learn is that the forces at work in the rural church are too big to be wrapped up. Young people moving to the city is not a fixable problem. (What would it mean to "fix" it, anyway?) Rural churches won't thrive by shifting into a higher gear. If anything, as Benedict cautioned in his Rule (quoting Genesis 33:13), we drive the flock too hard, and they die.[19] But that is not of God. We're not supposed to work the flock to death. We're called to abide.

Pastors sometimes fall prey to an illusion: the belief that we're paid for change. *Change* in this case is a stand-in for *results*, as if our work were to increase shareholder value. It leads to a propensity to constant tinkering. Insofar as this opens pastors to a broad-minded, teachable ministry, it can be positive. But instead, pastors often create a culture where everything is up in the air. The congregation becomes unsettled. There's a sense that, as one pastor I know put it, "the marbles are rolling all over the board." It's an anxious person's game that says more about our impatience with immovable objects than our genius as change agents.

And in rural congregations, particularly those with strong agricultural roots, this push toward change can awaken a deep font of resistance and resentment. This is not because rural people are culturally averse to change. It's not as if they're farming with mules. They've got snazzy GPS-guided tractors and field contours digitally imaged by drones. The problem is that rural congregations have seen it all before—in school consolidation mandated by state and federal powers and in distant denominational bureaucrats who pushed to eliminate small congregations in "overchurched"

19. Fry and Horner, trans., *Rule of St. Benedict in English*, 88.

rural communities.[20] It's the phenomenon of the visiting expert, embodied in Theodore Roosevelt's Country Life Commission one hundred years ago.

Writer Wendell Berry sums up the suspicion in his essay "The Work of Local Culture." He writes that beneficial change "comes not from the outside by the instruction of visiting experts, but from the inside by the ancient rule of neighborliness, by the love of precious things, and by the wish to be at home."[21] Berry has in his sights the whole Farm Bureau and university extension wing of rural revival. I wouldn't cast the same stones; I think it's nice to have the university agronomist stop by. But ultimately the visiting expert is only effective when the locals see him or her as an ally in their common endeavor.

I suspect that all too often, pastors have cast themselves in the role of visiting expert, more ready to shake the dust off their feet when their message isn't accepted than to take the time to become the dust of the earth in the place they serve. One rural pastor I talked to described the healing work he's had to engage in after his predecessor's run of "radical" agrarian preaching. The congregation was spent and tetchy after years of strident preaching of *everythingmustchangeism*. The new pastor found himself practicing a ministry of presence, returning to an expansive gospel vision that knows when to push and when to abide.

Abiding love

What makes abiding a true spiritual discipline is the same power that undergirds all practices in the way of Christ: love. To abide in a rural place is to stay long enough to love it. Forget the rush of the city. What we really need is time to be in a place, with a people, the years fermenting into affection and joy. We need time to love, and as Mark Twain put it, "Love . . . is the slowest of all growths."[22]

---

20. See chap. 3 in Kevin Lowe, *Baptized with the Soil: Christian Agrarians and the Crusade for Rural America* (New York: Oxford University Press, 2016).

21. Wendell Berry, "The Work of Local Culture" in *What Are People For? Essays* (Berkeley, CA: Counterpoint, 1990, 2010), 169.

22. R. Kent Rasmussen, ed., *The Quotable Mark Twain: His Essential Aphorisms, Witticisms, and Concise Opinions* (New York: McGraw Hill, 1998), 166.

Staying, on its own, is not abiding. Sometimes people are trapped in cycles of poverty, in bad relationships, in lack of agency. Sometimes we can't stay. Sometimes staying would be dangerous to our lives or our relationship or our souls. Sometimes we have to go in order to become the kind of people God is truly calling us to be. Jesus grounded abiding not in a geographic relationship but in living God's love through him. We can abide in Jesus, wherever we end up.

The apostle John knew this. He wrote in his first letter: "God is love, and those who abide in love abide in God, and God abides in them" (1 John 4:16). It is love that teaches us to abide. And honestly, sometimes it is abiding—even in the most limited sense of *staying put*—that teaches us to love. But this abiding is first a spiritual reality before it becomes a physical fact lived out on the ground. Without love, there is no abiding. Without love, there's just staying, and that's no great trick.

Saint Augustine, preaching on abiding love in 1 John 4, said, "Love, and do what you will."[23] Perhaps we could turn his statement on its head. What about this: "Love, and *go* where you will." When we take this seriously, I suspect that our going—and our staying—will be tempered by our loving.

A pastor who labored away in obscurity for years in small-town Maine was asked by his colleague, "Why have you stayed there so long?" Obviously, remaining in such a small setting required some sort of fortitude, something out of the ordinary—something even saintly. The pastor thought about it and responded, "I stay because I love the people."

That's the point we want to get to. Pastors stay because they love the church. The church stays because it loves the community. The community stays because God has loved it into existence in the eternal generosity of God's providence.

---

23. Augustine of Hippo, "Homily 7 on the First Epistle of John," in *Nicene and Post-Nicene Fathers: First Series*, ed. Philip Schaff, trans. H. Brown, vol. 7 (Buffalo, NY: Christian Literature Publishing, 1888), http://www.newadvent.org/fathers/170207.htm.

This is abiding: making our home among a people, heroically locating ourselves among real people in real places. It takes guts.

But then, that's what Jesus did. It's what, through us, he still does.

The Word becomes flesh, fashioned and formed from dust, and lives among us.

CHAPTER 4

Watch: Vida Painted on an Adobe Wall

With many such parables [Jesus] spoke the word to them, as they were able to hear it.
—Mark 4:33

The tiny community of Yarcaccunca perches on a verdant Andean outcrop two winding hours outside Cuzco, Peru. It's a hamlet at the top of the world, adobe and clay-tile-roofed houses surrounded by curving terraces of fava, potatoes, and massive white-kernel corn. There's also a little Mennonite church there, planted a decade ago when a couple of adventurous young guys trundled up in a van, stretched out a screen, and projected a Quechua-dubbed version of *The Jesus Film*.

We traveled to Yarcaccunca in our work with the Cuzco mission. As my wife and her Quechua-speaking colleague spoke about reproductive health to a group in the church, I wandered around the village. There was a gate hinged on the repurposed sole of a shoe. There were sheep, a path with rocks jutting out like the fringe of a massive turtle shell, and frizzy, tawny, clucking chickens. And there was a rough adobe wall painted with the word *vida*: life.

Current population trends in Yarcaccunca may sound familiar to rural North America. The young people are moving down to the city. There's a whole neighborhood of Yarcaccunca folks on the outskirts of Cuzco. Attendance at the Quechua service in the Cuzco church has swollen. But up in Yarcaccunca, it's mostly the elderly who remain, keeping watch over fields that younger backs and hands will come up to tend in the rainy season before returning again to the city. But there's life painted on the brown adobe of Yarcaccunca.

I didn't really need to have *vida* spelled out for me quite so literally, but I liked the straightforward symbolism. Potatoes, mountains, people moving away, adobe, *vida*.

I'll be honest: it's likely that *vida* was merely the hackneyed slogan of some political party. It sounds like a lot of the others I've seen: *pan*—bread, *trabajo*—work. *Vida* would fit right in.

But I'll take it anyway, regardless of how the original stencilist intended it. There's life right in the middle of our rural communities, and we need to learn to watch for it and to tell God's story about what we see.

"Watch" was one of the last commands Jesus gave his disciples in the garden of Gethsemane. This was no accident. His destiny was scheming and stomping from Jerusalem, and he needed his disciples to pay attention to what was going on, to what he was doing in that place. "Stay here," said Jesus, "and keep watch with me" (Matthew 26:38 NIV).

In the ancient church, "watching" was more than just looking out the window. To watch was to practice a core spiritual discipline, one necessary for triumph over sin and the devil. The Greek spiritual anthology called *The Philokalia* speaks of the importance of watchfulness: "Just as it is impossible to live this present life without eating or drinking, so it is impossible for the soul to achieve anything spiritual and in accordance with God's will, or to be free from mental sin, without that guarding of the intellect and purity of heart truly described as watchfulness."[1] This is what Peter was getting at when he said: "Discipline yourselves, keep

1. St. Nikodimos of the Holy Mountain and St. Makarios of Corinth, comp., *The Philokalia: The Complete Text*, trans. and ed. G. E. H. Palmer, Philip Sherrard, and Kallistos Ware (London: Faber and Faber, 1979), 181.

alert. Like a roaring lion your adversary the devil prowls around, looking for someone to devour" (1 Peter 5:8). Watch.

Learning to watch is especially important in the rural church, because we so often fall under the mistaken impression that there's not much to watch for. The city has lights and a curvaceous, gyrating economy of smokestacks and riverboats and jazz. Who wouldn't watch? It's hard to look away.

But gazing is not watching, and our hearts grow empty as our eyes fill up. We must learn to pay attention.

There's more. Human lives are storied lives, and our communities—country and city—are bundles of those stories, spinning out in relation to one another. To live in community is to participate in an eternal conversation in which the actors step on and off the stage but the conversation never truly ends. We are the stories we tell about each other.

This is why Jesus told his disciples to watch. He was telling a new kind of story just then in that garden: a story about what faithfulness might look like, about how we might live with God, about how evil would be thrown down—and not by the usual means. Jesus was telling the story of God's heart, which is ever and always the story of the cross, and he needed his disciples to get it, to see it, to pay attention. He needed them to watch.

This watching was no light assignment. No doubt the disciples would have preferred to look away. Rabbi Jesus was about to be murdered, and he was sweating blood (Luke 22:44). Indeed, Peter did look away a short time later when, in the courtyard of the high priest, he was driven to speak those fateful words: "I do not know him" (v. 57).

How many rural communities suffer the same fate? We never knew them. We never know the depths of stories, all the ways they're twined together. It falls to the church—and especially pastors, who often hail from outside rural communities—to be friends of stories. Sit with coffee, sit in living rooms, sit at the hospital or hospice or addiction treatment bedside, and ask, "What's your story?"

Watching will mean asking the simple question, "What's the story of this place?" It will mean sitting with people, listening to people, being present to people (which is why watching goes with abiding).

One woman tells how shortly after her husband died—amid all the platitudes that we chew like saccharine bubble gum—someone came to her, sat with her, and then said simply, "Tell me about your husband." She didn't need someone to say fixing words. (There are no such things.) She needed someone to hear their together-story.

Watching means becoming as a little child and asking *why*, and then becoming like a reporter and asking *who*, *what*, *when*, *where*, and *how.* John Adams, a longtime pastor to rural congregations, works for Village Missions, an organization based in Oregon that's committed to sending pastors to some of the most out-of-the-way corners of the United States and Canada. Adams speaks of the necessity of "showing up as a learner" and asking, "How do we do it here, and why do we do it that way?" Practicing this kind of attentive learning is a very human and humanizing thing to do. To pay attention to another is to give the gift of presence, which is ultimately the gift of love.

Jesus did this all the time. He was practiced in the art of paying attention, even when it didn't seem like there was much to pay attention to. He knew that where there's life, there's story. Think of blind Bartimaeus planted on the side of that road. "Jesus, Son of David, have mercy on me!" he cried. Easy enough for Jesus. He wouldn't even have to stop. He could do a walk-by healing. After all, he healed Jairus's daughter with a word and spoke the centurion's servant back into health from a distance. But not this time. Jesus stopped. Jesus spoke to the man who was blind. "What do you want me to do for you?" It's all too obvious. Except that it isn't, because what Jesus was really asking was that humanizing heart question: "What's your story?" Jesus' question to Bartimaeus was an act of watchfulness.

Rural churches and communities sometimes labor under the mistaken belief that they have no stories—or at least that their stories aren't as grand or important as city stories. How could rural stories be that important? There's no major-league sportsing of any kind going on.

But there are stories. If we don't learn to hear them well, they'll be rolled into some bland story—some nonstory—that knows nothing of the time the bank of lockers tipped over on the boy in the junior high locker room and the other boys strained together to heft them up so their friend could scramble out; or the great flood when everyone had to camp up on the hill and their lips swelled and chapped as their furniture bobbed away; or the truck that got trapped on the road in a blizzard while hauling a pink elephant, painted up for an advertising photo shoot. Driver and elephant waited out a week of snow in the local tow shop, and a stream of children came through to see the spectacle.

When we miss the storied fiber of rural places, we inevitably end up turning them into something quaint. We quaint them into a corner. We quaint them up. But quaint is the enemy of great in our small towns. We'll start to think that it's all one big Grant Wood painting out there, all amber waves of grain and straw bales rolled and resting on the hills. If we aren't careful, the stories of little places become jots and tittles hashed along the Great Big Story of the city and nation. We'll get quainted to death. This is why the church must learn to hear the stories of the rural community.

And then the church parabolizes them.

The word *parable* means "throw alongside." That's *alongside*—not on top of, not over and against, but alongside. When Jesus taught in parables, he told stories that invited further stories. He parabolized others' stories by inviting them to come alongside his story and be transformed in the process. This is why he asked so many questions. "Which of these three, do you think, was a neighbor to the man?" (Luke 10:36). "Whose head is [on] this [coin]?" (Matthew 22:20). "Do you see this woman?" (Luke 7:44).

Jesus was a parabolizer—he told stories that came *alongside* other stories. He invited and drew and showed the way into a different vision of life, a different kind of life. Jesus told God's story, and he told it crosswise so that others could find refuge in his telling.

The rural church is called to do the same. We're parabolizers, telling Jesus' story alongside the stories of our rural communities.

We don't run roughshod over the stories we hear around us. We listen for Jesus' story already present, and we draw it out. We bear witness to what God is doing. It's Jesus' instruction to his disciples in the book of Acts: "You will be my witnesses in Jerusalem, in all Judea and Samaria, and to the ends of the earth" (1:8). To witness is not just to watch, not just to see what happened, but in fact to speak the truth of what happened. It's to participate in that truth. It's to parabolize: to tell God's story alongside others' stories.

I see parabolizing happening in at least three ways: giving thanks, blessing, and mourning. Our rural communities need all three to thrive, and giving thanks, blessing, and mourning just happen to be the bread and butter of the church—rural or otherwise.

Give thanks: Reading Psalm 14 in San Jerónimo

It was nighttime in Cuzco, Peru, and I was chatting with a young missionary.

"You know," he confided, "I'm just tired of being here. There's just so much that I don't like here. Some people talk about learning to the love the culture, but not me. I'm developing a culture hate."

He and a clutch of other young people from their denomination had been sent into the Cuzco region with the instruction to plant churches. Multiple churches. Each. Before they hit the mission field, it must have sounded like terribly thrilling work, being sent off on God's errand, forging ahead into benighted mountains with a Bible in one hand and altitude pills in the other.

But as their term wound down, dreams were fizzling. Some congregations had been started, all right, but the labor of equipping leaders and navigating personality fuzz in a foreign language—languages, really, in the plural; Spanish has never displaced Quechua up in the old Inca heartland—meant that whatever success they experienced was tempered by a sense of weariness and failure. This individual had tromped right through despair and acedia and shoveled himself a nice spot of hate—culture hate.

And why not? I mean, the bus system was fidgety (system? I didn't know there was a system). You had to wash your fruits and vegetables in chlorine water to fend off typhus and cholera and ten million nameless bacterial squiggles. The sewer kept overflowing, boiling up and around the manhole covers at the bottom of the street. So yes, it was a little frustrating for a young man reared in a place where things just *worked.*

I listened pastorally and compassionately. Really, I did. I knew exactly what he was talking about. Those things bugged me too. I could have added heaps more to the list. But our conversation made me reflect later, what about the good things? Weren't there reasons to give thanks?

It turned out that there were.

Later in the week, the Mennonite mission team gathered in our rented apartment in the San Jerónimo neighborhood on the outskirts of Cuzco. We met weekly to study, pray, and support each other. I kept insisting on singing antiphonal verses while reading the Psalms. It was a high-churchy habit I had picked up along the way, and what better than to introduce it to our new friends?

The psalm for the week was Psalm 14. Verse 1 reads:

> Fools say in their hearts, "There is no God."
>
> They are corrupt, they do abominable deeds; there is no one who does good.

Except that this antiphon rendered it differently. The text was altered and the quotation marks moved. Fools didn't just say, "There is no God." They said in the same breath, "Everyone's corrupt, no one does good."[2] They weren't just foolish to not believe in God. They were foolish to not believe in people.

I invited our little gathering to name the ways we had seen God's goodness in the culture around us. We saw goodness on the packed combi buses when young people moved out of the way so that pregnant women or the elderly could have their seat. We saw goodness in the hospitality shown to us in the churches, how they would kill and roast the fatted guinea pigs in honor of our visit. We saw goodness in weddings and baptisms and friendships and celebrations.

---

2. Isaac Everett, *The Emergent Psalter* (New York: Church Publishing, 2009), 44.

It turns out that giving thanks for what we see is the first way we parabolize our rural communities. Through giving thanks, we tell people's stories as they mean to live them. Thanksgiving is our first and most essential posture. Indeed, we can do nothing without thanksgiving. If you can't give thanks for rural communities, don't try to transform them.

Jesus placed thanksgiving at the heart of the church when he left the church a thanksgiving meal, the Eucharist (literally "thanksgiving"). Give thanks in bread. Give thanks in cup. Give thanks for God's work among us along the train of history. Just like Jesus, we take the bread, give thanks (or *bless*; the words are nearly identical), and place it in one another's hands. I'm sure it's no coincidence that before Jesus transformed the bread that would feed those hungry five-thousand-plus people, he gave thanks (John 6:11). It was small bread and small fish from a small boy, but—thanks be to God—it was much more than enough.

This is one of the ways that coming to the Lord's table forms us, bit by bit, as people of thanksgiving. The early church in Jerusalem met regularly to give thanks at the table of the Lord (Acts 2:42), and that discipline propelled them into a life of glad sharing and generosity that was attractive to their broader community (Acts 2:46-47).

There is no church without thanksgiving. This is why Paul told the Colossian church, "Whatever you do, in word or deed, do everything in the name of the Lord Jesus, giving thanks to God the Father through him" (Colossians 3:17). Thanksgiving was Paul's mantra. He gave thanks for the churches he served and with which he was connected. "I thank my God every time I remember you" (Philippians 1:3). "I thank my God through Jesus Christ for all of you" (Romans 1:8). "I give thanks to my God always for you" (1 Corinthians 1:4). "I do not cease to give thanks for you" (Ephesians 1:16). And he commanded what he practiced: "Give thanks in all circumstances; for this is the will of God in Christ Jesus for you" (1 Thessalonians 5:18).

A posture of thanksgiving is especially vital in rural communities, where we're often conditioned to see lack and loss. There are no taco trucks, no Shakespeare in the Park, no picturesque streets filled with colorful, stylish people. Bah humbug.

But giving thanks is acknowledging what is already being God-touched, what is already part of God's story. It's refusing to buy into the myth that there's nothing good going on in a place (nothing good can come out of Nazareth, can it?). The opposite of thankfulness is all too often resentfulness, and this often shows up in the way rural congregations situate themselves alongside their communities.

In the first little rural town I served, I had to stop sniffing and start giving thanks. Literally. The place sometimes had a bit of a malodor. Depending on the wind, either a humid cloud of onion-processing emissions or the sharp stink of cattle manure hung in the air. But that wasn't all there was to the town. My first couple of years, I mostly saw need, brokenness, and all the ways that it didn't measure up to pretty much everywhere else I had ever lived. We had to filter our water because of farm runoff. We had two gangs, red and blue, Norteños and Sureños. They traded gang tags, graffitiing walls, doors, and the side of the Assemblies of God church. *Mine! No, mine!* There was a decommissioned nuclear missile silo west of town, massive doors permanently hinged up and open to the sky so the Russians would know we were serious about disarmament. If you had an earnest hankering to meet some needs, this town was perfect.

I developed a perverse joy in talking about it. Once, a traveling high school choir sang in our church. Before their performance, I hopped on the charter bus and took the mic. *Behold my rundown town!* It was all done in good faith. The choir youth had come to perform and serve. They walked around town picking up litter. They played with the neighborhood kids. But I wasn't giving them the full story. Seeing our community as a basket case of shivering needs was missing the point.

I was awakened to the error of my ways by a member of our church. One summer evening as he baled hay—him driving, me riding along in the "buddy seat" of the tractor—he said with a passion that took me by surprise, "I don't want people to think we're just a sorry little town!" He was kind enough not to direct his comment to me. I was smart enough to know whom he meant it for.

It was Jesus' question to Simon the Pharisee in Luke 7:44: "Do you see this woman?" Simon saw a sinner, an outcast drenching Rabbi Jesus' holy feet in tears. That was all there, but it wasn't the full story. Jesus saw something more complex: a woman seeking God, a woman of service, a woman of faith. *Do you see this woman?*

I wasn't seeing our town because I wasn't watching. Rather, I was engaged in a self-centered kind of seeing that made sense of the town by how I ministered in it. I saw it as a town that *needed* me. I was really just seeing myself, staring into the silver-slicked pond of my own vainglorious need to be needed.

I'm sure I'm not the only one who has done this. Pastors are especially at risk, particularly if we're youngish and have adorable children, because rural congregations all too easily idealize and idolize us. "You're our savior!" a woman told a bright young pastor friend in his early days of diving into rural ministry. He was grounded enough to deflect her praise. But sometimes we fall for it, swaggering in like heroes. We bring so much to the table! So much education! We've traveled! Let me regale you with stories of sleeping on dirt floors in the Andes!

Thankfulness is the cure, in part because it takes the spotlight off us and our abilities. We give thanks for all the ways that people and the church and our communities are God-touched and God-infused. We reposition the narrative in God and God's grace. We're not the center anymore. We start to recognize the good things in our community, and they all get tossed into the narrative pot. *Do you see this town?*

A pastor skilled in the tools of transitional ministry found himself tasked to serve a deeply troubled small-town congregation. Demographics had been against it for years, and sclerotic, intermittent conflict had set in as decline accelerated. Yet as he tells the story, everybody in the community surrounding the church always said, "They have great people over there!" The pastor felt God telling him and his wife to lay down the tools of congregational transition and instead to "just see them; just see the people." He and his wife said, "Let's just be with the people."

It turned out to be an inspired move, this adopting of an appreciative posture. It led to the congregation entering a process that would lead to its closure and the donation of assets to a thriving congregation nearby, which happened to be a daughter church from another era. The congregation dissolved not in acrimony, but in thankfulness for all that God had done among them and would continue to do through their generosity.

Thankfulness is fundamentally a hopeful posture. It's believing that there's something good going on, something worthy of Christ's blood and therefore worthy also of our own. To give thanks is to ascribe value, and it turns out that we cannot serve communities that we do not value first. A friend of mine said her pastor is "Pauline," referring to Paul's tendency to highlight the positive in a church. We have to get Pauline with our rural places: "I give thanks every time I think of you."

In my own ministry, I practice this by testifying on behalf of place. I never miss an opportunity to say something good about our town and church. I tell the story as we want to live it. Sometimes this means telling our congregation's story a little slant, more aspirational than strictly factual. I'm not shy about claiming that there are challenges, but I talk about the kids ministry and the new small groups and the neighbor who just up and started coming to church. I want mine to be a thankful telling. (You can find out about the other stuff later.) You should worship with us. You should move here. Really, you should. I don't know why anyone would want to live anywhere else.

Bless: Flubbing the health fair

The little sister of thankfulness is *blessing*. Sometimes blessing and thanksgiving are the same thing, or nearly so. The Greek words are used interchangeably in the accounts of the Last Supper. In Mark and Matthew, Jesus "blessed" the bread, while in 1 Corinthians and Luke, Jesus gave thanks—though in Luke 24, at the table in Emmaus, Jesus blessed. The Greek words are almost identical.

Our words *blessing* and *benediction* derive from the Latin verb *bene dicere*, which literally means "speak the good." When we bless, we are speaking good over something, speaking good into something or someone or someplace. It's seeing the good and saying "I like": thumbs-up. But it's more than that. Blessing is also transformative. Again, the supper of the Lord. It's upon blessing that bread becomes body and cup becomes blood. It's blessing that makes Abram *Abraham*—the "father of many nations" and Sarai Sarah—the one who would become the mother of many nations (Genesis 17:4-5, 15-16 NIV). It's blessing that makes Jacob the heir to the promise (Genesis 27). God's people are the blessed people (Joshua 17:14). Blessing is part of the Levites' core job description (Deuteronomy 10:8). Blessed is Mary and blessed is the fruit of her womb (Luke 1:42). "Blessed is the one who comes in the name of the Lord" (Luke 13:35), the Christ who is blessed forever (Romans 9:5). It's blessing that forms and sustains God's people. God blesses the good into being.

So do we. If our ministry in rural places requires us first to give thanks for what is, then authentic rural ministry will also require us to speak into being that which could be, to infuse God's dream into congregations and communities. This is blessing.

The apostle Paul did this at the Areopagus in Athens (Acts 17). Although Paul was "deeply distressed to see that the city was full of idols" (v. 16), he used the Athenians' traditional worship as a way to bless them. It's a perfect case of parabolizing. Rather than throw the Jesus story on top of the Athenian story, Paul found a way to come alongside them, even admire them, saying, "I see how extremely religious you are in every way" (v. 22). He blessed the gospel into the Athenians.

Athens was hardly a rural environment. Indeed, it was the preeminent *polis*. But what Paul did reflexively as an expression of the gospel impulse is what we're called to do in the rural church. We see this in the pastoral candidating process. So often, pastoral candidates come in, take a look around, and are deeply distressed that the church is full of the idols of ingrown and neurotic family systems. Yet if we persist, every vice can lead through to virtue. It's possible for pastors to accept a call to these rural places and say, "I see how extremely committed you are to the life of your church in every way." It's possible for pastors to tell the story of the rural church as the rural church would live it. This is parabolizing as blessing. It's "bringing out the best" in the church's identity.

Find out how your church understands itself, then play on that identity. Are you the welcoming church? Then welcome the down-and-out and marginalized and outcasts. Are you the church that cares for kids? Then host the vacation Bible school and start a children's choir and hand out sack lunches in the summer. Make the story of your identity into a blessing.

The rural church—and especially pastors and leaders in the rural church—is called to embody blessing in the community. We speak a good word into our towns and rolling farmsteads.

My wife served as a health promoter among rural Hispanic populations in eastern Washington. There were plenty of challenges, including drug and alcohol abuse, obesity, and a syrupy wave of diabetes. One model of health education that had been tried in other area communities was to put on a health fair. So we gave it a shot. It goes like this: reserve the high school gym, schlep in display tables, tape posters of the food groups to the wall, and sit back and watch as the health of the community improves. We pastors were even on hand with a booth on spiritual health, right next to the firefighters with their smoke detectors. It was a lovely event involving many health professionals volunteering their time to check blood pressure and talk about proper nutrition.

Except only a couple of dozen people from the community came. It turns out that telling everyone—nicely—to eat their broccoli doesn't work.

So after that first frustrating year, my wife mopped up her tears and went back to the drawing board. She rallied her plucky band of volunteers and started asking people, "What do you want?" She grabbed folks in the grocery store, in the school, at meetings. She asked, "What sort of event would the community appreciate?" She listened.

The next year, she and the other organizers threw a Children's Day celebration. It was a health fair in all but name (give or take a couple of piñatas), but it turned out that names matter. Children's Day factors brightly into Mexican culture. It's a family event. *Dad, you'll take us to the Children's Day celebration, won't you? ¡Sí, vamos, mijo!* Health fair? Not so much.

Five hundred people came to the Children's Day event—nearly a quarter of the community, and most of the families with school-age children. Between a game of Healthy Choices Plinko and a table on fire prevention, there was a game about the importance of eating your broccoli. The pastors ditched their table, mingled, and handled the piñata.

We're called to this sort of thing. We walk through the community and say, *I see you are very religious, very sportsy, very hardworking, very welcoming, very close-knit.* And then we speak and embody the gospel in and alongside what we see. *Bene dicere.* We bless.

The church's blessing in the community involves the usual works of mercy, the sorts of things that Jesus lays out in Matthew 25. Feed the hungry and give them a cool drink, clothe the naked, welcome, visit. Later tradition would add "bury the dead."

But the vocation to bless in rural communities takes on a special urgency because of their particular historical circumstances. Rural people often live with a profound feeling of loss. They're bereft. Young people's search for education and opportunity feels like rejection.

And so, by caring for our common rural life—by working "for the good of all" (Galatians 6:10)—rural churches play a special role. They value the community by being present to it and seeking its good. I know rural pastors who drove the school bus when the district couldn't find enough drivers, who coached the high school girls' softball team, and who sat on the library board. These are all ways of embodying blessing, of taking seriously that the good of the rural church will be tied up in the good of the rural community. If we bless one, we bless the other.

Mourn: We can't shoot our way out of this one

Mourning might not sound like much of a calling, but I'm convinced that the rural church misses out on its vocation without it. We thank and we bless and we mourn. We need all three.

Jesus taught, "Blessed are those who mourn, for they will be comforted" (Matthew 5:4). He assumed that we would mourn, that a life of following him would include a hearty awareness of all that is broken and wounded in the neighborhood. If we can't mourn, it's not because we're so chipper. It's not because we've moved beyond sadness or attained inner peace. On the contrary, a lack of mourning usually arises from the inability to care. Failure to mourn is often failure to love.

It's something of a gift to mourn—the gift of having a heart that breaks for what breaks the heart of God (to paraphrase Bob Pierce, founder of World Vision, in his famous prayer). It's this gift that allows us to see what's wrong in people's lives—what's broken in the world—and mourn. A heart that can't be broken—that does not know when and how to mourn—is often a hardened heart, and that's a fearful thing.

Think of Pharaoh in the book of Exodus. He heard of the plight of the Hebrew slaves, but his heart was hardened. Pharaoh's people suffered under the plagues, but his heart was hardened. Pharaoh's own firstborn died, and that shook him long enough to allow the slaves to go free, but then his heart was again hardened. Pharaoh ultimately arrived at a point beyond compassion where the Scriptures tell us, "The Lord hardened the heart of Pharaoh" (Exodus 14:8).

Hard-heartedness congests our capacity to love rural places deeply. We start to see them as projects needing a good manager. We tinker. They're fixer-uppers, and we've got a bigger hammer. But they're not people and communities to us. We're hard-hearted, and mourning is the cure. Mourning gets some heart-skin back in the game.

We mourn the usual things. We mourn *with* our rural congregations and communities at the loss of young talent to the city, the degradation of land and water through mass confinement livestock operations, the lack of jobs, the challenge of finding an opportunity to enter farming. And we mourn *for* our rural communities: the sometimes small-mindedness, the lack of meaningful diversity, the use of creativity not to try new things but to resist them. These are tropes, but true enough in many rural places.

Mourning is certainly better than judgmentalism, the usual go-to stance for pastors. Pastors hunch over their computers, the window air conditioner buzzing fiercely behind them, brewing up a mix of impatience and judgmentalism. "The church is going to die, and they won't change!" they sputter. "Seriously? This is what they choose to fight about?" But these pastors are trapped in a vicious cycle of their own: an inability or unwillingness to suffer with and for their people and thereby earn the trust that real change requires. For pastors, a return to mourning is the essential step in learning to play ball.

In congregations, hard-heartedness takes the form of grousing about their losses. It's factionalism, with our faction being the past. "Those young mothers don't come to the women's meetings. Why not? We always did. We lined the babies up on blankets right along the wall while we met. What's their problem?"

This is not authentic mourning. It's complaining. In both iterations—pastoral and congregational—it's a form of hard-heartedness that stands over and against the messiness of life. This is what Paul warned against when he talked about the "worldly grief" that leads to death, as opposed to the "godly grief" that leads to repentance (2 Corinthians 7:9-10).

It's no wonder that Paul tied grief to repentance, because repentance is the act of turning around. It's the process of reorienting ourselves away from loss and problems and edging toward God. Godly grief leads to transformation. Worldly grief—the sort that seizes upon us in our lowest moments—leads to backbiting and hypocrisy. It chases possibilities right out the door, and the people follow.

What we need is a renewal of mourning that leads to transformation in our rural churches and communities. This would mean telling the story of loss, naming it, but then turning back to Jesus as the source of our hope. A renewal of mourning means telling a different story about our rural communities, one in which there's room for sadness but not snark, grief but not grumbling.

Our community in Washington State was pocked with gang violence. About once a year for the last three years we lived there, somebody got shot. It wasn't Chicagoland violence, but hey, we're talking about a community of only twenty-five hundred people.

Gang tags proliferated. The house by the park was guys in and out, guys with red hankies hanging out of their pockets, guys crunching energy drink cans in the front yard, guys in red caps slouching low in souped-up, banged-up cars with motors that sounded like kazoos.

What to do became the talk of the town. They shot out the window of the Warden Community Church. *What to do?* They tagged the Assemblies of God church. *What to do?* They snatched a case of cheap beer and bolted out of the corner store, the owner puffing behind them. *What to do?* They planted a bullet, almost unnoticeable, on the book return box of the public library. There it was, brass and belligerent, their little middle-finger message: *Don't even think about collecting an overdue fine from us.*

There's a stereotype that the country is filled with guys in pickup trucks with a gun rack in the rear window. Sometimes, it's true. At the lowest point, the monthly city council meeting became a brouhaha of fist-shaking, irate citizens saying things like, "I have a gun, and I know how to use it!" And why not? People *cared*—about their community, their neighbors, their own families and property. I get it.

At one meeting of the Development Council—our local version of a chamber of commerce—the conversation again turned to gang problems. It quickly reached an angry register. "What do we do?" people asked.

I felt stuck. I was committed to nonviolence as the way of Jesus. I fancied myself a third-way sort of thinker: neither killing nor capitulating, instead plotting a creative alternative. But I had no idea what to do in this situation. I knew people in the gangs—or as was more often the case, I knew people whose sons were in the gangs. At our annual community celebration, I once approached a young gang member I knew as he stood on the margins, watching the event. He was a head taller than me and beefy enough to wring my neck. But I wrenched up my courage and said, "What are you wearing red like that for? You're going to get hurt. You're going to hurt someone else. Your mother cares for you. We care for you." He grinned dangerously, shrugged, and looked away.

I prayed. I connected with a group developing a community center for youth. I refused to be driven out of the park. We played there with our sons. It was our little civilizing act of defiance, our way of saying, "You can't have this park."

There in that Development Council meeting, the conversation again turned to guns. My heart started beating hard. I raised my hand, swallowed, and said, "You know, I don't think we can shoot our way out of this one." I went on to say that things were more complicated than that, that what we were facing wasn't so much the absence of law enforcement, but of community and imagination. It wasn't my bright formulation, but Samuel Wells's description of his own community's challenges in the book *God's Companions*. Wells writes: "I learned that poverty is not primarily about money. It is about having no idea what to do and/or having no one to do it with. To the extent that our neighborhood had imagination and community, we were not poor. But without imagination and community, no money could help us."[3]

I think he's on to something with that insight. Wells was speaking from his experience working with a low-income neighborhood in the United Kingdom, but the description rings true enough in our rural communities across the United States and Canada. We so often lack the imagination to tell a different story about rural places. In the case of our eastern Washington town, community had also crumbled.

In Warden, a lot of folks were telling a cowboy story, a pioneer story, an angry story. People were telling an "us" and "them" story, a good and bad story, a story that ends with a bang! and the

---

3. Samuel Wells, *God's Companions: Reimagining Christian Ethics* (Malden, MA: Blackwell, 2006), 7.

tinkle of spent brass shells on the pavement. Maybe the story we needed to tell was a *mourning* story. Maybe we needed to mourn the wreckage of generational poverty and the tensile stress of immigration and alienation. I'm not interested in describing every offender as a victim. Turning a crime story into a pathos story only gets us so far. But I am interested in telling a *different* story, one we can't shoot our way out of. Guns make a tempting story, because they always end with an exclamation mark.

But it's more complicated than that. Mourning is one way we acknowledge that complexity. Mourning is one way we learn to tell a different story.

Assume nothing

So much of what I'm saying starts with Jesus' question, "Do you see?" Do you see this woman who washes my feet? Do you see this community? Do you see this *vida*?

I talked to Todd Jones, pastor of the Hutterthal Mennonite Church in rural Freeman, South Dakota. He's been leading his congregation in a remarkable rejuvenation. During a phone call with Jones, I asked what advice he had for rural congregations seeking renewal. He paused long enough that I thought the connection had been dropped. And then he said, "Assume nothing."

Don't assume decline. Don't assume that everyone in the community is already connected to a church. Don't assume there's nothing going on.

We often do just that. We assume there's no story and nothing to say. We assume a deprivation story, a story flattened under the narrative steamroller of the *urbs*. We've become so used to hearing the city story that we forget to tell the country story. We neglect our redemptive imagination. It's a failure to watch with Jesus. We assume the wrong things and miss the *vida*.

To assume is the great temptation. It's to fall asleep and miss what Jesus is doing in our rural places. Christ is calling us to watch. It can be hard. "The spirit indeed is willing, but the flesh is weak" (Matthew 26:41). But learning to pay attention to the story of another is learning to love.

CHAPTER 5

Pray: Learning to Pray with Chickens

Jesus took Peter, James, and John up on a mountain to pray. And as he was praying, the appearance of his face was transformed.
—Luke 9:28-29 (NLT)

I like to fancy myself a rural contemplative, which is to say that I like to walk around town trying to pay attention to Jesus. I sing when I take out the trash. I recite Scripture when I hoe weeds. I liturgize when I mow the lawn.

And I pray with chickens.

It's not that I wrestle them down and force them to endure my contemplation as if they were some sort of feathered icons. I'm not that kind of chicken-keeper. I just pray, and our little flock gathers around me on the bench, clucking, preening, scratching, pecking. I should really say that the chickens *join me* in prayer.

This is my attempt at the contemplative life, a life of praising God amid the ordinary, of attending to God right where I am and in whatever I'm doing. It's what Brother Lawrence was getting at when he talked about "the practice of the presence of God." It's Ignatius of Loyola's *ad maiorem Dei gloriam*. It's what Eugene Peterson means when he says that following Jesus is "a way of living deeply and fully with the people here and now, in the place we find ourselves."[1]

All of this is about practicing the transfigurative discipline of seeing God in and through our present moment and circumstance. It's about being attentive to the *Jesusness* of any moment. That's contemplation. No work. No asking. No talking, even. Just being alone in the quiet with Jesus. Listening to him. Jesus shows up with those chickens. We're all sitting there together on that bench.

Or something like that.

I'm convinced that rural ministry is contemplative ministry, rooted in constant prayer that pays attention to Jesus. Perhaps one of the most important gifts that rural pastors and leaders can offer the church is modeling a life with a contemplative heartbeat. We demonstrate what it looks like to take time to *be* with Jesus.

Prayer is the special grace of the rural church. We see this in the gospel story of Jesus' transfiguration, which is a lovely and potent parable of the rural church. Jesus leads his closest friends and disciples, Peter, James, and John, away from cities and the crowds and takes them up on a mountain to pray. As Jesus prays, his face is changed, and the disciples peer into the depths of the kingdom. It's a clouded, confused moment. They don't know exactly what to do. The Father speaks his will over Jesus: "This is my Son, my Chosen; listen to him!" (Luke 9:35). And then the disciples are alone with their teacher, their ears ringing with startling, holy silence.

Leaving the city to meet God was Jesus' usual pattern. Jesus sought out empty spaces early in the morning to pray (Mark 1:35). He went up mountains alone to pray (Matthew 14:23). He spent the night in the countryside in prayer (Luke 6:12). Against the press of the hungry, needy crowds, Jesus withdrew to deserted places and prayed (Luke 5:16). It's a pattern that he set at the beginning of his ministry, when the Holy Spirit "drove" him into the lonely desert for forty days of fasting and wrestling with the devil (Mark 1:12). At the end of Jesus' ministry, he again prayed

---

1. Eugene Peterson, *The Jesus Way: A Conversation on the Ways That Jesus Is the Way* (Grand Rapids: Eerdmans, 2007), 33.

outside the city, in the garden of Gethsemane (Matthew 26:36). He died on the cross outside the walls of the city (Hebrews 13:12-13), still praying (Luke 23:34, among others).

Jesus took the disciples to a rural place to pray, but their prayer in the countryside wasn't a retreat. It wasn't about finding inner peace. Their prayer was struggle. It's like the labors of Jacob, who stayed behind, alone on the far side of the river, to wrestle with God (Genesis 32:24-32). It's why the ancient desert monk Abba Agatho said, "We need to pray till our dying breath. That is the great struggle."[2]

Leaders in the early monastic movement envisioned their monasteries as special houses of prayer sustaining the global church. They left the city and tucked themselves away in rocky nooks and crannies in the desert of Egypt. They didn't head for the sticks for fear of city life. Some of them, like the well-known theologian Evagrius, had cultivated successful ecclesiastical careers (though with a bit of scandal mixed in). Their stars were rising over the high altars of the city church. They had made it big. The city was good to them. They went out into the desert not as a flight but as a vocation—to pray on behalf of the city. They had a calling, and they took it with profound seriousness. Prayer was their struggle to their dying breath.

What if the rural church were to claim a special vocation to prayer like these ancient desert prayer warriors? Writer Kathleen Norris might be onto something when she labels the faithful in the rural church "monks of the land."[3]

In some ways, it's simply the racket factor. Go outside at night in any biggish city and you'll know what I mean. The heartbeat of the city is the drubbing of wheels and the passing slips of conversation and the urgent wailing of ambulances. The countryside is quiet, and quiet—*hesychia* in Orthodox theology (see 1 Timothy 2:2)—just happens to be why the ancient monks prized the desert.

---

2. Benedicta Ward, *The Desert Fathers: Sayings of the Early Christian Monks* (New York: Penguin Classics, 2003), 130.

3. Kathleen Norris, *Dakota: A Spiritual Geography* (New York: Houghton Mifflin, 1993), 110.

So often, rural congregations suffer from a sense of lack, defining themselves on the basis of what they are *not*. They're *not* big, *not* in an ideal spot for growth, *not* chock-full of the city's creative movers and shakers. It's time to reject this narrative of scarcity and encourage the rural church to begin to see itself as the caretaker of a different sort of abundance: space for prayer. What if we were to envision the rural church as the special house of prayer sustaining the global church?

We need prayer. We need the power of prayer to fuel the church's ministry. We need prayer that transfigures our reality so that we can discern what God is up to in the neighborhood. We need to take seriously that prayer is the central work of the church, work that releases us for long and patient abiding in our rural communities and holds us in the presence of God.

The secret fire

Of course, it's not that only rural churches can pray. God is in the city too. And without prayer, nothing happens in any church. Period. In a survey of some three hundred churches that experienced turnaround in vitality and growth, writers Ed Stetzer and Mike Dodson discovered that "strategic prayer" rated among the top three factors named for church turnaround (along with renewed love for Jesus and renewed heart for service).[4] One congregation described in Stetzer and Dodson's book organized "prayer labs"—worship services dedicated to prayer for their community, as well as twenty-four-hour prayer vigils held twice a year.[5]

This rings true to what I discovered in interviews with pastors of thriving rural congregations. Prayer factored highly in their accounts of congregational flourishing. One pastor named the importance of prayer walks around and through his community. Another spoke of three women who met faithfully every Saturday morning at seven o'clock to lift up the church in prayer.

---

4. Ed Stetzer and Mike Dodson, *Comeback Churches: How 300 Churches Turned around and Yours Can Too* (Nashville: B & H Publishing, 2007), 68.

5. Ibid., 60.

Prayer is the antidote to the washed-out, hopeless feeling that many rural congregations face. All too often, rural churches feel stuck, feel that they can't find their way forward, while newer, suburban models of church run rings around them. Prayer changes that dynamic. Prayer empowers, not least because it has a potential to restore our sense of self and agency. Prayer places us rightways before God. Prayer is our secret fire.

Our first months in Warden, Washington, were a little rough in a way that either confirmed or questioned our calling to the town. I crashed and corrugated our car when another driver blasted through a stop sign. I fell terribly sick. And the windstorm of the century knocked down the three massive pines growing along our house. Two fell beside the house. The third fell on it. Thankfully, it only cracked the overhanging roof. After a tense night camping out in our basement, we were grateful to emerge and not find a tree trunk in our living room.

After the downed trees had been sawed and pushed and piled, we had a mountain of limbs on the downslope of the parsonage lawn. The trunks were too big to haul off, and we were concerned that they would attract critters and insects. The consensus was to burn them. I called the local fire marshal.

"Well," he said after he heard our plan, "I can't tell you to do it. But I can tell you to be careful if you do."

That settled it. The fire would be our open secret. We would burn the logs. Carefully.

Of course, *careful* is a relative term. For us, it meant that we stretched some garden hoses down the hill—just in case—and threw a match under the logs. The dry brush caught surprisingly fast, flaring in a blazing heartbeat. Soon the fire was so hot and imposing that we couldn't quiet it with our hoses. It was like the furnace out of the book of Daniel, seven times hotter than what we anticipated. If we got any closer, we would have gone up like camp marshmallows. The flames swallowed the pile. They toasted a nearby tree. The fire marshal made a slow drive-by in his red pickup to make sure that all was well. It wasn't, but we tried to look calm, crouching behind scraps of plywood that we used like shields to protect ourselves from the heat while sniping at the fire with squirts from our inadequate hoses. It's all under control. Nothing to see here.

A day later, the logs and the open flame were gone, but if you kicked at the ash, you could find smoldering specks of ember, lines of grinning flame, crackling, charred branches. There it was, the secret fire.

Thomas Merton, the famous monk from the Abbey of Gethsemani in Kentucky, wrote in a poem that "the whole world is secretly on fire."[6] His experience of prayer was an encounter with the God who is a "consuming fire" (Hebrews 12:29). Merton discovered the love of God smoldering beneath reality. The world looks ordinary enough, but kick at it in prayer and you find secret fire.

Our rural congregations need to be places of secret fire. Beneath preaching sermons and leading vacation Bible school and schlepping groceries at the food pantry must be the sustaining power of prayer: always burning, always smoldering, always rising like incense before the throne of God (Revelation 5:8).

Transfigurative prayer: Apocalypse in the sticks

The gospels tell us that while Jesus prayed, "the appearance of his face changed, and his clothes became dazzling white" (Luke 9:29). He was transfigured. In the Greek, Matthew says he was "metamorphosized" (17:2)—a word like the one we use to describe tadpoles becoming froglets.

By prayer, the disciples saw through a superficial reading of their context and caught a vision of Jesus. They didn't see an alternative reality, but Reality—the Really Real. The God of the universe was present and at work in Jesus, and Jesus was present and at work among them in a way that they couldn't wrap their heads or hands or words around. Their strategies fell flat. Peter didn't know what he was doing or saying (Luke 9:33).

6. Thomas Merton, "In Silence," in *American Religious Poems: An Anthology*, ed. Harold Bloom and Jesse Zuba (New York: The Library of America, 2006), 346.

We find ourselves in a similar position, perplexed by the structural challenges of rural communities. But through prayer we do the transfigurative work of discernment.

Rural communities are characterized by a certain kind of stability—what some experience as inertia: multigenerational business relationships, friendships, and marriages. And feuds. Many aspects of rural life are fixed and immovable. It's a complicated relational landscape that takes years to understand, let alone traverse. *How are you related again?* I had never heard of "double first cousins" until we moved to rural Kansas.

Rural communities have *structure*. Just as soil possesses a structure, bound together by bacteria, fungus, and plant roots with the potential to create a nutrient-cycling, erosion-resisting matrix, so too do rural communities. Strands of trust hold people together like mycelium. It's a cheerful arrangement that cycles social capital and keeps rural communities from eroding.

Rural communities also have rules. This is hardly unique to rural places. But what makes the countryside different is the endurance and prevalence of the rules. In fact, as sociologists Patrick Carr and Maria Kefalas have discovered, in many small Midwestern towns, folks take a kind of comfort from "being surrounded by people who understand the rules of local life instinctively because they are the direct descendants of the people who created these standards."[7]

Because cities are composed of sets of overlapping communities, the rules don't play as big a role. You might break the rules of one community, but that won't mean the end of your social life. People move in multiple circles, and no one circle dominates the city.

The rules are really about lines of predictable behavior and the trust that comes with them. People have an understanding of what's expected of them, and when they follow through, others can join forces with them. It works great.

Until it doesn't.

---

7. Patrick Carr and Maria Kefalas, *Hollowing Out the Middle: The Rural Brain Drain and What It Means for America* (Boston: Beacon Press, 2009), 16.

It can be as small as not knowing which school door is open during summer break (hint: it's not the one that's open during the school year). There's no sign, but who needs a sign? Everyone and their grandparents know which door to use. Only rank outsiders would be so obtuse as to rattle them all and rap on the windows for help.

One pastor told me how an elderly woman in his congregation caught him by the arm one morning. "Pastor, can I give you a piece of advice?" she asked. "Don't ever speak bad about anybody in this community, because they're all related." It's good advice, a rule aimed at fostering good relationships. But the shadow side of this fishbowl courtesy is a circumspection that sometimes lacks the fiber to confront bad behavior.

As outsiders, pastors fit into a premade social slot within the community. We're often allowed to enter into privileged spaces of birth, death, and calamity. However, when pastors get themselves in trouble in rural churches and communities, it's often because they've failed to recognize and respect the structure.

Take church pews. Just try to move them or (gasp!) *remove* them, and you'll find yourself in hot water. The sacred geography of the sanctuary mirrors the structure of the congregation. As Carl Dudley has pointed out, people are sitting alongside the memories of those who have passed on or moved on.[8] Removing a church pew harms those invisible memories and damages a structure that transcends the grave.

A similar mentality operates in the broader community. There are boundaries that must be respected, not as an exercise in rigidity, but because to do so is a sign of good neighborliness. In one congregation I know, the newly appointed mission committee proposed sending invitational postcards to every home in the church's zip code as part of a broader campaign to extend a fresh invitation in the community. However, their church council warned them off, sensing that the mailing would be perceived by those in other

---

8. Carl S. Dudley, *Effective Small Churches in the Twenty-First Century*, rev. ed. (Nashville: Abingdon, 1978, 2003), 41.

congregations as an attempt to steal sheep from their churches. It wasn't the kind of thing good neighbors would do.

The rules of rural community can be bent, but they can't easily be changed, least of all by a church vote. The rules sustain community and promote trust, and breaking them damages pastors' and leaders' capacity to function and creates an unhealthy disequilibrium in the system.

In this environment, pastors and leaders won't be able to find their way by strategy and smarts, picking their moves as in a good game of checkers. Strategy rearranges the elements of what *is*. Transfigurative discernment sees ways that God is present and at work beyond our own clever planning and prays its way into those realities.

Strategy is a temptation, and it will come at us on subtle tiptoe. There will be no whiff of sulfur, no spatter of diabolical brimstone, no click of cloven feet. The temptation won't seem all that bad. We'll think that if we can just hire the right people, all will be well. We'll believe that a new program will save us. We'll imagine that our "problem" is that we don't have enough young families with children.

But these are deadly temptations. I'm convinced that the church needs less strategy and more prayer.[9] On the one hand, strategy—in the sense of thoughtful intentionality—is vital. But strategy as reliance on human programing and initiatives is deadly. In my experience in small-town ministry, it just doesn't work. Life in the church is more complicated than our strategies can get a handle on. There are too many things beyond our control, things happening behind the scenes that can only be touched by God's Spirit and prayer.

The work of the rural church is transfigurative because it begins with looking beyond the surface and structure to see Jesus. Where's he at? What's he doing? That kind of seeing is *apocalyptic*.

Apocalypse is a word commonly associated with the sinister: gas masks, nuclear weapons, and zombies. But in the New Testament, apocalypse simply means "unveiling." It's what John sees

9. More on strategy in chapter 6.

in *the* Apocalypse—the Book of Revelation—when Jesus unveils through symbolic figures what's really going on behind the world scene. The dragon may seem invincible, but in fact the Lamb wins. Bank on it. Jesus' transfiguration was a local apocalypse, the pulling back of the gauzy-thin curtain that passes for reality to catch a glimpse of Jesus' true identity and work.

Seeing like this requires the work of discerning prayer. It's learning to operate in God's structure and play by God's rules. We need prayer that unfolds into transfiguration, that finds ways in and through the structure and rules of our communities. It's seeing God as the One who has to make many of our most urgent tasks possible—we can't do it by our own devices.

Sometimes there will be a supernatural element. In the early 1950s, Mennonites in Paraguay, many of whom had settled in South America less than a decade earlier after fleeing war and displacement in Europe, longed to address poverty and poor healthcare in their new country. A plan developed to start a small hospital aimed at treating leprosy (Hansen's disease)—an illness with profound social consequences, especially among poor and indigenous folks already marginalized in so many other ways. The question was where to locate the hospital. Most Mennonites lived in rural colonies outside the capital, far from the populations most in need of treatment.

And then Mennonite Central Committee service worker C. J. Dyck had a dream.[10] In it, he saw a green, hilly stretch of land perfect for both a hospital and grazing cattle. A short time later, while traveling the roads outside Asunción, around the 81- kilometer marker, Dyck was surprised to find himself looking at the hill he had seen in his dream. It was for sale, and the land was quickly purchased—along with a herd of three hundred cattle intended to support the hospital. The Mennonite Hospital Km 81 was born, and it has since expanded its purview to include treatment of tuberculosis and HIV/AIDS.

---

10. Edgar Stoesz, *Like a Mustard Seed: Mennonites in Paraguay* (Herald Press: Scottdale, PA, 2008), 237–38.

I've experienced this sort of transfigurative discernment. Once, while praying for a young couple in need whom I had recently met, I heard voices outside my window. I stood to look and saw them passing by right at that moment. I hopped off my couch and caught up with them on the sidewalk. A short while later, we ended up back in my office. Through our ensuing conversation, I was able to help them out with a material need and talk through some of their struggles.

But most of the time, prayerful discernment relies on the much more mundane spiritual gift of wisdom. It comes through abiding attentiveness to God in prayer. We listen to the beloved Son, and his will and ways come upon us bit by bit.

Once, after I had talked through a decision of great importance that I had made, an elder in the church asked me, "How did you know?" I responded with something suitably pious. But what I really wanted to tell him was that I didn't *know* anything. I had returned to the conundrum multiple times and worked it like bread dough. I had sat with it and talked to others I trusted and ultimately mustered up my thimbleful of God-formed wisdom to come to a decision. I discerned. There's no other way.

Forget knowing. We're called to enter the cloud and do the transfigurative work of discernment. It's deep, prayerful seeing, our apocalypse in the sticks.

Coworkers with Christ: Watching the sweat pool in our belly buttons

According to legend, Isidore the Laborer, patron saint of agriculture, day laborers, and farmers, was able to dedicate substantial portions of his life to prayer and attending worship because when he did go out to work in the fields, God would occasionally supply angelic helpers and oxen to plow beside him.[11] God was at work through his prayers, multiplying his effort. Isidore didn't have to do it all by his own hand. It's something like what Paul was getting

11. Daniel Stewart, "An Everyman Saint: St. Isidore the Farmer," Catholic Exchange, May 15, 2014, http://catholicexchange.com/isidore-the-farmer-everyman-saint

at when he told the Corinthian church that he was a "co-worker in God's service" (1 Corinthians 3:9 NIV).

Nowhere is this more the case than in the rural church. I'm convinced that prayer is the central work of the rural church. Especially in smaller congregations, there aren't myriad volunteers, staff, and programs to be overseen. We have the luxury of time for prayer. I, for one, relish it. I take a day each week to fast and pray. I do other things on that day, but my focus is prayer. I spend significant time each morning in prayer. I pause in the afternoon, often in the cool of our darkened sanctuary, to pray.

Once, in the dead of winter, I was praying. A young man with the boiler-inspection service stopped by. I pointed the way to the boiler and got back to my prayer work. On his way out, he stopped by my office. "So," he said. "Nothing going on today, huh?"

"Some days are busier than others," I said. "Today, I pray."

He shrugged. "I guess prayer is something."

Prayer is indeed something. Sure, it may just be the marginally articulate way that I justify holing up in my office. Yet I'm convinced that prayer is key to moving the church forward. Prayer is what makes ministry something more. It makes it *ministry*. Without prayer, pastors and church leaders may be managers and counselors and public speakers, doing tasks and tasks in an unending series, one thing after another, just pushing paper. But with a vision of ministry where work and prayer meld seamlessly together, we become something different: people of destiny even, freed from the grind. We're no paper pushers. God sends teams of angelic oxen to plow alongside us. This isn't to give up on vision and elbow grease. Rather, it's seeing prayer as an essential component of vision and elbow grease.

Ministry is always going to be a puzzle for the world. The world will always imagine the church to be a civic organization, one in which the pastor's job is to maintain the good order and proper functioning of said organization—sort of a club secretary engaged in overpaid, light clerical (in the derivative sense of the word) duty. The world will always be more impressed by light shows and bass thump than it will by humility and prayer and the way of the cross.

The reality is that without prayer, we cannot flourish as coworkers with Christ. Without prayer, we're just workers. Without prayer, wrote the Orthodox saint Hesychios the Priest, "we merely hunt after earthly things."[12] This will never do. It doesn't accomplish what God is about in the neighborhood. And it's not satisfying. For ministry to matter and hold true to the calling of the Good Shepherd, it has to be less a job and more a way of life. Authentic ministry is a kind of presence—to God, to the church, and to the community. This requires prayer.

My point is simple: we need to take seriously that prayer is work—not a cop-out, not thumb twiddling, but the essential work of rural ministry—and then throw our best time and discipline and energy into it. Do the work of prayer.

And prayer is not one work among others. It's the singular work that permeates and sustains all that we do. In the teaching of the Catholic Church, it's "the only occupation: that of loving God, which animates and transfigures every action in Christ Jesus."[13]

Author and gardener Fred Bahnson writes of his experience in the Mepkin Abbey in rural South Carolina. Meditating on the twinned monastic ideals of *ora et labora*—pray and work—Bahnson claims that "among these men, prayer was itself a form of labor, and difficult labor at that. It is prayer that keeps the world from spinning off its axis."[14]

I don't know if I can claim to have kept the world from spinning off its axis, but I have prayed my way through some pretty rough spots in rural ministry. Stuff happens. People happen. There was that apologetic phone call after everything had been shaken down and shaken up. *Lord, have mercy!* And the problem just disappeared. There were the immigration papers—*Just one more step, just one more thing, even though I don't have it all. But*

12. St. Nikodimos of the Holy Mountain and St. Makarios of Corinth, comp., *The Philokalia: The Complete Text*, trans. and ed. G. E. H. Palmer, Philip Sherrard, and Kallistos Ware (London: Faber and Faber, 1979), 194.

13. U.S. Catholic Church, *Catechism of the Catholic Church*, 2nd ed. (New York: Doubleday, 1995), 703.

14. Fred Bahnson, *Soil and Sacrament: A Spiritual Memoir of Food and Faith* (New York: Simon and Schuster, 2013), 30.

wait, I do! There was the disagreement and the hard conversation and the open space of possibility that followed. I prayed my way through it all. Thanks be to God.

Ministry is prayer territory. We can't plan for a lot of the most important events in ministry. We can't heal the deepest wounds. Like the apostles on Mount Tabor, we cannot wrap our heads or hands or words around the most important work. Through prayer, we bring the resources of God's power into the complicated structure of rural life. Ours is a call to become coworkers with Christ. It's *ora et labora*: pray and work.

I think that the prayerful work required in the rural church can be especially suited to folks on the introverted end of the personality spectrum. After all, rural ministry affords much time alone, allowing introverts the space to bring to bear their special gifts of reflection and vision. Adam McHugh, in his book *Introverts in the Church: Finding Our Place in an Extroverted Culture*, writes that "introverts are often drawn to [contemplative] spirituality, as it involves a quieter, more reflective lifestyle."[15] McHugh structures his day to maximize his giftings as an introvert, with generous dollops of silence and time alone.[16]

Extroverts may be challenged by small-town pacing. Rural ministry doesn't conform to the jaunty, charismatic ideal of leadership held in many suburban churches, with their bustling campuses and legions of staff, coffee cups in hand around the foosball table.

A young summer intern traveled out to a rural congregation located in the middle of wheat fields. The congregation had pulled a travel trailer into the church yard for him to live in during his internship. It was a gracious act. But they forgot the air conditioner.

"I wonder what he did all summer," said a friend upon hearing about the experience. "He probably just sat in that trailer, watching the sweat pool in his belly button."

He may indeed have been watching the sweat pool in his belly button. But I bet he was doing a whole lot more than that. I bet he

15. Adam S. McHugh, *Introverts in the Church: Finding Our Place in an Extroverted Culture* (Downers Grove, IL: InterVarsity Press, 2009), 70.

16. Ibid., 80–81.

was calling on the church's elderly, visiting the sick, diving into the Bible, stalking a sermon into the wee hours of Saturday night. I bet he was praying—a perfect internship in rural ministry.

Prayerful patience: Doing cloud work

Peter offered to build three shelters, or tabernacles, on Mount Tabor, one each for Jesus, Elijah, and Moses. It seemed sensible enough: honor the men, preserve the moment, harken back to the wilderness wanderings of the Israelites. That's plenty of work for anyone. But Luke tells us that he did not know what he was saying (Luke 9:33). Instead of the certainty of work that they could take hold of with their hands, the apostles needed to enter the uncertain cloud of prayer with Jesus. They forgot that Jesus didn't take them up the mountain to build, but to pray.

Entering the cloud requires patience. In the church, we so often favor the concrete work before us rather than the cloud work of moving forward in prayer. No doubt this is why church building projects become popular when congregations lose their bearings. Building projects are a way to transmute adaptive challenges (How do we grow? What's our calling?) into something tangible, something that can be broken down into a checklist. They're a way to turn the uncertain cloud into something concrete—literally.

The patience required in the rural church is an expression of faith in the face of uncertainty. We don't know where our congregations and communities are headed. There's risk and doubt. But in the cloud, we cling to Jesus and follow the command of the Father: "This is my Son, my Chosen; listen to him!" (Luke 9:35). We pray our way through.

Here's where prayer becomes a form of abiding. It's praying in place—and for people in a place—long enough that transformation happens. It requires us to play a long game. Think about it. What worth doing can be completed in our lifetimes, let alone the span of a pastor's tenure? Pastors are mayflies in so many congregations. They sparkle in for a few days and then are gone in the blink of an eye. It takes at least five years for the church to begin to trust that we're solid, that we won't disappear at the first hint of trouble.

All too often, pastors and church leaders have little patience for the kinds of work required in rural congregations. It takes time. Agricultural rhythms are sometimes cited. Supposedly, rural congregations develop an ethos of risk aversion due to some combination of the wisdom of the land and backwoods stubbornness. According to this interpretation, rural communities hold a cyclical vision, rooted in the plant-harvest, rain-sun, boom-bust cycles of agriculture. Wheat prices rise and fall. Rain comes and goes. We better just hold steady. Hang on to those pews.

But the reality is that few rural congregations are actually rooted in agriculture. True, agriculture factors into the construction of a rural mentality. But only a scant 6 percent of residents in rural communities are directly employed in agriculture.[17] Rural churches are made up of similar percentages of teachers and factory workers and truck drivers, and each job moves to its own rhythm.

Likewise, the city mouse, country mouse vision of rural communities imagines them as "sleepy" or "slow." Supposedly, things happen at a different pace out here. It can seem true enough. A traffic jam means waiting for a grain truck to pull into the elevator. But the reality is probably less one of pacing and more one of brute movement. Ten lanes of traffic give the impression that things are moving faster, as opposed to two. Perhaps everyone's moving equally fast; there's just more people moving in the city.

Indeed, social psychologist Robert Levine, writing on how different societies, and even different cities within those societies, experience time, notes: "The greater the variety, the more rapidly time seems to move."[18] Could it be that the greater variety (of people, of vehicles, of stores, of restaurants) found in the city leads us to believe that things are moving faster?

Observing the hours that people work and the level of community involvement they engage in doesn't suggest small-town

---

17. U.S. Department of Agriculture, "Rural Employment and Unemployment," USDA Economic Research Service, last modified November 17, 2016, https://www.ers.usda.gov/topics/rural-economy-population/employment-education/rural-employment-and-unemployment/.

18. Robert Levine, *A Geography of Time: The Temporal Misadventures of a Social Psychologist* (New York: Basic Books, 1997), 44.

slowness to me. As far as speed goes, I suspect rural congregations are holding their own. In any case, I'm not so sure the brutal pace of modern life is something to emulate.

In my mind, the real rhythm of rural communities and congregations is not so much agricultural or slow as it is communitarian. The cycles of high school sports events, school, town festivals, fairs, and church meetings sustain the communitarian structure of rural communities. It's got a beat to it. It's got a rural groove.

Of course, even in small towns, there are multiple rhythms going on. There's no one drummer or one beat. But it's not the cacophonous rhythm of the city.

In our congregation, June is wheat harvest. July and August are vacation months: expect attendance to be down. We start new programs or classes in September, when the air just begins to crispen with autumn and the kids head back to school. Be ready for the Christmas Eve service. Everyone comes back as families get together. Make sure it's a bang-up event.

When we move along with the rhythms of community and congregation, we build trust. By valuing the local time signature, we're valuing the local people. We're declaring with our participation and presence that the things they do, and the time they do them in, matter. This takes patience.

It's no accident that Jesus often spoke of the kingdom of God with metaphors of slow development. The kingdom is the germinating mustard seed in the field (Matthew 13:31). It's yeast slowly lofting the bread (Luke 13:21). Kingdom work is process work. It's patient prayer work. I've been slow to learn this.

Several years ago, we sidled up to a new family on the sidelines of a kids' soccer game. Our sons were both on the same team, so we had a natural conversation starter. Over the next two years, we got to know the family bit by bit, conversation by conversation—at the farmers' market, over garden talk, through the bleacher seat rhythm of soccer, football, basketball, baseball. We prayed. Nothing frenzied or focused, just our usual prayers blessing and interceding on their behalf.

And then one Saturday morning, the mom called up wanting to talk to my wife about life. In the conversation that unfolded over the next several weeks, they decided to launch a women's Bible study together with another woman. Our new friend revealed that she felt God had been working on her to deal with some stuff in her life, and she felt my wife could help hold her accountable to the changes she wanted to make.

In my mind, the source of this movement was clear: prayer. That was our secret fire. Two years is a painfully long time to wait, but it's clear to me that in this situation, faithfulness meant patience. There was no way we could have talked her into a Bible study any earlier. The fruitful conversations came about in the context of a relationship that had eased its way into trust, and we had prayed our way into that trust.

Patient prayer believes that God is at work. It does not mistake slow growth for lack of growth. Patient prayer trusts in God's timing. It does not "lose hope in God's mercy."[19]

Patience is not so much merely waiting as it is knowing when to act. At times, patience can also require us to move quickly, to recognize that a "door for the word" (Colossians 4:3) has opened and that we must walk through it. Now.

It was like that with one of our neighbors. We knew his wife, his grandkids, his daughter, and his cats—but we didn't know him. We prayed for them all (not so much the cats), and after a couple of years, I got the inkling from his wife that our neighbor might want to talk. That wanting to talk part is still fuzzy, because she didn't just up and say it. She and I had a series of texts and conversations that intimated her husband might want to connect with me. Or something like that.

Then, on a chilly day before Christmas, I found myself sliding open the door on their back porch, stepping over a cat, and sitting down at the kitchen table as I met our longtime but new-to-us neighbor.

---

19. Timothy Fry and Timothy Horner, trans., *The Rule of St. Benedict in English* (Collegeville, MN: Liturgical Press, 1981), 29.

"Pastor," he said, "something's missing in my life, and I think it's Christian community."

"Yeah!" I said. That was easy.

We've been walking together ever since, as he and his wife became church members and a vital part of our Christian community.

This is patience work. It's entering the cloud in prayer, even though we don't know where exactly we're headed or how long it will take to get there.

Contemplative prayer: Learning to pray with chickens

In the rural church, we need to *do* less and *be* more.

The transfiguration teaches us this. Jesus took the disciples up the mountain to pray. The disciples were in a hurry to launch a tabernacle building project—to do the Lord's work—but they needed to slow down and learn to simply be present with Jesus in prayer.

Being present with Jesus in prayer may be the most important thing we do in the rural church. We will always be tempted to build holy tabernacles on the mountain rather than listen, but like Peter, we don't know what we're doing. Unless everything we do unfolds from a basic commitment to meet Christ in prayer, our ministries will miss the mark.

The sort of prayer I have in mind is traditionally called "contemplative prayer." *Contemplare* is Latin for "observe" or "be attentive to." In contemplative prayer, we're observant of and attentive to God's presence. Our minds descend into our hearts. The Russian Orthodox saint Theophan the Recluse writes that we stand "before God, in an opening of the heart to Him in reverence and love."[20] We bring Jesus to mind and focus on him. We are "in Christ" as Paul so often speaks in his letters—"alive to God in Christ Jesus" (Romans 6:11). In contemplative prayer, we abide in Jesus as a branch in a vine (John 15:4-5).

We pray, attentive to Jesus. If a few chickens happen to sit in on our prayers, well then, thanks be to God.

---

20. Timothy Ware, ed., *The Art of Prayer: An Orthodox Anthology*, comp. Igumen Chariton of Valamo, trans. E. Kadloubovsky and Elizabeth Palmer (London: Faber and Faber, 1966), 72.

It's not that we get jazzed up by prayer so that we can go do something else—no doubt something social justice-y and urgent. We don't meet Jesus as a way to improve our effectiveness at meeting our neighbors in evangelism. It's meeting Jesus as the core of what we do—and what we're calling others to. Don't build tabernacles, Peter. *Be* the tabernacle!

This is the special grace of the rural church: we can pray out here. That broad, expansive sky is an open window to God in the cathedral of the world. In our moment of spiritual rootlessness, this is a grace we can offer the world. It's one more reason why globalizing, urbanizing Christianity needs the rural church. Maybe our rural churches can become hotbeds of prayer. Maybe this is our *thing*. We pray. With chickens.

Sometimes, when I walk out at night to lock my roosting flock into their coop, I stand looking up into the dark sky. There are no high-rises to block my view, no din of ambulances, no industrial piston hiss and factory clank. It's just me and God and a couple of chickens. I stretch my hands upward to embrace the unembraceable God. I breathe. I pray. And the world is transfigured, inch by inch.

CHAPTER 6

Grow: Weirding the Axes

You must worship Christ as Lord of your life. And if someone asks you about your hope as a believer, always be ready to explain it. But do this in a gentle and respectful way.
—1 Peter 3:15-16 (NLT)

Can the rural church grow?

In a lot of ways, the question is not can it grow, but where is it growing? Rural congregations *are* growing in many communities. This may come as a surprise, since the dominant narrative, as we saw in chapter 1, is of rural decline. Farms got big and populations got small, we explain. The kids moved to the suburbs. Thus our churches are empty. Blame it on the twelve-row combine.

The decline of the rural population is an old concern. One Missouri farmer who responded to a survey put out by Theodore Roosevelt's Country Life Commission, the results of which were reported to Congress in 1909, wrote that it was hard to find enough help on the farm. Although he and his wife had eleven living children, when asked if the "supply of farm labor in your neighborhood [is] satisfactory," the farmer responded: "No; because the people have gone out of the baby business."[1]

1. *Report of the Country Life Commission* (Washington: Government Printing Office, 1909), 10.

But the reality is that rural population shifts have been uneven, and while some communities have experienced decline or plateau, others have held their own or even grown.

Many heartland communities have not experienced the population decline that is said to have accompanied mechanized farming. Church conference and congregational leaders have long employed a narrative of rural decline due to mechanized agriculture as a shorthand for explaining why congregations have bottomed out. However, looking at the data, we can see that it's simply not the case that most of our rural communities have declined. On the contrary: they've grown. Our alibi won't hold.

For example, population data for some communities that are heavily Mennonite, the tradition to which I belong, shows steady growth in the century between 1910 and 2010.[2] My own Moundridge grew from 626 people to 1,737. Hesston, Kansas, home to Hesston College and multiple thriving industries, grew a striking 605 percent—graduating along the way from the "rural" designation to the U.S. Census Bureau's "urban cluster" category.

A similar story plays out in other Mennonite heartlands. Mountain Lake, Minnesota: 95 percent growth. Henderson, Nebraska: 154 percent growth. Kalona, Iowa: 407 percent growth. Arthur, Illinois: 88 percent growth. Shipshewana, Indiana: 165 percent growth.

Yet despite this impressive population growth, many historic congregations in the heartlands, Mennonite and others, have disappeared or experienced a steep drop in membership. Many counties and communities that have held steady population-wise have declined congregation-wise. An article in the *Des Moines Register* found folks in one small town were more likely to slide into convenience store benches than into church pews on Sunday mornings.[3] Clearly, whatever is happening in rural churches is

---

2. Data for this and the following statistics based on 1910 and 2010 U.S. census figures.

3. Mike Kilen, "Why Fewer Iowans Are Going to Church," *Des Moines Register*, October 23, 2015, http://www.desmoinesregister.com/story/news/2015/10/23/christian-churches-face-decline-rural-iowa/73993340/.

more complicated than simply church population tracking community population.

What do we make of this? Apart from making rural congregations feel even more guilty about being on the wrong end of the population slope, the facts compel us to complicate our story. Something is going on that can't be explained by sheer population trends.

Growth is possible in rural congregations. Taking our cue from the apostle's advice in 1 Peter 3:15-16, we can begin to rethink how we measure success in the rural church and reclaim the ancient Christian practices of relating and listening people into the kingdom. Along the way, we'll discover that the growth of the church is ultimately rooted in our own growth as we become more authentically ourselves in Christ.

Time to get weird: Finding a new way to measure growth

We need to complicate our understanding of growth and what it takes to achieve growth in rural congregations. We need new metrics to measure our work. It's time to get weird.

The word *weird* describes things that don't jive with the norm—people and situations that are a little off-kilter. Weird is a blizzard in May and adding tomatoes to the fruit salad and putting pickles on peanut butter and jelly sandwiches. That's weird. Weird is anything that strays from our definition of normal.

But the word *weird* comes from an ancient Germanic word, and before it came to mean "uncanny," weird meant "to turn, bend." "Weirding" is changing the direction of something from the expected line. In that definition, bending a fence or metal rod or tree trunk makes it weird. The object strays from the usual form.

I think it's time we got a little weird with how we measure growth in the rural church. We need to bend away from the usual graphs, away from growth over time plotted out along axis A and axis B. We need new *axes*, the plural of *axis*: weirded axes, axes that bend, curve, and stretch our graph and measure success in our churches by more than merely how full the sanctuary is. In fact, if we use the word *success* at all, we'll need to redefine it.

This may be the first thing we should take to heart about rural congregations—success should be measured along a multi-axis scale, one that takes into account all the ways that congregations faithfully love God and neighbor and inhabit their communities. Pastor and author Tim Suttle puts it this way in his book *Shrink: Faithful Ministry in a Church-Growth Culture*: "Success is the kind of metric we simply don't know how to handle. It's above our pay grade."[4]

Inevitably, whenever we talk about success, we come back to numbers. We scan the sanctuary for new faces, and our hearts sink if it's the same old, same old. Just the usuals. We end up nodding to what Eugene Peterson calls "King Number." In his book *Christ Plays in Ten Thousand Places*, Peterson writes, "How has it come to pass that after twenty centuries of rejection, North American Christians assume that acclaim by numbers is a certificate of divine approval? The significance of the church has never been in King Number."[5]

But what if we began to plot what God is doing among us along the axis of prayer, the axis of cruciformity, the axis of love of God and neighbor, the axis of neighborly abiding? How might those axes change our assessment of rural congregations? We'll have to learn to look for the ways that our congregations are growing in goodness and beauty, faithfulness and hope. Are we becoming more Christlike? These might be our new metrics for growth.

Yet what I'm suggesting is more than simply looking for refined growth metrics. Weirding the axes gets at a deeper question. We're challenging whether the fundamental reality of the church can be measured in the usual ways: by counting heads and checking the bottom line of the budget. The question is this: What is the norm?

Somewhere along the line, we began to use the world's axes to measure the church's growth. We've gone about it all wrong. The ways we've measured growth in the past have missed the mark.

---

4. Tim Suttle, *Shrink: Faithful Ministry in a Church-Growth Culture* (Grand Rapids: Zondervan, 2014), 41.

5. Eugene Peterson, *Christ Plays in Ten Thousand Places: A Conversation in Spiritual Theology* (Grand Rapids: Eerdmans, 2005), 288.

You see, the old metrics are the problem. They're actually what's weird. Anything we do now to redefine how growth is measured is simply getting us back to the true norm found in Christ.

And yet, while I'm convinced that we need fresh metrics for measuring the growth of our rural congregations, I also think we need to get serious about not baptizing our current no-growth malaise and calling it good. I'm convinced we can do better.

Spending all you have without getting better

Our problem is not demographic, so neither is our solution. We do not need to pine for a nostalgic vision of the past when the countryside was filled with farm families who had bushels of children. Remember when? They all went to church, every time the doors were open.

Like most churches in our rapidly de-Christianizing age, rural congregations have suffered. We perform more funerals than baptisms. The anxiety of decline has given birth to a cottage industry of turnaround: books, conferences, and techniques meant to stem the tide and reenergize the base. It's a whole lot of strategy.

Not all of it's bad. But the products of the turnaround-industrial complex have one thing in common: the belief that we can do something about our situation if only we hone our strategy.

But strategy won't get us where we need to go.

The challenges to growth that face the rural church cannot be fixed by simply importing church growth strategies from the suburbs. Like the woman in the gospels who had suffered hemorrhages for twelve years, the rural church has "endured much under many physicians, and had spent all that she had; and she was no better, but rather grew worse" (Mark 5:26).

Indeed, much that afflicts the rural church is bigger and more intractable than what we can fix through strategy. I interviewed some dozen pastors of thriving rural congregations for this chapter, and one recurring response to my questions about their strategies for turnaround—their "secret sauce" for growth—was silence. They didn't really *do* anything. There was no strategy. It just happened.

Of course, church growth doesn't just happen. At the risk of sounding glibly pious: God does it. God blows through congregations and stirs people up and sends them out. God taps new lives and loves them right into the body. These realities are bigger than strategy and can only be touched by the Spirit and by prayer. "I've got no church revitalization stories that don't start with prayer," said Brad Thie, director the Thriving Rural Communities Initiative at Duke Divinity School, when I asked him about growth among rural congregations. "I've got none. Zero. There comes a time when churches reach the end of the rope, and they just say, 'God, we need you.'"

Among the pastors I interviewed, there was another commonality. In all their congregations, they sought to get back to basics, which is to say, Jesus. They made Jesus the center of their lives and teaching. They lived the gospel and shared the gospel.

True, living and sharing the gospel is a kind of strategy. It is doing something. But like prayer, this is the Strategy of strategies. Or maybe it's an anti-strategy. Either way, it's intentional Christian living in the way of Jesus: nothing more, nothing less. It's adaptable to any situation or cultural context. You don't buy it in a boxed set. In the storehouses of the church, we already have the tools we need. It's a matter of bringing out of the treasure, as any good steward does, "what is old and what is new" (Matthew 13:52).

Like the woman whose fingertips brushed the soft threads of Jesus' power, our rural congregations—hemorrhaging people, especially the young, for years—have been wounded by our constant seeking after doctors. They have poked us and prodded us and made us drink nasty radioactive liquid chalk for their scans, telling us that if we would just believe the right things, pay to attend the right conferences, and buy their books in bulk, we would be well. We would grow. But so many of their prescriptions have ended up being little more than leeches and bloodletting. Many rural congregations have been left in the lurch, feeling guilty that they haven't been able to grow like that new church in the suburbs.

Not least, we see this in the way so many churches have entered a profound malaise. They've tried it all, and nothing has worked. Pastors too. They come juiced up on church growth theory spiked with liberation theology and find that congregations are not infinitely malleable. The new wine bursts the old wineskin. And the pastor moves on, claiming (as we all do) that the congregation didn't really want to grow. Out of this wreckage, so many congregations, pastors, and lay leaders have come upon a hunger and a searching for a way forward.

But the challenge is that we're all suffering from the same illness. We're all hemorrhaging, and whether we're consulting the experts or self-medicating, we're all essentially experimenting on ourselves. The conditions of our healing are changing even as we're popping new sorts of pills. We've been infected with the same ailments of modernity as those we're trying to heal: individualism, consumerism, the loss of fundamental truth claims, and the disparaging of authority beyond our own cultural conventions. It's often precisely these cultural maladies that so many models of church cater to, fomenting a consumeristic mentality that appeals to our desire for the new and comfortable over the ancient and vulnerable.

What's more, so much that is touted as growth strategy in fact amounts to taking folks whose faith has been lovingly handcrafted in one congregation and transferring them to another—this time with a smoke machine and bass thump. It's the phenomenon of planting new churches in already highly churched small towns and declaring that no one was really doing church until we showed up. The existing churches weren't relevant. It's exploiting the fissures and discontents present in every congregation to carve out a new church. This may be good marketing technique, but it's shabby treatment of the bride of Christ.

I suspect we're nearing the end of an age. It's the fading of a certain American Christianity—one aligned with the powers, one earnestly ethnocentric and unthinkingly (post)modern. All too often, the suburban model of church is the natural outworking of American civil religion. But it's also the death of that religion. In many churches, we see the final stage of acculturation. The biggest dinosaurs were also the last. The next stage is a shrug and a changing of the channel.

Yet to be honest, our scruffy rural congregations are often scarcely in better shape. We're just little dinosaurs.

Bright spots in the sticks

Growth is possible.

Looking for bright spots in rural ministry, I contacted conference, denominational, and parachurch leaders. I wanted to know about congregations that had found ways to grow and thrive—however they defined growth and thriving in their context—despite the challenges faced by many rural congregations and communities. I corresponded with pastors by phone and email, asking them to tell their story and share what they'd learned along the way. I talked to folks like Todd Jones at the Hutterthal Mennonite Church in Freeman, South Dakota. Jones told me how in his first year at Hutterthal, a young family began relating to the congregation. Then, by what he described as a "movement of the Holy Spirit," more young families began to show up. The first year Todd was involved with vacation Bible school at Hutterthal, they had a smattering of kids—maybe thirteen. Now they have fifty to sixty. When Jones calls kids up for the children's time during Sunday morning worship, some twenty to twenty-five come forward.

Jason McConnell, a pastor in rural Vermont along the border with Quebec, has experienced growth in both of the congregations he serves. One of them, the Franklin United Church, has tripled in size over the thirteen years that Jason has led the congregation, to about 120 people. In his communication with me, McConnell emphasized clear, expository gospel preaching, intentional outreach and community involvement, and discipleship. He's a believer in patience, and he urged rural pastors to make a commitment to longevity.

Kent Rogers, former pastor of Evangel United Methodist Church in Holton, Kansas, talked about how Evangel launched a children's choir and how he began serving as the sports announcer for the local team, the Holton Wildcats.[6] The congregation's defining moment came, however, in a massive ice storm that knocked out power to their small town. The Evangel church took the lead in providing temporary housing for storm-displaced residents and became the base of operations for the Red Cross. With some fifty locals sleeping in Evangel's classrooms, Rogers joked that the church had become the "Evangel Hilton." Evangel's hospitality was a redefining moment, and the congregation grew as community members came to check out this welcoming church.

There are more stories. God is at work in rural places. The narrative of rural decline does not tell the whole story.

Sacrificing success on the threshing floor

One consistent factor among pastors of thriving rural congregations was their hesitance to define success solely by numbers. They named congregational engagement in the life of the church throughout the week, work with local and international relief efforts, connections between members throughout the week, and other metrics that pointed beyond the numbers on Sunday morning. One pastor, James Ralph at the Ark Bible Chapel in Pennsylvania, spoke of measuring growth around a set of eight qualities, among them "opportunities to be involved with one another beyond Sunday morning."[7] Margaret Ewen Peters, who together with her husband serves two congregations in rural Saskatchewan, described a shift from the language of numbers growth to faithfulness. Another pastor preferred to speak of "health" rather than "growth."

We would do well to remember what happened to King David when he relied on strength of numbers in 2 Samuel 24. In an effort to quantify the military power available to him, David sent Joab

---

6. Rogers spoke at our Holy Week services in Moundridge in 2015. His and Evangel's story is also told in Paul Nixon, "The Good News Church," *We Refused to Lead a Dying Church! Churches That Came Back against All Odds* (Cleveland: Pilgrim Press, 2012), 15ff.

7. Ralph drew on the book by Christian Schwartz, *Natural Church Development: A Guide to Eight Essential Qualities of Healthy Churches* (Bloomington, MN: Churchsmart Resources, 1996).

and the commanders of his armies to take a census of the Israelites. For nine months and twenty days they passed through the land, counting men of fighting age. But when the commanders made their report, David was convicted by what he had done. Rather than rely on the King of the universe, he had trusted in King Number. At the end of the story, David had to sacrifice his ambitious counting on a hastily constructed altar on the threshing floor of Araunah (or Ornan in Chronicles) the Jebusite. In the books of Samuel and Kings, this is the last of David's acts. The first book of Samuel begins with a warning to Israel against desiring a king, and the second book ends with David's repentant sacrifice for doing what kings do: measuring the success of their rule by numbers.

There's more. David decides to locate the temple of God at the altar on Araunah's threshing floor (1 Chronicles 22:1; 2 Chronicles 3:1). In a very real way, the temple, which would become the center of Israel's worship, is a monument to resisting the narrative of success-by-counting. It's a monument to counting on God. The temple of Israel is a visible reminder that our success does not rely on numbers and that in fact it can be dangerous for leaders of God's people to hang their hopes, self-worth, and the worth of their ministry on numbers.

Yet this is just what most churches and church leaders do: they count. Tim Suttle writes that most churches "have been captivated by the values of a culture that demands progress toward the goals of bigger, better, stronger, higher, faster—cultural markers that are foreign to the gospel story."[8]

Our very use of the word *success* belies our dependence on this cultural narrative "foreign to the gospel story." The word *success* comes from a cluster of Latin words that also mean "come after." At its root, success is the great "What's next?" Think of the way that we talk about "successive regimes"—the governments that come after one another—or a prince "succeeding" a king. The prince has come after the king and become the new king. This language is ill-suited to the church, for what comes after the church?

8. Suttle, *Shrink*, 29.

Nothing. The Scriptures speak of the church as the place where God's vision for humanity is fulfilled, as the body in which God is adored and glorified, just as God is in Jesus (Ephesians 3:21). There is nothing successive to the church, no plan B (bigger, better, stronger, higher, faster). Nothing comes next. Besides, the measure of the church's success has already been met—and continues to be met—in the life, death, and resurrection of Jesus. Success is a word that twists in the hands of the church, the people who must discover their purpose and progress not in the next big thing or in their own accomplishments, but in the fullness of Christ's life and accomplishments (see 1 Corinthians 3:11).

Talk of success in the church comes not from the cruciform vocabulary of the gospel but from the world's fixation on victory and ranking. We lionize the successful entrepreneur, the successful athlete, the successful politician—so why not the successful pastor? Jason Rains, pastor of the thriving Grace Crossing church plant in my community, reflected that in seminary he was taught that if you start with one hundred attendees and end with one hundred, the year was a wash. "But," said Rains, "that's just business analytics." In the church, much of what's most vital—particularly the way of the cross and costly love of God and neighbor—does not conform to the ideals of the American narrative. Like King David, we may need to sacrifice our false vision of success on the threshing floor.

Jesus anticipates our confusion when he asks, "What do you benefit if you gain the whole world but lose your own soul? Is anything worth more than your soul?" (Matthew 16:26 NLT).

If there is a biblical word for *succeed*, it's the one Jesus uses here. We usually translate it as *gain*. It's the same word Matthew uses in his gospel for the servants who shrewdly invested the money given them to "gain" more (Matthew 25:16-17). It's the word the apostle Paul uses to speak of "gaining" new people to the faith (1 Corinthians 9:19-21). But even there, Paul understands this word in the light of the cross—becoming weak to save the weak—much in the same way that Jesus used it. Paul has given up everything and regarded it as rubbish, that he might "gain Christ"

(Philippians 3:8). It's succeeding as shedding, succeeding as humility, succeeding as becoming smaller in order to be in and with Christ. "He must increase," said Jesus' cousin John the Baptist, "but I must decrease" (John 3:30). So it is with us.

What this means is that the suburban megachurch is not the measure of God's victory. That model is not going to be a workable model for the country. Much of the growth of the megachurch depends on discontent—the same discontent that advertisers actively seek to cultivate in their target audiences. It's the discontent of the consumer, who is encouraged never to settle for anything less than the biggest and best.

But this will not do in rural places, where we must learn the art of loving dying things and dying people, and where we must do the hard work of remaining in community even in the face of disappointment. In rural places, we don't have the luxury of pitching our gnarly community and starting over in a better circle of relationships where the grass is greener and the music better. It's just us out here. We're going to be working and shopping and rubbing elbows with the same group of people for a long time. We all share the same neighborhood.

We cannot content ourselves with defining success based on numbers, but there is one way that numbers matter. There comes a time when, after we have done the work of weirding the axes, we (carefully, hesitantly) count heads—not because numbers equal success, but because numbers point to human lives, and the church is in the business of embodying the gospel among human lives. We will ask ourselves whether we are effectively reaching out into our communities, and if not, we ask why. We'll remember that "day by day the Lord added to their number those who were being saved" (Acts 2:47). The Lord did it. Not the talented preachers. Not the amazing program directors. Not even the apostles. The church lived the gospel and shared the gospel, but it was the Lord who added to their numbers. Their success came in the preceding verses, in the ways that they embodied the gospel.

How can we embody the gospel among new people? It's a question of growth that can only be met through the humble practices of relating and listening folks into the kingdom, even as we deepen our commitment to authentic Christlikeness.

Relating: Getting beyond The Wave and neighboring the present

In our community, as in a lot of rural towns, there are no stop signs on side streets. The streets simply cross each other, and when we meet an intersection, we have to figure it out on our own. There's nothing to instruct us, not even a yield sign. Moving through the intersection requires an interpersonal interaction. We go by watchfulness and a wave. The Wave.

We wave to people on the side of the street. We wave on the country roads (there are no signs out there, either). We greet each other in the grocery store. It's all about acknowledging and reinforcing relationships.

On a recent trip to Chicago, we didn't get The Wave. We relied on signs and traffic lights and turn signals. Moving through the intersection required a lead foot. People were friendly enough, but the city operated on a different scale and relational logic.

Rural communities are profoundly interrelated through work, blood, and general neighborliness. My granddaddy and yours were friends (or rivals), and so are we. These communitarian sensibilities lend themselves to a sense of interconnectedness, but they also lead to at least two dangers. In the first, we can believe that vague friendliness and familiarity is the same thing as authentic relationship. In the second, we can glom on to an idealized past community instead of embracing the neighborhood of the present.

In the first danger, we fall under the mistaken belief that The Wave constitutes a relationship. We can think that because we're generally friendly with one another—because we allow someone to go before us in line or we talk about the weather in the post office—that we're in relationship, even in communion. But it's not so. The Wave is not relationship. Of course, The Wave can lead to talking on the sidelines of the soccer game, to deep sharing over coffee, and thus to relationship. But The Wave, on its own, is not enough.

In the second danger in our rural communities, we end up living in the community of the past rather than welcoming and neighboring the present. Occasionally, elders in the community will point out how much things have changed, how many new people have moved to town. "I don't recognize the family names of half the kids on the basketball team," they say. It's an observation tinged with longing for a past in which we knew everyone and could place them in the appropriate family tree. There's a bit of pride too. Our town has attracted new people. This is a good place to live.

The problem is, sometimes this idealized past community stands in as the true community. It's the good old days gone bad. The real town exists sometime way back when. The present is a sort of weak reflection of that true community, a colony of the motherland past.

We see this in the way shared community memory maps the town. It's the classic statement: *You live in the old Galle house.* One pastor I interviewed lovingly chided his people. "Folks can name who lived in the house fifty years ago," he noted, "but they can't name who lives there now." Too often, our rural congregations neighbor the past, but they lose sight of neighboring the present.

An elderly woman once invited my wife and me to visit her in her home. It was out on an unpaved road, a destination our GPS feared to tread. But no worries: she had told us a sure way to identify her house—it was the one with the green mailbox.

When it came time for our visit, we drove up and down her road several times, unable to find the address. Our GPS refused to plot coordinates beyond the known world. And that green mailbox? It was nowhere in sight. Finally, we made our best guess and pulled up carefully to a mailbox at the end of a driveway. It had a couple of peeling numbers that roughly corresponded to her address. And right along the steel edge of the box we made out the barest hint of green paint. There it was: the green mailbox, circa 1950.

All too frequently, our rural congregations risk getting stuck in a relational network that belongs to the past. We see our communities through retro glasses that don't allow us to plot out a new community with new names. Developing (or recovering) our capacity to relate to people is vital to becoming the kinds of congregations God needs in the rural neighborhood. It's not the old Galle house anymore. It's the Martinez house. And their mailbox is orange.

Living the gospel and sharing the gospel presume relating. In growing congregations, people are open to forming new relationships. Folks aren't limited to superficial niceties or stuck in the community of the past. They're relationally oriented.

Look at the apostle Peter's first letter. Peter reminded the church: "If someone asks about your hope as a believer, always be ready to explain it" (1 Peter 3:15 NLT). This asking presumes that followers of Jesus will find themselves—will actually place themselves—in situations where others will bump up against them and notice their Christian faith. There will be wonder. There will be puzzlement. There will be questions. *What's your hope?* "Be ready," says Peter, "to explain it."

This means that in our rural communities, we have to be ready and open to forming relationships. This might not sound like much, but authentic relationship requires us to glance up from the smartphone, look away from the television, and be with people. If the last chapter was about staying in to pray, this chapter is about going out to connect. The gospel is about connecting people into the community of Christ. The kingdom is lived into being one relationship at a time.

Connecting with people will require us to hold a full-bodied vision of neighborliness, not a shallow view of people based on their value to us as evangelistic targets. We care about them as human beings, not as warm bodies in the pews. We don't count them, we relate to them.

Jesus demonstrated this sort of relating in his own life. He was constantly relating people into the kingdom. Through a mix of pastoral acumen and prophetic foresight, he tapped men and women for discipleship. He saw Simon and Andrew on the beach and said, "Follow me." He spotted Matthew in the tax booth and said, "Follow me." He found Philip and said, "Follow me." Jesus said, "Let the dead bury their own dead"; "Take up your cross"; "Pick up your mat"; "Follow me" (Luke 9:60; Mark 8:34 NLT; Mark 2:11 NLT; Matthew 4:19 and 9:9 and John 1:43). His invitations were intentional and targeted.

Where it gets interesting is in the encounters Jesus had with people in which he *didn't* call them to discipleship. He simply related to them as human beings, and that relationship opened the door to another level of encounter. Think of the Canaanite woman who dogged Jesus, seeking relief for her demon-tormented daughter. "Have mercy on me, Lord, Son of David" (Matthew 15:22). But Jesus did not even answer her. It was only after she persisted—to the great annoyance of Jesus' disciples—that he turned and met her request. "Her daughter was healed instantly" says the gospel (Matthew 15:28).

The scene can strike us as odd, because it would seem an encounter ripe for discipleship: a woman with a need meets the man with the power to meet that need and call her to the kingdom. She was hungry. She had faith. Bring that lady to Jesus.

But no. Something about the way the encounter was presented signaled to Jesus that the request would not lead the woman into the kingdom. She came looking for a solution, not a savior. Perhaps as she wrestled with her situation, she was able to recognize her deeper need, not just for God's power, but for God's love and mercy. Who knows? What's interesting is that Jesus cast no invitation for the woman to follow him. He simply related to her in mercy.

This is a snapshot of the ways Jesus not only calls people to follow him as disciples but also recognizes their full humanity as people with unique stories. Of course Jesus always points people—in a way that is appropriate to where they're at—to himself and to the kingdom of God. But he doesn't do this in a way that detracts from their humanity. They don't lose their agency. Rather, they're sent out to do the same—to become "fishers of men" (Matthew 4:19 KJV), to "make disciples of all nations" (Matthew 28:19). People become *more* in relationship to Jesus, not *less*. For Jesus, discipleship is inviting people into ongoing relationship. Jesus relates them into the kingdom.

Among the pastors I interviewed, relationships factored heavily into congregational growth. One pastor, Richard Early out of Lacey Springs, Virginia, has led a rural church plant since 1997. The congregation has grown to some 275 folks on a Sunday morning—this when the population of Lacey Springs is only about 150. During our interview, Early emphasized human connections. He noted that there's often a sense of defeatism and apology among many rural congregations, but he maintains that small congregations have a tremendous ability to connect with people. "Don't try to get someone to come to church before they come to you," Early said. First connect people to you through relationships; then connect people to the church.

Pastor Jimm Wood of the Hope Vineyard Church in small-town Paxton, Illinois, said that in his experience, "It's only . . . in being a part of people's lives that you get to share Jesus with them."[9] In the anonymous swirl of urban areas, we may bump into someone only once. We only get one shot. But in our rural communities, it's ongoing relationship that creates a safe space to share the gospel.

I've had to grow into this reality in my own ministry. I've moved from a caffeinated desire to invite everyone I meet to church and have learned instead to simply relate to people as people. I've developed more of a willingness to give the relationship a chance to grow. I've come to trust that God won't drop the ball. Learning this lesson has saved me from alienating folks. Spring the church invitation too quickly, and they peg you as just another salesperson more interested in getting them into the pews than in getting to the heart of their stories. It's not hard for people to figure out. If all I care about is inviting them to church, then they know exactly what I am: just another mercenary.

Our neighborhood has been a source of growth for our congregation, though it's not because I've pursued any sort of strategy to get people in the door. Conversations about Jesus have followed conversations about whose class the kids are in. My family and I

9. Michael Houle and Jimm Wood, "How to Do Evangelism in Small Towns" (lecture, 2016 Small Town Church Planting and Doing Church Conference, Lancaster, OH, May 19–21, 2016), https://www.youtube.com/watch?v=_J_SqQjA64E&feature=youtu.be.

have simply taken the time to relate to the folks next door. We've done the human work of becoming neighbors.

Listening: Evangelism means sitting down in the dark with someone

Just as we can relate people into the kingdom, so too we can listen people into the kingdom.

Just look at Jesus. Even in the most obvious situations, he took time to listen. "What do you want me to do for you?" he asked blind Bartimaeus (Mark 10:51). His call to discipleship had an invitational air: "Come and see" (John 1:39). He spent time alone, sharpening his ability to listen to God (Matthew 14:13, for example), and thus to others. For Jesus, listening was an act of openness to the *other*. It was an act of love.

Think again of Peter's words on sharing faith. He told the church to testify to their hope in a "gentle and respectful way" (1 Peter 3:16 NLT). I like the literal translation of the word for "respectful" here: *phobos*, fear. It makes me think of Paul's reminder that we must work out our salvation with "fear and trembling" (Philippians 2:12). We walk carefully up to the burning bush of other people's stories. We're a little afraid to stand before something so holy and powerful. We take off our shoes.

We speak with "humility." This means not barging in. It means not interrupting and pushing our way to the front of the narrative line, but rather creating spaces where people's authentic hope comes out as testimony, as response, as openness. It's like James's words: "Be quick to listen, slow to speak, slow to anger" (James 1:19).

This is about hearing people's stories and, when we have heard them, humbly identifying that-of-God we've heard in them. We don't watch for the slipups and stumbles and sin so that we can convince them of their need for redemption. That's all there, but it's not our focus. Our goal is to listen. This person is precious in God's sight. So is her story.

I've never known anyone to find their way into the kingdom without first being listened to. People don't want to be indoctrinated. They want to be heard. Remember that neighbor I went to visit before Christmas, the one who found his way into the life of church? I spent most of my time listening to him. Then, at a couple of places, I tentatively—with humility and fear—connected God's story to his.

Think of Jesus' interaction with the Samaritan woman at the well. He spoke, and he listened. She asked questions, and he responded. He initiated the conversation not with a doctrinal statement, but with a statement of his sheer need: "Will you give me a drink?" (John 4:7 NIV).

This was not the usual way for a teacher to interact with a Samaritan woman. In fact, she would have been doing entirely too much talking for most rabbis. The woman asked: "How is it that you, a Jew, ask a drink of me, a woman of Samaria?" "Where do you get that living water?" "Are you greater than our ancestor Jacob?" (John 4:9, 11-12). She told her story: "I have no husband" (John 4:17). She shared her deeply held belief: "Our ancestors worshiped on this mountain, but you say that the place where people must worship is in Jerusalem" (John 4:20).

In all of this, Jesus certainly spoke. He certainly taught. But he did so in such a way that the woman at the well was heard. Her story became a doorway for God's story.

Part of what this means is that in rural congregations, we don't need to learn some sort of "effective" evangelistic strategy; we need to learn to listen. We need to cultivate an openness to the stories of others. We need to ask questions, keep quiet, value their story, and then with humility and fear speak our truth. Evangelism isn't about getting up on a soapbox and preaching at someone. It's about sitting down next to that person and turning down the volume.

At the congregation I served in Washington State, it was the pastor's job to pull the trash bins to the street on Monday nights. With everything else going on, that was often the last thing I did: a quick dash down to the front of the church and into a dark cranny formed by an outstretched arm of bushes.

One evening, as I made my usual sprint between putting boys to bed and snatching some quality time with my wife, I slipped out of our house and down across the lawn to the church. I stepped into the shadows at the front of the church and grabbed the back of the trash bin. And I froze. There, in that darkness, I could feel someone watching me. As my eyes adjusted, I made out the silhouette of a young man sitting in the far corner, face lost in the shadows of a hoodie. Cigarette smoke wafted my way. It was just me and him and a trashcan.

Several thoughts went through my head. Our town was being torn up by gang violence around that time. Was this young man in a gang? What was he doing down here? Maybe I should just pull out the trash and keep right on going—pretend I didn't see anything.

But I set the bin down, brushed off my hands, and walked over to introduce myself. It turned out that he was a teenager looking for a peaceful place to escape from it all. Where better than in the dark embrace of the church? Um, okay, well, good to meet you.

It became our little routine—or at least my little routine. Each week as I went down to take out the trash, I looked to see if he was there. Sometimes he was. Sometimes he wasn't. At one point in our running nighttime conversation, I sat down beside him in the dark. We talked about life, how he lived with his mom, how he wasn't from around here, how he didn't know anyone his own age. And then one night, in humility and fear, I popped the question: "So, do you know who Jesus is?"

I'll admit, the conversation didn't get much further than that. He didn't have much use for faith just then, and I'm not a very good evangelist. Eventually, he stopped coming around. Maybe I scared him off. I bumped into him sometimes around town during the day, but it was never the same, nothing like our smoky nighttime conversations by the trashcan.

Nevertheless, this is what I think of when I think of evangelism. It's waiting and patience. It's taking the time to listen to the other person's story. Evangelism means sitting down in the dark with someone.

Authenticity: With God's help, becoming ourselves

I once bought a fake Rolex watch.

I knew it was fake. The real deal sells for a bit more than the twenty dollars I put down, and you tend not find them on the corner at a Venezuelan cheap goods market. But I was a kid on a mission trip, and I was fascinated by the idea that a fake Rolex existed. And hey, it didn't look half bad.

According to my youth pastor (who claimed to know about such things), the motion of an authentic Rolex doesn't tick. It *glides*. The second hand traces a clean arc, as smooth as Ben Franklin's rounded cheek. My gold-tone watch, with its herky-jerky tick-tock, was thus, conclusively, a fake.

In the apostle Peter's advice on evangelism, he told his readers to share their faith in "a gentle and respectful way" and to "keep your conscience clear" (1 Peter 3:15-16 NLT). They weren't to ladle on the details and concoct a dramatic conversion story. Keep it simple. Keep it authentic. Keep your conscience clear. This is no place for fakes.

No doubt this is good advice for Christians at all times and places, but I suspect it's particularly vital that rural congregations hear Peter's call to authenticity. So often, rural congregations have forgotten the art of sharing their faith. In the absence of a gentle, humble evangelistic idiom, they flail about for something and end up latching on to a salesmanship model. At its worst, it's the slick pitch of the televangelist. It's the altar call week in and week out. It's emotionalism and manipulation.

Or rural congregations become apologetic, thinking that since they (presumably) can't run with the big dogs, they should stay on the porch. We see this in the disheartening phenomenon of inviting the new neighbors to *someone else's* church rather than our own. This actually happens. Someone will say, "You wouldn't be interested in my church. We're old. Go to that young church down the road. They have a smoke machine."

But we want to be the church down the road (though maybe without the smoke machine). We want to be the church to which others invite their new neighbors.

I think this starts with being willing to claim our congregation's identity. What are special gifts that God has given this church in this place, and how can we celebrate that identity and play to those strengths? This doesn't mean the tribalism into which many of our congregations retreat: unless you're part of the tribe, you're not likely to be interested. I once saw a church sign that read "If you're looking for good Lutherans, they're here." It had never occurred to me to be on the lookout for good Lutherans—I thought they were all pretty good. I wasn't in on the tribe-speak, so I walked on by.

But I believe that we can claim our heritage in a gentle and respectful way. We can authentically be who we are. Denominational names and histories ground us. They're like last names. We came from somewhere. We're part of a family. We belong to a story that's bigger than ourselves.

There's a further risk to cultivating authenticity, and we hear it in the constant chorus that "everything must change." It has a ring of faithfulness: change happens, so work with it rather than against it. Adapt to the needs and expectations of society to reach people for the gospel. The idea would seem dabbed with a bit of sacred gilt by Paul's words in 1 Corinthians: "I have become all things to all people, that I might by all means save some" (9:22). Yet in our righteous desire to contextualize the gospel—to "become all things to all people"—we inevitably fall prey to our own and our culture's worst impulses. We end up shaving anything from the gospel that might offend or inconvenience those we seek to win. In our tinkering with the gospel chemistry, however, we rarely know what the effects will be on the church in years to come. Think about it: What does it mean for the identity of a people and the life of a congregation when Mother's Day has become a holy day higher than Easter?

I recognize that I'm putting my foot across the line into contested territory. These are old archetypes—Christ and culture—and I'm scarcely doing them justice. Yet I fear the effects of *everything-mustchangeism* upon our rural congregations. Almost inevitably, instead of finding ourselves more deeply loving and challenging our communities, we accommodate in subtle ways to our culture's underlying ways of thinking.

For instance, our culture tells us that true leaders exercise visionary, top-down leadership—like a CEO. Meanwhile, many churches in rural communities have strong indigenous leadership. It's well known that in churches smaller than about fifty people—and the leadership habits of small, rural congregations likely have less to do with their being rural than with their being small—authority tends to concentrate in the hands of a patriarchal or matriarchal figure (or both). This dynamic has challenged pastors who land in small rural congregations. Either they learn to play ball with these folks or they go home. No appeal to pastoral authority or credentials will change this dynamic. (Trust me.) It's just part of the local structure. Coming in as the outside professional and declaring "Everything must change" will simply rock the boat, and we're likely to be the ones who fall overboard.

There are reasons that congregations take the shapes they do. Congregations adapt. They find ways to survive. Small, rural churches develop strong indigenous leadership because they often spend long periods without pastors, or with young pastors-in-training, or with retired, part-time pastors. Not everybody has the gumption to move to deepest, darkest Arkansas, or North Dakota, or the Yukon. But the elders of the church, who have poured their blood, sweat, and tears into the church—like their granddaddy and daddy before them—remain. As one woman said during a conversation about some changes being discussed in her congregation, "Pastors come and go."

A commitment to authenticity gets us at least part of the way to where we need to go. Authenticity is this: claiming our own story and then living it out into the future. Authenticity touches on care for place and particularity. It's remembering that there is no *church* in the abstract that we can commit to and love. Just as we marry *this* woman or *this* man, so too we inhabit *this* church, with its rich (and occasionally sordid) history. We claim it. We claim our congregation's particular history, our musical style, our distinct way of doing church, and we imaginatively live out that identity into the future.

But this is not a junior high graduation speech. "Be yourself" will not do. Authenticity only works as a gospel principle when we come to understand it as claiming and living our story as a unique expression of Christ's story. It's something like what the Danish philosopher Søren Kierkegaard meant when he wrote in his journal, "Now, with God's help, I shall become myself."[10] This is recognizing that what we are becoming with God's help in our rural communities will often look very different from what a congregation is becoming in the city or the suburb. David can't fight in Saul's armor. Our authentic Timex will be more dignified than a knock-off Rolex.

God has given us permission to become ourselves. What's more, God is calling us to become ourselves in the rural communities we inhabit. I think we should see our congregations' particular local stories not as baggage to be shed but as unique expressions of God's providence. We're here in this place at this time for a reason.

Think of the story of Esther. Esther's life came down to a key decision: What story would she claim? Would she enact the story of the Persian queen or that of the Jewish woman in solidarity with her exiled people? Hers was the story of the whole Jewish people, embedded in the foreign Babylonian (and later Persian) culture. From whom would she take her cues? What lines would she riff on? And what's more, was it even possible to truly live out the Jewish story in the Persian world? Could she "sing the Lord's song in a foreign land" (Psalm 137:4) so removed from the markers (temple, Jerusalem, land, law) that *placed* their story? With a little help from her uncle Mordecai, Esther recognized that she had been brought to her place of authority "for just such a time as this" (Esther 4:14). She learned that by living out her people's particular story in that time of crisis, she would find a way forward for them all. With God's help, Esther became herself and claimed the story of her people.

And so must we.

You're the bait: Become the gospel

In the 1995 film *Waterworld*, Kevin Costner plays a mysterious man called the Mariner who has gills on his neck and webbing between his toes and is trying to make his strong-but-silent way

---

10. Quoted in John Ortberg, *The Life You've Always Wanted: Spiritual Disciplines for Ordinary People*, expanded ed. (Grand Rapids: Zondervan, 2002), 11.

across a flooded world. An armored atoll, post-apocalyptic pirates on Jet Skis, and a whole lot of rough-stitched rawhide clothing follow.

At one point in the movie, the Mariner has rescued a young girl and a woman. They're on a boat in an endless ocean, and they're hungry. In desperation, the woman attempts to angle in some fish with a cobbled-together rod, but the Mariner grabs their flimsy rod and chucks it overboard. "You'll never catch anything with that!" he shouts in their faces. "It's useless!" Instead of a rod, the Mariner scoops up an enigmatic double speargun, wraps a cord around his wrist, releases a winch, and jumps into the ocean, where he is trolled along behind the boat. A sea monster promptly strikes, and from inside the beast's throat, the Mariner fires his speargun. In the next scene, we see the three castaways gathered on the deck as the sun sets, enjoying a massive sea monster cookout—all that's missing are a few tiki torches. It turns out that the Mariner was the bait.

When Jesus called Simon Peter and Andrew into a life of discipleship, he told them beside the sea that he would make them "fishers of people." It seemed straightforward enough. Before, they had cast nets for scaled, silvered fish, tugging and wriggling and straining. Now they would cast for people. There would still be some tugging and wriggling and straining—just no nets.

But it's more than that. Jesus would send them out without boats and nets and gear. They took nothing to share the good news (Luke 9). They had no tools of the trade ("You'll never catch anything with that! It's useless!") They had only his message and anointing. They had only themselves to offer, selves formed in their time spent trailing Jesus and picking up his life and way. They weren't just "fishers of people." It turns out that they were the bait.

Living and sharing the gospel is less about doing and more about becoming. We are the gospel. Or, as writer Michael Gorman puts it, we *become* the gospel.[11] Our lives are the message.

---

11. Michael Gorman, *Becoming the Gospel: Paul, Participation, and Mission* (Grand Rapids: Eerdmans, 2015).

If you're anything like me, that's a scary thought, because most of us aren't all that gospel-ish. If sharing our faith means we have to out-nice, out-grace, and out-good everybody around us, most of us are likely to turn around, draw the blinds, and hunker down. We just don't got it.

But that's not what sharing the gospel is about. The only one who's got *it* is Jesus, and he's given us everything we need to live and share the gospel. What Jesus needs is for us to be willing to get in there, cast off all pretenses and useless tackle, and become what he's making us. Go, live, speak, share. Jesus has the boat and net and gear. He just needs us. We're the bait.

The growth of the church is ultimately about our becoming more Christlike and, in that becoming, offering ourselves to the world. Christlikeness is the measure of our growth. Even as we seek to relate and listen new people into the kingdom, the deeper question is always whether we are becoming more authentically ourselves in Christ. It's about how we're embodying the Jesus way in our rural neighborhood. Jesus gives us what we need to do it. That's weirding the axes. That's what it means to grow.

CHAPTER 7

Work the Edges: Stepping across the Barbed Wire

He is our peace; in his flesh he has made both groups into one and has broken down the dividing wall, that is, the hostility between us.
—Ephesians 2:14

My grandfather kept cattle. Each morning, a string of Black Angus would lumber out of his barn and across the pasture, through an underpass, and up into a wooded area. They would spend the day wandering the gullies and brush, making the return journey as evening fell. Part of my grandfather's weekly routine involved checking the fences. He made the circuit on a small three-wheeler, removing fallen limbs and testing electricity flow with a screwdriver as he went.

He knew his business. The fence was taut and electrified, and my brothers and I treated the fence with respect. When we had to cross, either we ducked under or, as we got bigger, one of us held the barbed wire down with a dry stick so that the others could step across. Without the barbed wire, it would have been impossible for my grandfather to keep cattle. We did not want to get the call saying, "The fence is down and the cattle are out!" The fence going down and the cattle escaping was an emergency, a danger to the cattle and—more importantly—unwary passing cars. Good fences make good neighbors, but also good farmers. We knew the importance of the wire to making my grandfather's life as a farmer possible, but we also knew how to cross the wire when we wished.

In many ways, the history of barbed wire is the history of the rural West. After being invented in multiple locations and successfully industrialized in DeKalb, Illinois, in the 1870s, barbed wire made the leap to the Great Plains frontier and down into Texas, where it was used to fence off vast swathes of territory that had been previously open range. In the process, it cut off trail drivers and their longhorn herds from watering holes and pasture and blocked the movement of Native Americans.[1]

Some free-rangers responded to the changing circumstances with violence, igniting what became known as the "fence cutting wars," an escalating series of conflicts across the Old West in which aggrieved vigilantes donned hoods and snipped barbed wire by night while large landowners employed bands of armed men to quash the cutting. It was a battle to control land and water, people and cattle. Two forms of mapping the earth collided—one bounded, one open—and the modern West was born in the struggle. The frontier was closed—literally. It was *enclosed* with barbed wire.

Barbed wire is great, until it isn't. As settlers in the Old West discovered, barbed wire created boundaries that made possible one form of life while simultaneously cutting off other forms. Ranchers' cattle were kept safe, but the range was closed.

There's a lesson here for the rural church. Boundaries snaggle throughout communities and congregations. As pastors and leaders, we can often stumble over them, slung like barbed wire along the ridge of a hill. We must learn the art of discerning these boundaries—where they are, what they represent, and when to challenge them. It will require us to learn to work the edges—the art of stepping across the barbed wire. This is a boundary-transforming spirituality that flows from the meaning of our baptisms.

---

1. Alan Krell, *The Devil's Rope: A Cultural History of Barbed Wire* (London: Reaktion Books, 2002), 27–45.

We live in an age that despises boundaries and regards their demolition as a moral imperative. "Transgressive" behavior is regarded as innovative, perhaps even as morally superior. Something there is about our age that does not love a wall. But I'm convinced that not all boundaries can be removed, and that oftentimes when we believe we're tearing down walls, all we're really doing is moving them or making them more subtle.

There will always be boundaries. Just as the walls of houses can be exclusionary but also give strength and security, so it is with community. As leaders within congregations and communities, we have to approach the edges with respect. It's true that sometimes the edges are capricious relics of a forgotten age. The barbed wire is still up, but the cows are long gone. Or worse: sometimes the edges are a malicious concertina wire of isms—racism and sexism and nativism—slicing spiked lines of prejudice. But often the barbed wire edges snaking throughout our communities and congregations serve purposes that are not always obvious to us. We have to approach them gingerly. As author and pastor James Nieman points out, "Whenever we encounter something in a congregation (or really any group) that makes no sense to us, it's easy to conclude that it makes no sense at all."[2]

Cultivating a barbed-wire-crossing spirituality means coming to see boundaries not as offenses that must be eliminated or overcome but as the natural outworking of a centered community. The church takes a transformative view of the margins. The question isn't whether boundaries exist. They do. They will. But we come at those boundaries differently. We look for places where people can cross over and join us in the life of the church. We're oriented toward the margins. The real question is how we become an Ephesians 2 community that's always moving toward the boundaries (its own and the boundaries of the larger community), always graciously helping others over the barbed wire fence.

2. James R. Nieman, "What a Congregation Knows: The Deep Wisdom behind Odd Practices," *Christian Century* 133, no. 9 (2016): 27.

Where's our newspaper ad? Discerning community structure

Rural communities have boundaries because they have structure. They're made up of human connections spread across generations. People who share a common history, common family bonds, and common faith connect and form a tightly knit pattern of relationships. Sometimes this structure can make it hard for newcomers to connect.

Often, descriptions of the past, the "good ol' days," are descriptions of these community structures. "We just took care of each other," says one man, speaking of his youth. "If we needed some sand for our construction business, we went and got a load from the trenching business's pile. We'd settle up later."

Trust is important in any community, but I'm often struck by how rural communities in particular run on trust. Folks grab the two-by-fours they need out of the lumberyard and then let the owner know what they took after the fact. The owner puts it on their tab. There are no attendants checking receipts under a barbed-wire-topped fence. Another local man sells pork sausage out of a small building beside his house in the country. The sausage is wrapped and coiled in the freezer. There's a scale and a cash box on the table. Customers weigh out the sausage they want, work out the cost with tax using the supplied calculator, and leave payment. There's change in the cash box if they need it. The transactions—whether two-by-fours or sausage—are upheld and protected by the communitarian structure of trust.

Noting the ways that smaller, rural communities differ from mass, urban societies, German sociologist Ferdinand Tönnies coined the terms *Gemeinschaft* and *Gesellschaft* in the late 1800s. These loanwords are used to describe two types of community: communities structured and regulated by trust, relationships, and social boundaries (Gemeinschaft), in contrast with a social order structured and regulated by institutions, contracts, and prescribed roles (Gesellschaft).[3] Rural communities are Gemeinschaft. Cities are Gesellschaft.

---

3. David Brown and Kai Schafft, *Rural People and Communities in the 21st Century: Resilience and Change* (Malden, MA: Polity Press, 2011), 37.

Of course, that's a simplification. Rural communities are also bound together by laws, contracts, and prescribed roles, and folks are neighborly in the cities and suburbs. But the dichotomy can be a helpful shorthand for summarizing basic characteristics of rural community. Trust and relationships are key.

Community structure and boundaries are created and reinforced through family bonds, favors given and received, friendship, and general neighborliness. Central to community structure is the local school, in which everyone has a stake by way of children, grandchildren, sports, or at a minimum, property taxes.

Another place communitarian values and structure are enacted is the local newspaper. I stumbled upon this reality when our congregation's mission team proposed removing our church's one-inch ad in the "church" section of the paper. The team reasoned—correctly, I think—that new residents were unlikely to visit our congregation on the basis of a small, nondescript ad tucked away in the center of the newspaper. Honestly, newcomers were unlikely to subscribe to the paper. So we yanked the ad.

The reaction was cordial but persistent. Older congregational members noticed immediately and expressed their disappointment at the ad's removal. They approached the mission team. They talked to the deacons. They cornered members of church council after worship. And they talked to me. Interestingly, members of other churches approached me in the grocery store aisles, at sports events, and around coffee at the retirement center. "We noticed your ad disappeared," they'd say. "Everything okay at your church?" After a couple of months of this, the mission team relented and reinstated the ad.

Why the fuss? It turns out that the purpose of our diminutive newspaper ad isn't to attract newcomers. In fact, it's not an advertisement at all. It's a block in the structure. You see, our ad doesn't stand alone on the page. It's nestled in a pattern of squares, each one representing a congregation. With local sports reporting above and the police report below, a newspaper reader is literally seeing the structure of the community. The ad signals our congregation's support for that structure. Removing the ad dinged our Gemeinschaft.

Rather than resist the ways our local newspaper supports this structure, I've come to embrace it. I began writing a monthly column in which I reflect on how I see God in our rural neighborhood. It's become a way to demonstrate that I value the community—especially folks on the older end of the spectrum who tend to be newspaper aficionados—and it's a writing outlet. I'm contributing to our community's structure and story. There it is, month in and month out: our Gemeinschaft, black and white and read all over.

Another place we see community structure created and sustained is at estate auctions. When an elderly member of the community dies or moves into a retirement home, the house must be emptied and put on the auction block. The fast-talking auctioneer perches on a high chair above a lifetime's worth of knickknacks and kitchenware and sells off the estate. In one way, it's purely utilitarian, an essential step in converting unnecessary household objects into liquidity. But there's more going on. Large segments of the community turn out to bid. Local churches sell pie and hamburgers as a fundraiser. People chat in the shade and make guesses as to how much the house will go for.

It's the closing of a chapter in the life of an individual and the community. Purchasing bits of the household isn't just about getting something that we want. It's also about caring for the person and family. It's helping them make the transition. We walk off with our little treasures, the accumulations of their life, now our mementos. I have a hoe from one of the renowned elders of our congregation, now passed on. Every time I use it, I think of him. Saint Alfred's hoe.

Estate sales are also a great missional opportunity. We rub elbows with people from all over the community. I make an awkward glad-hander, but this is my chance to connect with folks in between bidding on pickle crocks. I hear the latest, and I traffic in stories. I work the edges of the auction and the community.

The margins make me sick: The challenge of working the edges

That rural communities have a center and structure means that they also have margins. That shouldn't surprise us: every community has margins and folks on the edge. The question is, how does the church approach those margins?

Margins are a fact of life. It wouldn't be possible to live in a boundaryless world any more than it would be possible to live in a wall-less house. But sometimes boundaries are unjust. Think of our society's "White Only" water fountains and pools, the malevolent boundaries of segregation and Jim Crow. We're called to resist these sorts of boundaries, break down these dividing walls, snip these fences and mash them out of the way. These sorts of edges require us not only to cross but also to challenge or even cut.

However, boundaries are often more complicated affairs, places where the congregation or community has staked out its identity. Boundaries can be sources of strength.

Regardless of how the edges got there—or how they seem to us—faith in the Crucified One calls us to work the edges. It's not that we try to demolish every boundary. Fence cutting wars redux won't do. Instead, we take a transformative, fence-crossing view of boundaries. We approach the edges differently.

The apostle Paul took up the edges in his letter to the Ephesians. As Paul makes clear, Jesus has given the church new life. He has "raised us up with him" (Ephesians 2:6). He has saved us by grace through faith. Out of all of this, we have been formed as the church, the very body of Christ (see Ephesians 2:5-6, 8; 5:23). And it's the church that now continues God's redeeming work in Christ Jesus. The nature of the church plays centrally in Paul's thematic development in Ephesians; the word *church* is mentioned nine times in the letter's six chapters.

We see the centrality of the church in Ephesians 2, where after detailing the work that Christ has done in bringing salvation to all people, Paul sets about describing how those people are newly related to one another. Jesus has saved Jews and Gentiles and formed something new: a mixed body made up of previously unmixable parts. It's a "new humanity" forged "in the place of the two" (Ephesians 2:15). It's the earthly expression of the "household of God" (2:19), and just as Jesus promised in John 14:2, it's got many rooms. They're spacious enough to encompass the whole of humanity, Jew and Gentile. It's a new structure imbued with the power of growth, like a body (Ephesians 2:21).

The key to making this new body/household/structure/humanity possible is the reconciling work accomplished in Jesus' life, death, and resurrection. Jesus has "broken down the dividing wall" in his own flesh (2:14). Paul has staked everything on this message of reconciliation, risking life and limb on spreading the gospel among the Gentiles (3:1-2). They've got to hear it.

And it's not just what Jesus has done but what he is doing through the church. The church is the reconciled reconciler, the body that by its very nature and calling works the edges, a church oriented toward the margins. We hold the barbed wire down so that folks can step across and find their way into life with Christ. We continue the vision of Ephesians 2, becoming the barbed-wire-crossing church.

This is nothing particularly radical. Half the time, it's just greeting visitors at the church picnic. It's just talking to our new neighbors. Yet such boundary crossing can be harder than it would seem, because the visitor at the church picnic voted for the other candidate, and the new neighbor just dragged a plush sofa onto the front porch. They don't conform to the values of our Gemeinschaft.

Becoming a barbed-wire-crossing church will mean identifying and encouraging what small-church researcher Carl Dudley refers to as "gatekeepers" in the congregational system: people who welcome outsiders and interpret the life of the church to them, thereby helping new folks find their way in.[4] These gatekeepers are folks who work the edges and chat with newcomers. They open up the structure of the congregation so that others can find a place.

Crossing the barbed wire will also mean challenging our own comfort. So many of us suffer from BFF syndrome. We're deeply

---

4. Carl S. Dudley, *Effective Small Churches in the Twenty-First Century*, rev. ed. (Nashville, Abingdon: 2003), 51.

committed to the friends we already have: our "best friends forever." It's a beautiful thing. But it means that sometimes we don't have enough emotional energy or will to reach out to that new neighbor.

One pastor I know struggled to connect an established church family with their neighbors. "Would you mind dropping by to visit them?" he asked. Despite living just around the block from the new family, the church family would ask the pastor for updates on the neighbor's health. They couldn't seem to go over and knock on the door themselves. It wasn't that they were mean. On the contrary, they're compassionate folks, nice to a fault. But invisible barbed wire separated them from their neighbors. Too many communitarian boundaries prevented them from becoming a part of their neighbors' lives.

Another pastor I interviewed spoke of a family that began to connect with the congregation he served. The family came from a socioeconomic background different from those in the congregation, and they brought with them difficult family dysfunction. The oldest of the two daughters began attending church through the efforts of a woman in the congregation who picked her up and brought her along. Others in the family started to attend intermittently, and the pastor reached out to them. "It was hard for me to visit them at home," he said. "The man was a chain-smoker. Sitting across from him at the table drinking coffee, we would have invigorating conversations, but I would go home smelling of smoke and would be sick the next day. It wasn't easy to do. If I had my druthers, I would rather not have gone." Going to the margins made him sick.

Yet the pastor persisted. The family had a long way to go and many struggles, but they also received much welcome and encouragement from the congregation and were eventually received into the church. If shepherds should have the smell of the sheep on them, as Pope Francis has suggested, these sheep smelled like menthols.[5]

---

5. Pope Francis quoted in Dennis Coday, "Pope's Quotes: The Smell of Sheep," *National Catholic Reporter*, October 29, 2013, https://www.ncronline.org/blogs/francis-chronicles/pope-s-quotes-smell-sheep.

Do you allow visitors? Working the edges in rural post-Christendom

Sometimes, people ask me if our church allows visitors. I figure it's a Mennonite thing. No doubt many wonder if they'll have to arrive in a buggy or don special headgear. Maybe they're afraid they'll have to grow a beard or wear a cape dress.

In part, the question is simply a gauge of our openness to new people. It's a test thrown out to see how I respond. Are we the kind of church that's welcoming to new people? You have thirty seconds to state your reply.

But I suspect the question runs deeper, especially as churches of all sorts find their influence slipping and their standing at the cultural center getting swept to the edges. It's a symptom of the decline of Christendom.

In the Middle Ages, European society was for the most part governed by the dual authority of the Roman Catholic Church and the Holy Roman Empire. It was a partnership of church and state, what we now refer to as Christendom—what the medieval church called the *corpus Christianum*—a system that embraced its citizens' lives completely, body and spirit. For the most part, if you were born in Christian Europe, then you would be baptized as an infant as a matter of course. Baptism was both an entrance into the church and a mark of citizenship. The rite was not just about faith, but a sign of belonging to the fabric of secular society as well.

The Christendom model survived even the breakup of unified Europe that accompanied the sixteenth-century Reformation. Rather than loyalty to a distant emperor, allegiance was simply transferred to local Christendoms. The prince's faith—Catholic, Lutheran, or Reformed—determined the faith of the people.

Christendom had its discontents, but a veneer of Christianity, however thin, guaranteed society a common ethical and theological fiber. People instinctively took their bearings from Christian faith. They thought in terms of the Christian God. Society adhered—or gave lip service—to a basic Christian morality. They swore on the Bible and showed up in church for Easter and at least wanted to be married and buried in a Christian service. But changes are afoot as a new attitude toward the church has emerged.

Describing this new historical period we're entering, Stuart Murray and others have popularized the term *post-Christendom*, a "culture that emerges as Christian faith loses coherence within a society that has been definitively shaped by the Christian story."[6] Post-Christendom is what happens when a "Christian" society gives up claiming that it's Christian. It's what happens when people become estranged from the Bible, don't bother to show up for Easter, and would rather have a "celebration of life" service in the local pub when they die than a proper Christian funeral rite.

The trend is sharply visible in places like the United Kingdom, where the Church of England once held a foundational place within British society but now finds itself struggling to connect with a culture increasingly alienated from and unaware of Christian faith. Something similar is happening in much of western Europe, but also in Canada, in Australia, and in cities along the U.S. coasts. Christian faith no longer makes up our shared cultural framework.

It's been a long time coming. Christendom has been on the decline for centuries, replaced by a mosaic of congregations set among folks of many faiths and none at all.

The process is something we most often associate with urban areas with a state church history. Think London, Stockholm, or even Massachusetts, with its onetime Congregationalist micro state church. Yet post-Christendom also describes what happens when many different sorts of churches find themselves suddenly alienated from a culture that they had assumed was their own. Post-Christendom can happen even without an official state church. And it can happen in rural places.

You see, many rural communities in the United States and Canada were not so much settled as colonized. Whole congregations picked up shop, crossed the Atlantic, and set about replicating themselves in the so-called New World. It was new to them, in

---

6. Stuart Murray, *Post-Christendom: Church and Mission in a Strange New World* (Milton Keynes, UK: Paternoster, 2004), 19.

any case, and they did their best to make it look like the "Old World" they had left behind. In places like Kansas, many Mennonite congregations migrated from German-speaking colonies in the Ukraine or Russia. They plotted out towns and farmsteads just as they'd had in Russia. These communities on the Great Plains became home to multiple Mennonite churches with successive waves of migration. Other Anabaptists arrived (where there are Mennonites, expect to find other Anabaptists—Amish, Hutterites, or Brethren groups—nearby). Until the spasmodic backlash against all things Teutonic during World War I, people spoke German as their main language. Towns like the one I live in were almost exclusively Mennonite. Even today, people refer to Moundridge as a "Mennonite community."

In the absence of state educational oversight and curricula, these communities ran their own country schools. School boards, local government, and core businesses were dominated by Mennonites. They were ethnic enclaves, ordering their affairs and caring for their own. People intermarried. In many ways, they were mini-Christendoms: communities homogeneous in ethnicity and faith, fusing state and church in practical (if not official) ways, differing from the *corpus Christianum* mostly by scale.[7]

This was hardly a phenomenon limited to Mennonites. Stephen Rasmussen, a Lutheran pastor with long experience serving rural congregations in western Minnesota, described the profoundly Nordic character of the congregations he has served: Danish, Swedish, and Icelandic Lutherans each preserving their distinctive cultural styles and theological approaches. One newcomer, seeking mightily to fit in with Rasmussen's congregation, once threw up her hands in despair and asked, "Do I have to go to Iceland in order to get in?"

Granted, in Anabaptist circles it may be jarring to speak of Mennonite-heavy geographic areas as little Christendoms. Christendom has become a code word for oppression, religious illiberality,

7. Cf. Alan Kreider, "Tongue Screws and Testimony," in *Fully Engaged: Missional Church in an Anabaptist Voice*, ed. Stanley Green and James Krabill (Harrisonburg, VA: Herald Press, 2015), 38–39.

and a rigid cultural homogeneity that oppressed minorities—particularly Jews, Muslims, and folks at odds with the state church. For Anabaptists, Christendom sums up everything that was wrong with the Middle Ages. Christendom is tongue screws, burning stakes, and dungeons packed with religious dissenters.

But that's not what I'm getting at when I talk about rural communities as little Christendoms. I'm talking about the way these communities operated according to a set of assumed values that included a shared faith. In Pastor Rasmussen's words, the Christendom system was "just the way people took care of each other." And it was good. Besides, even in the most homogeneous communities, not everyone was Mennonite or Lutheran or Dutch Reformed or Catholic. The unique chemistry of the American scene meant that there was room—at least in theory and by constitutional guarantee—for varied expressions of faith.

And in the Mennonite case, belonging to a little Mennonite Christendom did not mean furthering the state's ends, as it had in the medieval model, especially when it came to war making. Belonging to a little Christendom didn't guarantee cultural dominance, or even safety. Many Mennonites found themselves despised and under threat in their own communities, particularly during World War I war bond drives. In central Kansas, some Mennonites faced tarring and feathering, mob action, and the desecration of church buildings with yellow paint. Before he was rescued by the leader of the Anti-Horse Thief Association, John Schrag of tiny Burrton, Kansas, was nearly hung for refusing to purchase war bonds.[8] In Kalona, Iowa, the Mennonite bishop was hung in effigy and dynamite was exploded outside some Mennonite homes and businesses during World War II. Strikingly, the local Catholic priest in Kalona spoke out against these threats to the Mennonite community.[9] In many places, patriotic tensions strained communitarian values.

8. James Juhnke, "Showdown in Burrton, Kansas," in *Gathering at the Hearth: Stories Mennonites Tell*, ed. John Sharp (Scottdale, PA: Herald Press, 2001), 81.

9. Franklin Yoder, "Tension on the Homefront: One Mennonite Community's Experience during World War II," *Mennonite Historical Bulletin* 61, no. 4 (October 2000), 1-6.

In any case, the centrality and dominance of one or two faith traditions and ethnicities in rural communities persisted into the twentieth century. Whatever its benefits and faults, that system has been breaking down for the last fifty-some years. In the Mennonite case, the emigration of Mennonite young people and the immigration of folks with different backgrounds has led to the formation of new "Bible" or nondenominational congregations. Multiple factors contribute to the presence of these congregations, but one important reason new congregations have found a niche where they can thrive in rural communities is latent hostility to the old-guard churches. It's not just that people feel they can't connect with a Mennonite church because they don't have the right last name, or can't worship with the Icelandic Lutherans because they don't know the old recipes or understand the loanwords. It's because they reject the established order as oppressive, antiquated, or uninteresting. Established churches in rural communities are often not seen as bastions of strength or as guardians of communal values. Rather, they're the face of Organized Religion, the great bugaboo of our age. The whole problem with the established churches is that they're the Establishment. People don't want to pray with the Man.

For established rural congregations, then, it will be vital to come to a deeper awareness of the boundaries that keep them from connecting with newcomers. It means actively questioning the blood-is-thicker-than-baptismal-water mentality that binds many congregations together in a shared structure. The church leadership diagram cannot double as the family tree.

This is not to criticize the deeply intertwined family character of small, rural congregations. That's a fact of life, and it can be a source of strength. But there are family structures, and then there are family structures. Rural congregations, especially when they're small and composed of a few central families, grow by *adopting* newcomers into the church family. It's no accident that in laying out his vision in Ephesians of the margin-crossing, boundary-stretching church, Paul employs the language of adoption. God "destined us for adoption as his children through Jesus Christ" (Ephesians 1:5). God adopts us. We adopt others.

Congregations that understand this throw baby showers for the pregnant mom who recently showed up and find camp scholarships for the kids who plop down in the back row without their folks. They invite the new family over. They share meals and play board games. My friend's traditional Mennonite congregation threw a German-Mexican fusion *quinceañera* for the daughter of a new family. The congregation I serve pushed its own envelope by marrying a new couple during the morning worship service and throwing a celebratory potluck reception afterward. These are acts of adoption. There are more. I'm convinced that there's a lot of love in these little congregations that's just waiting to be tapped.

This is the vision we have to recover and encourage in our established rural congregations. It's a moral imperative, a way of living out God's own commitment to those on the margins. But it's also a pathway to revitalization. You see, folks who are deeply embedded in the communitarian structure through family and business ties will rarely make a lateral move within the community. When they do, it's often a sign of turmoil within the community's system. But folks on the other side of the fence, newcomers or misfits or both, don't have an automatic place within the community. They're open to invitation. Sometimes they're even seeking it.

Because boundaries are great, until they aren't. What gives strength and identity to one community—the traditional foods, shared family names, and churchy acronyms—is a barbed wire fence to those on the outside. It can seem all but uncrossable.

The most prickly boundaries are seldom the most obvious to outsiders. We initially assumed the community we served in eastern Washington was divided along straightforward racial-ethnic lines: Mexican and white. That was true enough, in some ways. But we gradually picked up on something far more subtle. There was no one "Mexican community." True, most of the town was of Mexican descent, but the much more important division was between the earlier migration of folks from Los Ramones—a small town in Nuevo León, Mexico—and those who had come in later waves. *Ramoleños* were deeply ensconced in community life. Their native sons and daughters included the mayor, the director of the migrant daycare, and leaders within the Catholic church and Assemblies of God. They were great folks, bound together by family ties stretching back to ancestral lands in Mexico. They were on the inside of a communitarian structure that also included Mormons and other white folks who had pioneered and cut open the sagebrush tilth when irrigation came in. And they weren't moving. They embraced Christian faith, or they didn't; either way, they were secure in their identity and in large part held by the inertia of tradition and family ties.

Newer migrants, however, were much more open to connecting with an earnest young pastor and his wife. They might try the Spanish-language Bible study. They were interested in the whole-grain tortilla cooking class in the church basement. They were free radicals, open to forming new connections and relationships with those who were willing to reach out. They were open to adopting and being adopted.

This pattern of adoption was repeated among other pastors I talked to. Connie Stutts, a Methodist minister serving a rural congregation near New Bern, North Carolina, described how members of her aging congregation began to pray for children. They sensed that the church was dying. The younger families had moved to the city and suburbs. The older members who remained had little hope left. So they began praying that God would bring them young families with children.

A surprising thing happened. The federal government began to resettle Burmese refugees in the area. After a tragic car accident in which several refugees were killed, Stutts's congregation performed funerals and became involved in the grieving families' lives. Refugee families and children began connecting with the church. There were challenges: noise, uncertainty about appropriate behavior in church, a bit of a learning curve on the use of flush toilets. But the church had prayed for children, and God had sent them children.

The congregation welcomed their new neighbors into the life of the church, eventually launching English as a second language classes, summer programs for the kids, and incorporating a Karen language greeting and Scripture reading into worship. They didn't just allow these visitors. They adopted them. And the congregation was adopted, in turn, by their new neighbors.

The water's edge: Transforming boundaries in baptism

Learning to work the edges is not about strategy. It's about spirituality. We've got to cultivate a barbed-wire-crossing spirituality that points us toward the margins and tells us what to do when we get there.

This is a baptismal spirituality. Baptism is the fundamental sign of Christian identity, the moment when, as Paul puts it to the Colossians, we are "rescued . . . from the power of darkness and transferred . . . into the kingdom of his beloved Son" (Colossians 1:13). Baptism marks the moment when followers of Jesus are welcomed fully into the household of God. It's the place of adoption.

What this means is that baptism is also about margins. The boundary between the church and the world runs right through baptism. This isn't as simple as saying *world = bad, church = good, and baptism is the door between the two*. It's more complicated than that, because baptism doesn't remove us from life in the world. We still live in the neighborhood, and the world is still our neighbor. What baptism does is *reorient* us in the neighborhood. It sets us up to come at the world differently. We're reoriented toward love of God and neighbor. We're reoriented toward Jesus as the source and center of our life. Nowhere are these new orientations more stark than in worship, where adoration of God takes center stage and the church's exaltation of Jesus as Lord pushes back against all the other gods clamoring for our allegiance.

Baptism reorients us toward the margins. What's more, baptism creates a new margin between an old way of life and all the behaviors and commitments that go with it, and the body of Christ with its way of life (Ephesians 4:17-32). Baptism draws a new line around and among believers. But it also draws an arrow pointing believers out into the world. It's no wonder that Jesus gave the apostles a baptismal mandate when he sent them out on mission into the world (Matthew 28:19). Baptize and preach. Baptize and teach. Baptize the world into a new way of life, a rebirth into the kingdom through the water and the Spirit (John 3:5). In the name of the Father, and of the Son, and of the Holy Spirit, go get 'em wet.

Ephesians is a baptismally centered letter. We are called into church through the "one baptism" (Ephesians 4:5). We are made holy through "the washing of water by the word" (5:26). Baptism makes us who we are in Christ Jesus and sets us at an odd angle to the world. Baptism is edgy.

Rowan Williams, former archbishop of Canterbury, reflects on the reorienting power of baptism in his book *Being Christian*. Williams writes that baptism does in miniature what Jesus did on the world stage: he entered into the messiness of the world in order to restore humanity to what God had created it to be. Where will we find the baptized? "In the neighbourhood of chaos," writes Williams. Baptism doesn't make us superior to the unwashed masses. Rather, it lays a claim upon us to enter into "a new level of solidarity with other people."[10]

Where does this baptismal spirituality take us? Here are three ways forward.

First, baptism means we have to reclaim our essential identity as those who linger at the edges of the community. Especially in our small towns, this will mean connecting with folks who, for whatever reason, find themselves on the wrong side of the Gemeinschaft. We'll have to embrace the edge. We're edge people.

Second, baptism means that we will have to become a church that's open to risk. Life in the rural church is risky. If you mess up with the neighbors, it can be hard to recover. Churches that gain a bad reputation have few opportunities to redeem themselves. It's not as simple as calling a fresh-faced pastor and hanging out an "Under New Management" sign.

But life in the rural church is also risky in that we're opening ourselves up to the messiness of community, with all its needs and hurts. We're pouring ourselves out for the life of the world, which just happens to be the concrete life of the neighborhood.

---

10. Rowan Williams, *Being Christian: Baptism, Bible, Eucharist, Prayer* (Grand Rapids: Eerdmans, 2014), 4–6.

Of course, the church can do this in the city. But there's something different about the way it plays out in a small town. The needs are right there. You can't escape across town on the subway. They know where you live.

Third, baptism transforms how we see the boundaries. Baptism is inherently boundary crossing, because baptism transforms us and places us in new relationship with Christ and with one another in the church. Rather than attack boundaries, baptism sets us up to transform them. This means less fence cutting and more pushing the fence down with a stick. Give people a hand over.

My friend and colleague Brett Klingenberg found a way to do this in his congregation. He pastors a country church in small-town Nebraska. He describes the key role that the traditional bread *semmel* plays in the culture of his church. Semmel is part of the congregation's Mennonite heritage, a bread carried along with them on the trek from West Prussia to the Great Plains of Nebraska. It's an identity marker bound up with layers of family tradition. Clearly, for the church's outreach, semmel could be a big problem. Semmel is not a part of the wider culture. People don't buy a dozen semmels at the corner gas station. It could easily be just one more strand of barbed wire keeping the neighborhood out.

But Klingenberg's congregation has developed a powerful way to use semmel to push down the barbed wire. During the final session of membership class, candidates for membership are treated to a semmel breakfast. As they eat, the deacons and pastor share the church's history. It's a way that the congregation helps "newcomers navigate terrain that is foreign and yet attractive."[11] Semmel—and all that it represents to the people and history of that congregation—becomes part of *their* story. Klingenberg labels encounters like this "creek crossings": moments when the church acknowledges its boundaries, yet finds ways to help others across.

This is a transformation of how we see the boundaries. I'm convinced it's the only clearheaded thing we can do. The boundaries are still there, but their meaning is transformed. We find ways

11. Brett Klingenberg, "Creek Crossings" (paper presented at Western District Conference Rural Church Reference Council, Beatrice, NE, April 23, 2016).

over and through. We value them even as we turn their meaning on its head.

Baptism calls us to become people who go beyond ourselves and a church that goes beyond itself. We are often most preoccupied with how boundaries keep people out. But boundaries also keep us in. Stepping across the barbed wire means reclaiming our birthright identity in baptism. It's asking God to renew the grace of our baptisms in each of us and to lead us out from that water's edge.

Baptism helps us over the fence, allowing us to face the other not as a scapegoat or threat, but with hope. Baptism is the centrifugal force that propels us outward from our own inertia. We're centered in Christ and sent out in Christ, the pilgrim church that steps over its own barbed wire. Baptism swings us perpetually outward, where we move not only to the margins but also to the horizons of the kingdom.

My son and I once took a walk with a little band of brothers. While their mother chatted with my wife inside our house at the edge of town, we walked down to the end of a lane and up over a hill clothed in dun winter sagebrush. It wasn't far, but for those boys it became an epic hike. This was no mere walk. It was a journey to the very edge of society. Who knew what might lie over that hill?

When the dirt path ended, we struck out through the sagebrush and weeds and waded our way up the hill. The wind battered us. The cold pinked our faces. And then we had to pause under the tungsten globe of the sun, because barbed wire ran the length of the hill and cut off our little path. Should we cross or not? The wire was ancient and low, weighed down by years of forgetful neglect. But it was still there, marking where *open* and *closed* began, *mine* and *yours*. Easy does it. Careful now. Just don't get hung up and trip.

We crossed the barbed wire edge of the world and walked on.

CHAPTER 8

Learn to Die: Congregational Ars Moriendi

Lord, if you had been here, my brother would not have died.
—John 11:21

Not every story has a resurrection.

You wouldn't pick this up from a stroll through a Christian bookstore, where the central preoccupation is church growth, revival, and turnaround. Much has been written on how to make your congregation live again. People travel great distances to attend conferences on that sort of thing. Little, however, has been written about church death. Denominational offices have produced some helpful guides.[1] But the work of congregational hospice and funeral—caring for and "burying" dying congregations—is not bestselling material. No one wants to buy such depressing stuff.

1. Such as "A Resource for the Closing of Congregations," produced by the Evangelical Lutheran Church in America in 2011 (http://www.lss-elca.org/wp-content/uploads/Documents/Closing_Congregations.pdf), and the *Choosing the Faithful Path* curriculum used by United Methodist leaders.

Yet I'm convinced that in order to live fully and vibrantly in the rural church, we must also learn to face congregational death faithfully, hopefully, and lovingly. In order to tend the living promise of the rural church, we also must learn to find meaning in death.

In order to learn to live, we must learn to die.

At various points in history, Christians have taken the task of learning to die with deep seriousness. An entire genre of literature arose in the Middle Ages to help Christians die well. It was called the *Ars Moriendi*—the "art of dying." This self-help genre was widely read, what writer Allen Verhey refers to as a sort of *Dying Well for Dummies*.[2] The *Ars Moriendi* gave instruction on—among other things—the imitation of Christ's death as well as prayers for use with the dying.[3] The works analyzed the special temptations facing the dying and recommended virtues to be cultivated—at the time of death, but also over the course of life. The *Ars Moriendi* were a way to train Christians in the faithful art of dying, an art whose practices were ultimately rooted in imitation of the dying Christ.

Without buying into the detailed specifics of fifteenth-century death manuals, might something similar aid the contemporary church—not just for individuals but also for congregations? What might a congregational *Ars Moriendi* look like? Learning to die well is no small feat. At the very least, developing a congregational *Ars Moriendi* will require us to recover the dying role in our congregations and deepen our understanding of the meaning of resurrection. Developing a congregational *Ars Moriendi* will mean learning to love the dying, fear the Lord, and depend on God.

Don't ruin the church's death: Dying and the heart of the gospel

In the 2004 Disney movie *The Incredibles*, the superhero career of Mr. Incredible takes a turn for the worst when he saves a man from death after he leapt from a skyscraper. In a comic spin, the

---

2. Allen Verhey, *The Christian Art of Dying: Learning from Jesus* (Grand Rapids: Eerdmans, 2011), 79.

3. Ibid., 87.

man hires an attorney and sues Mr. Incredible for having foiled his suicide attempt. Standing indignantly before TV cameras in a neck brace, the man accuses Mr. Incredible: "You didn't save my life! You ruined my death!"

This sounds familiar. Pastors come in like superheroes bent on resurrection, yet our turnaround efforts in shaky churches frequently don't amount to saving the life of the congregation, but rather ruining its death. Learning to die is not a task impressed upon the church by unfortunate circumstances. Just as with individuals, learning to die is a vital skill that all congregations must squarely face and master.

Learning to die—to self, to evil, to the false promises of power, wealth, and security—is at the heart of the gospel. Dietrich Bonhoeffer, martyred under Nazi Germany, wrote, "When Christ calls a man, he bids him come and die."[4] He was right, of course. Jesus said as much: "Take up [your] cross and follow me" (Mark 8:34). Jesus said, "Those who want to save their life will lose it" (Matthew 16:25). Jesus said that it's the grain of wheat that dies that "bears much fruit" (John 12:24).

Jesus' disciples perceived all this as too much loose talk of death. They got a little worried and tried to correct Jesus' theology. But you'll remember Jesus' sharp words for Peter: "Get behind me, Satan!" (Matthew 16:23).

It is only in dying to self, to our petty messiah complexes and distorted notions of our own importance, that we can return to the true source of our life in God. We have to go out into the desert and crash, Elijah-like, under the broom tree (1 Kings 19). Otherwise we'll never shed our false selves, our false hopes, our false beliefs in our own abilities to fix the world. We have to learn to die.

At the very least, I think we begin from the point of view that death happens. Congregations have life cycles, and while there's not an exact parallel to the human life cycle in that congregations can be renewed and transformed for centuries, congregational mortality is not extraordinary. You may have noticed I'm avoiding

---

4. Dietrich Bonhoeffer, *The Cost of Discipleship* (New York: Touchstone, 1995), 89.

the word *natural*. In the Christian point of view, death is never "natural." Death is the result of sin (Romans 6:23), an affront to the goodness of all that God has created. Death is not built into the natural order of things but is a result of the natural order having gone existentially haywire. The "natural" lifespan of a congregation is eternity. Yet death happens, and as followers of Jesus, we have resources that we can bring to bear on understanding death and journeying with the dying.

In developing our congregational *Ars Moriendi*, we'll delve into the theological basis for dying well. We won't make a checklist of factors meant to determine if it's time for a congregation to die. We won't lay out a list of loose ends that must be tied up at the end of the life cycle. Denominational bodies have their own resources that address these issues. What's more, every context is different, and congregations may have wildly variant views on what makes for a "viable" church.

In a 2015 article, writer Angie Mabry-Nauta relates the experience of her congregation, the Reformed Church in Plano, Texas. The congregation had declined to some 135 members "strongly committed to their church" with vibrant worship.[5] Yet the church perceived itself to have lost vitality and a sense of mission and voted to close its doors. Few rural congregations I know would close at 135 strongly committed members with vibrant worship. We would be happy to break 100.

Our congregational *Ars Moriendi* begins in reclaiming the dying role for congregations.

Ennobling death: Recovering the dying role for congregations

No doubt the church's reluctance to probe congregational death and its focus on turnaround is a reflection of our culture's idolatry of growth, fear of death, and disdain for the dying. Death is regarded as failure. Pity those who do not "fight" cancer with every available tool, regardless of the chances of success. As the

---

5. Angie Mabry-Nauta, "The Last Sunday: When It's Time for a Church to Close," *Christian Century* 132, no. 1 (2015): 22–25.

late writer Allen Verhey put it in his book *The Christian Art of Dying*, "people may be sick, quite sick, but to admit that they are dying seems a betrayal of the confidence we have in medicine and technology."[6] This attitude is a symptom of the broader medicalization of death in our culture, in which, as Verhey observed, "the 'dying role' is lost; only the 'sick role' remains."[7] The sick role prescribes passively submitting to medical advice, consulting physicians and specialists, and often clinging to life even when there's only a whisker-thin chance of success. Above all, the sick role prescribes *not giving up*. There's always one more treatment, one more physician, one more heroic moonshot that might put off the inevitable. Who knows? Not trying everything at one's disposal would seem a betrayal of confidence—and in modern medicine, there is much at our disposal. It's no wonder that the search for a cure, especially when diagnosis is sketchy, is often embraced by patients as a "medical odyssey"—a kind of quasi-spiritual journey that has given birth to the genre of cancer-survivor memoir.

I suspect that something similar has happened with congregations. This same loss of the "dying role" and wholesale conversion to the "sick role" has taken place, but to the nth degree. Congregations may be sick, quite sick, but to admit that they are dying seems a betrayal of the confidence we have in turnaround strategies. Especially to those on the inside who have invested vast sums of life and treasure, it can be extremely difficult to admit that a congregation is dying. The dying role has been lost to congregations, having been replaced by the turnaround role. There's always one more program to try, one more music style to adopt, one more visioning meeting to hold. You can always hire a young pastor.

On top of that, our society disparages dying churches. While dying individuals can be afforded compassion and the ministrations of medical personnel, family, and clergy, dying churches are looked at with scorn. In the minds of many, churches don't die; they fail. The dying role is lost.

---

6. Verhey, *The Christian Art of Dying*, 4.

7. Ibid.

The difference between death and failure is not trivial. Death can in some ways be ennobled by ritual and Scripture and tamed by friends and compassion.[8] Death points to our ultimate dependence on God as the source of life, and through Jesus' death on the cross, death can be invested with theological meaning. Failure, however, is procedural. It's about doing or not doing. A business can fail. A plan can fail. An employee can fail at his duties. But failure is not existential. It doesn't reach down to the fundamental human mystery. Death does. The vocabulary of failure, on the other hand, leads to disparagement.

A man once dropped by my office to sell us something churchy. He was amiable, asking several questions about the congregation and my role. Then he launched into an extended paean to his magnificent megachurch in a nearby city. It was so big. It had so many youth. It was starting up new campuses in neighboring small towns. He was so confident in the superiority of his congregation that he even invited me to come and attend (that is, he invited me, the *pastor* standing in my own sanctuary, to attend his church). But that wasn't what bothered me. I love it when folks are jazzed up about their church. What got me was the language he used to talk about the village churches in the small towns where his congregation was launching new campuses. Yes, there were some well-established churches in those communities, but they weren't anything like his grand church. They didn't have his church's drive and creativity. No. They were, in his words, "fuddy-duddy." In his eyes, those country churches were washed-up *failures*.

I suspect that this disparaging language lies just below the surface in many discussions of the rural church. It clouds the air and prevents congregations from speaking frankly and openly about their circumstances and what might lie ahead. It causes churches to engage in just the slightest bit of number fudging and creative storytelling. Things are great out here! We're not failures!

The ascendance of the language of failure and the diminishment of a meaningful vocabulary of congregational death make the work of bringing dying congregations to a graceful end all the

8. See Verhey's discussion of "tame death" in *The Christian Art of Dying*, 11.

more difficult. Lyn Sorrells walks with congregations through the dying process. Sorrells leads the Church Legacy Initiative out of the Western North Carolina Conference of the United Methodist Church. The initiative works to guide congregations as they shut down, help members find new church homes, and direct the dying congregation's resources into new, life-giving ventures in the broader church. According to Sorrells, congregational leaders who understand their congregation's death as a failure are often angry. They seek someone to blame: other congregational members, the church hierarchy, a previous pastor. Part of the essential work that Sorrells and his team do with congregations is to help them reframe what they had named a failure as death. Life goes on in the larger church. God is still faithful.

But the problem of the loss of the dying role for congregations runs deeper than just the disparagement our society lobs at dying churches. It's a theological conundrum as well. The problem goes something like this:

> There is life where Jesus is.
> There is no life in your congregation.
> Therefore Jesus is not in your congregation.

It goes back to Martha's faith-filled profession in John 11:21. She believed in Jesus' life-giving power. "Lord," she said, "if you had been here, my brother would not have died." Indeed, Jesus affirmed her faith, telling her, "I am the resurrection and the life. Those who believe in me, even though they die, will live, and everyone who lives and believes in me will never die" (John 11:25-26). Where Jesus is, there is life and resurrection.

Thus, it would be all too easy to conclude that when a congregation dies, it must have been because Jesus wasn't present. If the Lord had been there, your church would not have died. Jesus has, obviously, left the building. Add to that the bickering and infighting that often accompanies congregational death, with its heightened anxieties, and you have a perfect blame-the-victim mix. The church died because of all the fighting, all the bad decisions, all the lack of missional outlook. They were a bunch of old fuddy-duddies. Jesus wasn't there. Good riddance.

But this is a scandalous treatment of the bride of Christ, not to mention a heretical understanding of Jesus' resurrection. In the words of Romans 14:4, who are we to judge the servants of another? We must remember that whatever the faults of leaders and folks in the pews, every congregation is mysteriously the bride of Christ. Even troubled congregations must be treated with care and respect. They're all Jesus' beloved.

The resurrection is not a happy ending

The resurrection is not the "happy ending to the gospel," to use Sam Allberry's phrase.[9] Yet happy endings are precisely what most of us long for. We want things to turn out all right—or better yet, to turn out the way they used to be. When it comes right down to it, most of us don't want resurrection, which is messy, risky, and forward-looking. We want a renewal of that golden age in the past when the nursery was full. But that's just embalming.

So if resurrection is not the happy ending of the gospel or the guarantee of renewal, then what is it?

The simple equating of Jesus' presence with guaranteed life is at best a misunderstanding, at worst heresy. The church in Thessalonica seems to have misunderstood the gospel on this point. In Paul's first letter, he spent considerable time (much of chapter 4) explaining how it was that faithful believers had died. At least some in the church seem to have imagined that Jesus' resurrection power meant they would not have to face physical death. But Paul writes, "We do not want you to be uninformed . . . about those who have died" (1 Thessalonians 4:13). We grieve, but not as those who have no hope. We look forward to Jesus' resurrection power awakening even the dead on the last day.

In Ephesus, Paul confronted some who believed that the resurrection had already taken place. He named Hymenaeus and Philetus among those who were "upsetting the faith of some" (2 Timothy 2:18). Their bad theology was spreading "like gangrene" (v. 17). Paul is light on the specifics of their error; his audience knew

9. Sam Allberry, *Lifted: Experiencing the Resurrection Life* (Nottingham, England: Inter-Varsity Press, 2010), 17.

who they were and what they were teaching. But it seems that some believed themselves to be walking in the fullness of Christ's resurrection *already*. This is it. The resurrection is now. No more dying here; we are going to see the King.

Strikingly, Paul's corrective involved the assurance that the Lord knows his people (v. 19) and that there are many utensils in a big house, "not only of gold and silver but also of wood and clay" (v. 20). Paul named the heresy for what it was—not merely a theological difference, but also a matter of some who were "successful" disparaging others who were "struggling." It's not unlike the struggle Paul faced in his own ministry, with some "super-apostles" criticizing his proclivity for suffering and weakness (see 2 Corinthians 11–12).

For Paul, these leaders had committed the classic sin, what he named a lack of "discerning the body" (1 Corinthians 11:29). It's the sin that divided the church at the Lord's table, the core of its worship. And it happens to be the sin that led many to be "weak and ill, and some have died" (1 Corinthians 11:30). Of all the troubles faced by the early church, Paul singled this one out for special concern and opprobrium. There are no fuddy-duddies; there are merely utensils set apart by the Lord for different uses. Success and superiority are not signs of Jesus' resurrection life inhabiting an individual. Or a congregation.

So what is?

The heresy of Hymenaeus and Philetus was the classic one, a variation on the heresy the church has struggled with and against since the beginning. It's gnosticism.

The details of what makes gnosticism *gnosticism* are fuzzy. The term is a blanket one used to speak of teachings that arose in and around the ancient church and had roots in a philosophical framework that contended that the mind needed to break free of the body. It goes back at least as far as Socrates, who awaited his death with a dispassion that the ancients lauded as heroic, as if death were merely the shedding of his bodily husk. For Socrates, freedom lay outside the confines of his jail cell—and the cells of his body.

Gnosticism was a philosophy of spiritual success that led to a particular view of the body. Proponents focused on attaining *gnosis*—knowledge—and valued the life of the mind, or spirit, above the life of the body. For some, the body was not as real as the mind. It was a source of trouble, irredeemable, of no use to those truly seeking salvation. What's more, some gnostics saw the body as a product of a vicious and vindictive creator god of the Old Testament, not the God of love who sent Jesus. Gnostic disparagement of the body led to disparagement of morality lived out in the body, of the hope of bodily resurrection and that of the body of the church. Gnostics divided the church into categories: those who were fleshly and those who were spiritual. Some got it, some didn't.

Here we are again, still thumb wrestling with gnosticism's latest iteration. There are myriad ways that our society is gnostic to the core, treating bodies as vehicles for pleasure and entertainment, for pills and scalpels and gamma rays, but having scant grasp of the *holiness* of all that God has writ in human flesh.

For churches, death-defying gnosticism comes disguised as renewalism. Like Hymenaeus and Philetus, we come to believe that if we just had the proper technique and strategy for renewal, we would attain the resurrection now. We believe that congregations don't have to die, that they won't face their own disintegration and mortality. It's the sneer at the fuddy-duddies. What makes it all the worse is that it's wrapped in the idiom of renewal and thought to be justified by resurrection. But it's heresy all the same. The disparagement of dying local Christian bodies is just gnosticism dolled up in black lipstick, mouthing the devil's empty promise to us that the Lord will not allow us to "dash your foot against a stone" (Matthew 4:6).

This is not the meaning of Jesus' resurrection. It's no happy ending to the gospel. The two-part Luke–Acts series makes this abundantly clear. Jesus' resurrection does not mark the end of the disciples' troubles. Jesus defeats death at the conclusion of the gospel of Luke, and a scant few chapters into the book of Acts, the disciples face persecution, dispersal, contention between

Greek- and Hebrew-speaking believers, and the death of both a deacon (Stephen, Acts 7) and an apostle (James, Acts 12). So much for happy endings. The resurrected Jesus calls Saul into his service with the not-so-winsome invitation, "I myself will show him how much he must suffer for the sake of my name" (Acts 9:16). Saul-who-becomes-Paul, the great preacher of resurrection (see 1 Corinthians 15), thinks this makes perfect sense. "If I must boast," he writes, "I will boast of the things that show my weakness" (2 Corinthians 11:30).

Thus the promise of the resurrection is not a guarantee that everything will turn out all right or that wherever Jesus is present, his church will be shielded from disappointment and trouble and persecution. Resurrection does not exempt the church from death. Something deeper is going on. For congregations, just as for individuals, the promise of the resurrection is a promise that God gives new life and that God is faithful beyond death. Resurrection is so much bigger than church renewal.

Yet it is also true that where Jesus is, new life is. People are healed in all the ways that people need healing. Things get turned around, surprisingly, improbably. Old Lazarus's graveclothes slip off. He doesn't need them anymore.

No doubt this is what Jesus meant when he told Martha, "I am the resurrection and the life. Those who believe in me, even though they die, will live" (John 11:25). The life Jesus gives endures beyond physical death. It's the ancient promise of resurrection on the last day, the promise Daniel talked about when he prophesied, "Those who sleep in the dust of the earth shall awake" (Daniel 12:2). It's the book of Revelation speaking of the judgment and the "second death" (Revelation 20:14) for those who do not share in the "first resurrection" (20:5). But it's also the day-in and day-out promise that there will be fresh sprigs of resurrection poking up in our lives whenever Jesus is around.

The point hardly needs arguing, for without Jesus' resurrection power, there would, quite simply, be no church. As G. K. Chesterton put it, "Christianity has died many times and risen again; for it had a God who knew the way out of the grave."[10] And we do. The church has arisen improbably from beneath the weight of old gods and dead religions too many times to count. In many ways, dying is just as characteristic of Christianity as rising, and less surprising.

It's God who gives new life to the church in every age, as God chooses, and none of it depends on the church's worthiness or relevance or even faithfulness. Jesus just shows up, and the gravestone rolls away with a crack and a rumble.

But this does not imply that every congregation will be revived. Even faithful Smyrna and Philadelphia, commended among the seven churches of Revelation, lie in ruins. Resurrection is a promise to the church universal, not to any individual congregation.

The resurrection attests to God's faithfulness beyond death. All too often we come to believe that resurrection is a response to *our* faithfulness. If we play our doctrinal cards right and keep ourselves free from sin, God will reward us with resurrection, which really just translates into continued existence. This is to drag Jesus' warning in Revelation 2:5 that he will "remove [the] lampstand" of unfaithful congregations into America's culture wars. According to this reading, conservative churches are said to thrive, while liberal mainline denominations who have made confetti of the church's traditional beliefs die a slow death, mottled with controversy.

Except that this is not true, even in broad strokes. The landscape of American Christianity is more complicated than a simple equation of faithfulness = growth, apostasy = decline (as handy as it would be to use *existence* as a test of faithfulness). Nowhere is this more apparent than in rural areas, where "traditional" and "liberal" don't always have the same valence as in the city, and where powerful demographic currents have emptied faithful congregations of all stripes.

There are no deathless churches, no Church of the Perpetual Spring. But neither are there churches not marked by the hope and ongoing power of the resurrection. Resurrection does not mean

---

10. G. K. Chesterton, *The Everlasting Man* (Seaside, OR: Rough Draft Printing, 2013), 160.

that God will just keep on keeping on, doing the same things that God has always done in a congregation or community. Resurrection is not renewalism. A congregation may stumble, may crumble, may die, but God's kingdom ministry will continue forward, by hook or shepherd's crook. God won't give up on the church or drop the work of resurrection, but God's future won't necessarily be identical to God's past. God doesn't guarantee our projects. God guarantees God's glory.

We see this in the story of Lazarus. When Mary and Martha sent a message to Jesus that their brother Lazarus was dying, he responded simply, "This illness does not lead to death; rather it is for God's glory, so that the Son of God may be glorified through it" (John 11:4). It all seems straightforward enough. Jesus shows up in the nick of time (or shortly thereafter) and resurrects his friend with a word. It all turns out okay—a happy ending. Maybe there's still some sheet cake left over from Lazarus's funeral lunch.

But something deeper is afoot. Jesus timed his visit. He conspicuously showed up *after* Lazarus had died. Jesus shifted the focus to God's glory over and against the simple binaries of alive or dead, good or bad, success or failure. This illness does not lead to death. It doesn't really even lead to resurrection. It leads to God's glory.

It was true for Lazarus, and it's true for our congregations. The point of resurrection isn't just continued life. It's glory. It's God winning glory for himself by trampling down Death by death. When Jesus showed up at Lazarus's craggy tomb, days late for the funeral and intent on premeditated resurrection, he had God's glory in mind. Jesus promised Mary and Martha that they would see "the glory of God" (John 11:40). When, a short time later, Jesus turned toward his destiny on the cross, he said, "The hour has come for the Son of Man to be glorified" (John 12:23).

Learning resurrection means learning to glorify God in all things, whether life or death, things present or things to come. For the church, this means that though our local ministry will come to an end, we place our hope in Jesus' universal ministry, which never ends. God's name is glorified in the church to all generations

(Ephesians 3:20-21). We aim to glorify God even in congregational death.

In the most simple and concrete terms, churches can glorify God in their dissolution by how they treat each other and what they do with their assets. Congregations can catch a resurrection vision by committing their remaining funds and sometimes their building to the ongoing mission of the church, such as through new church plants or revitalization efforts. Lyn Sorrells spoke of how a church building can be reopened as a new congregation with a new pastor and seed group that better reflects the transformed neighborhood. Pastor Meg Lumsdaine, who walked with her congregation at the end of its life cycle, talked about how churches find meaning "when the life of the congregation can be transformed to help the birth of something new." One church I know found the courage to pull the plug on their current ministry because they were donating their building and assets to become a campus of a growing congregation. Resurrection was a real and tangible possibility for them. Just sign on the dotted line.

But this understanding of resurrection also means recognizing that not every church can be turned around—because of circumstances, because of personalities, because the neighborhood has changed and God is doing a new thing. Believing in resurrection will not mean believing that good congregations never die. It will mean trusting that God's life-giving power is sufficient to accomplish God's mission, through and beyond death. It's this kind of resurrection trust that gives us the space we need to truly love the dying.

Learn to love the dying: On not pretending things are other than they are

Shortly after graduating from seminary, I signed up for some unspecified "service" at a church convention in a big city. My assignment came in: go to the Alzheimer's wing of a local nursing home and hang out with the residents. I had been imagining something with a little more pizzazz—like playing with a bunch of vivacious and suitably multiethnic kids. I could go to the nursing home any day of the week. I wanted something more *life giving*. So I tried to change my assignment. Thankfully, the volunteer coordinator would have none of it. "We can't change it," she said. "You'll just have to go."

I'm embarrassed about it now. I had a lot to learn: about accepting challenges rather than avoiding them, about caring for people in all stages of life, and especially about learning to love the dying.

I mean dying people, whom I loved in theory but, in this case, didn't love in practice—at least not at first. I figured it out with their help, after a few crafts and a bit of halting conversation and singing. Their lives were just as valuable and worthy of my attention as any child's. But I also mean all that is dying: dying dreams, dying plans, dying churches. Especially dying churches.

While the bride of Christ will never die, and God is an expert practitioner of resurrection, local congregations die all the time. Good people with good intentions watch as their congregations gray and dust gathers on the cry room changing table. There's a bang or a whimper or, if a few people manage to hear the Spirit, a gracious wrap-up.

What then?

I'm convinced that a core Christian virtue is learning to love the dying, including dying congregations. In fact, I think that a lot of the church hopping that characterizes our contemporary moment has to do with a fear of being associated with death. It's the same reason we avoid the cemetery and the nursing home. We don't want death to rub off on us. We don't want to be associated with decay and defeat. Check out that new church down the road! They're so young!

I admit my own complicity in the pursuit of the congregational fountain of youth. I'm more apt to highlight our outreach efforts and the new young people who are connecting with our congregation than our bevy of faithful eighty-year-olds. While researching this chapter, one of the pastors I interviewed asked if my interest in dying congregations was merely academic or if it was because my own congregation was dying. I demurred. *My church? Oh, no! [Insert nervous laughter.] I'm just doing research.*

Methodist writer Paul Nixon published two books in 2007 and 2012. The first, *I Refuse to Lead a Dying Church!*, is a manifesto on turning congregations around. In the book's description, Nixon confidently declares that "God has called all leaders . . . to lead healthy, *growing* spiritual movements."[11] The second book, *We Refused to Lead a Dying Church!*, tells stories of congregational leaders who, with a mix of pluck, optimism, and the power of the Spirit, managed to get their congregations back on the road to growth. (I mentioned pastor Kent Rogers's story in chapter 6). Both book covers feature pastors in defiant poses, arms crossed and chins jutting out as they stare down death and congregational inertia.

But why refuse to serve dying churches? Dying churches need our gifts and compassion too. Perhaps our hesitancy points to a weak spot in our theology, a place where our love is rather conditional. We'll love you, unless you're dying. I wonder about this. Do we believe that Christ is the Lord of the church? Do we believe that "in the Lord [our] labor is not in vain" (1 Corinthians 15:58)? Do we believe that "if we live, we live to the Lord, and if we die, we die to the Lord; so then, whether we live or whether we die, we are the Lord's" (Romans 14:8)?

We need to recover a deep faith rooted in Christ's love. Our faith is not that everything will work out, or that if we believe the right things, our dreams for congregational resurrection will be fulfilled. We hold on to something a little subtler—and a lot harder. It's this: that if you follow brokenness all the way down, it will always hit the seam of God's love. This is a love that, in Wendell Berry's words, "is folded and enfolded and unfolded forever and ever, the love by which the dead are alive and the unborn welcomed into the womb."[12] It's the love that compels us to love the dying.

---

11. Paul Nixon, *I Refuse to Lead a Dying Church!* (Cleveland: Pilgrim Press, 2007), 13 (italics in original).

12. Wendell Berry, *Andy Catlett: Early Travels (Port William)* (Emeryville, CA: Shoemaker and Hoard, 2006), 130.

Pastors are especially prone to stumble at this point, because we stake so much of our self-image on congregational success. If the church does poorly, it reflects on us. If it does well, it's points for our résumé. If it dies, well, then we (or at least our careers) might just die too. Indeed, all the pastors I spoke with who had journeyed with their congregations to the grave found that they had to take time to recover spiritually and emotionally. It's often easier to move forward with naïve optimism than to face the reality that a congregation is dying. But this must change. Perhaps Nixon could publish a third book: *I Embraced Serving a Dying Church*.

All too often, our optimism and church turnaround efforts are a mask for our fear of death. We don't want that mark on our soul—or worse, on our ministerial résumé. Our efforts amount to experimental chemotherapy. It may or may not work, but at least we're doing something. And many pastors bail out with a parachute before the end.

But we must learn to love the dying. We must love them not just in theory but by being present to them, which is the true meaning of the word *compassion*: suffering with. We must stand with dying churches, crossing our arms and jutting out our chins against those who would disparage them. We must be able to say in the same breath, "My church is dying. I love my church."

Pastor Norma Duerksen shared how the small Ohio congregation she had recently begun to serve first faced the possibility of its own death. Between the motions made and seconded in the annual business meeting, a woman piped up and raised the question, "Can we talk about closing?" It turned out to be a defining moment in the congregation, not one evoking anger or resentment but one allowing the church to frankly assess its position. Duerksen led the church, which numbered around twenty-five congregants at the time, to write what she called their "living will." The document laid out a series of decreasing benchmarks in funding, attendance, and energy that would prompt the process of the congregation closing its doors. After the congregation completed the living will, they filed it away.

Then an amazing thing happened.

The process of facing the church's mortality gave the congregation a renewed sense of life and purpose. They recognized that congregational death wasn't the worst outcome. Together, they could handle it. The uncertainty of the future was assuaged by the clear benchmarks of the living will. They began to live more hopefully as a congregation. They celebrated more and became more relaxed. New families with children showed up and stayed, attracted to the congregation's lightness of spirit. Duerksen attributes some of the turnaround to the fact that through the process, the congregation "got to a place of enjoyment." They were no longer worrying about death. They were just loving being church together. They were just living.

We don't want to draw the wrong conclusion. Death is not a growth strategy. But facing mortality courageously allows us to just *be*, to just *live*, to just *care* for one another. Duerksen's congregation learned to love their dying self, and Duerksen loved them as their pastor.

Writer Kathleen Norris, reflecting on her experience of rural North Dakota, with its tumbleweed depopulation, says this: "Maybe the desert wisdom of the Dakotas can teach us to love anyway, to love what is dying, in the face of death, and not pretend that things are other than they are."[13] We accept congregations where they're at, don't "pretend that things are other than they are," and then love them as we love all those dear to us: unconditionally, through thick and thin, come what may. Even death.

Learn the fear of the Lord: You're just another church

I once chatted with a pastor who was working at planting a new congregation in a rural community. The church was thriving, even bringing in folks from neighboring communities who were attracted to the pastor's style of preaching and the worship band. In contrast to other congregations in town, he explained, their church was different. They were doing something new, something relevant, something that drew in folks disaffected from the

13. Kathleen Norris, *Dakota: A Spiritual Geography* (New York: Houghton Mifflin, 1993), 121.

old-guard congregations. He summed it up like this: "We're not just another church."

It's an interesting claim. This pastor looked around at the area established churches, at their thin attendance and graying leadership, at the aches in their liturgy and their dependence on antiquated technology like hymnals, bell choirs, and printed Bibles. They probably still used dial telephones. He saw churches that had reached ripe old age. Some of them were dying. He didn't want to be just another one of *those*.

The pastor's words may have had the ring of fresh mission and energy, but it was really a statement about mortality: the belief that somehow the fate that has befallen other churches will not befall us. We will not grow old. The community will not change around us and become estranged from the people who nurtured it. We will not die. Because we're not just another church.

Of course, this is precisely the myth that most of us concoct about ourselves, especially when it comes to death. We create the imaginative fiction that we will remain young, hale, and hearty forever. No sagging for us. It's our private mythology: that we will beat death's imposing odds and somehow manage, as writer Katie Roiphe puts it, "the incandescent defeat of death itself."[14] Perhaps someone will develop a vaccine for death. Even if we don't imagine the possibility of our personal immortality in a literal sense, we believe it in a functional sense by avoiding speaking of our own deaths. We think that God smiles on us and the trials of life will pass us by. Onward and upward!

But life happens to all of us—the good and the bad—and it's not because God looks away or falls asleep at the wheel. Things are scarier and more complicated than that. "The Lord kills and brings to life," sings Hannah. The Lord "brings down to Sheol and raises up" (1 Samuel 2:6). The Lord declares, "I bring prosperity and create disaster; I, the Lord, do all these things" (Isaiah 45:7 NIV). Says God through Moses, "There is no god besides me. I kill and I make alive; I wound and I heal" (Deuteronomy 32:39). There's

14. Katie Roiphe, *The Violet Hour: Great Writers at the End* (New York: Dial Press, 2016), 51.

more. This is just a smattering. We worship the God of Elisha. Our God has she-bears, and he's not afraid to use them (2 Kings 2:24).

The vision of God that we see in the Scriptures is fiercer and wilier and holier than our tame and huggable god. After its emphasis on God's mercy, love, and kindness, perhaps Scripture's next largest theme is on the fearsome bigness of God. We're dealing with the God who was willing to see his people carried off to the white-hot soul foundry of Babylon. This is the God who abetted the razing of his own temple. Twice. Letting old First Church downtown die sort of pales in comparison.

God's providence runs so much deeper than our individual or congregational survival. It's not easy to come to terms with this. One common question Lyn Sorrells hears from dying congregations is this: "Why doesn't God intervene and turn this thing around?" It makes sense. Couldn't God, in God's infinite goodness and infinite power, save our congregation? Shouldn't God?

When we realize that God is willing to let us die for God's own ends, there's really only one response. It's what the Scriptures speak of as the "fear of the Lord." God will not guarantee the outcome that we dream—even in the church, even when it's good, even when it seems we're doing God's will. God is willing to choose harder things for us than we are for ourselves. It's like what the lion Aslan told young Jill in C. S. Lewis's book *The Silver Chair*. "Do you eat girls?" asks Jill. The lion responds flatly, "I have swallowed up girls and boys, women and men, kings and emperors, cities and realms."[15] We could add *churches* to Aslan's list.

Yet the fear of the Lord is not based merely on, well, *fear*. It's also about trust. It's about where we ground our ultimate hope. This is why Proverbs 19:23 reads, "The fear of the Lord is life indeed; filled with it one rests secure and suffers no harm." God is not a mindless hurricane destroying everything in his path. God is good, and that goodness goes all the way down. We don't flee God in the whirlwind. We gird up our loins and stand before God in prayer (Job 40:6-7). We adore this almighty and dangerous God.

15. C. S. Lewis, *The Silver Chair* (New York: HarperCollins, 2002), 21.

All of this is to say that God's faithfulness to us and our relationship to God will not depend on things going the way we plan. In the mystery of God's good providence, churches—even good churches—will die. It has happened before. It can happen to us. We're just another church.

Learn to depend on God: God takes back his breath, and we return to the dust

The church is not our creation. We can forget this in the annual shuffle to fill open positions on the church council. We think that because we set the budget—and give to meet it—that the church is this thing we've fashioned by our own hands. We've designed and organized it, and the church is held together by our willingness to continue gathering—or at least to put up with each other.

But no. The church is God's gift, sustained by God's Spirit. When God sends forth his Spirit, it is created. When God takes back his breath, we return to dust (Psalm 104:29-30). The two major images of the church in the New Testament—the body of Christ and the people of God—both attest to the church's absolute dependence on God. As the body, the church is renewed from within by Jesus' living Spirit. As the people of God, the church is called together at God's initiative. There is no church without God's Spirit or call, which is to say there is no church that does not depend on God.

We often try to avoid this truth. Tim Suttle makes a powerful critique of so many current expressions of the church growth movement when he writes that "the megachurch is an attempt to flee vulnerability through size."[16] This pretty much describes the Babel project. Make a city, erect a tower "with its top in the heavens" so that we can avoid being "scattered abroad upon the face of the . . . earth" (Genesis 11:4). No enemy can bring us down. No foe can conquer us. No tribe can overwhelm us. Here in our big city with our big tower and our pristine Proto-Indo-European language with its regular verbs, we're all set. So long, vulnerability.

---

16. Tim Suttle, *Shrink: Faithful Ministry in a Church-Growth Culture* (Grand Rapids: Zondervan, 2014), 55.

The problem was that by trusting in their own ingenuity and words, the people of Babel lost the capacity to be open to God's destiny and God's word. They lost their vulnerability. So God destroyed their well-considered plans and set the stage for his own greater dream. God made them vulnerable again.

It's not that God despises all that is big and strong. After all, God made the Behemoth and the Leviathan (Job 40; 41). God ignited the sun that crosses the sky with the zest of a just-married man (Psalm 19:5). But God has chosen "what is low and despised in the world" (1 Corinthians 1:28) to carry out his plan of salvation. God's delight is "not in the strength of the horse" but rather "in those who fear him" (Psalm 147:10-11). Again and again, God chooses smallness and weakness to show God's power. God chooses an unwed mother and manger and shepherds. God enters the great city on a borrowed donkey. God chooses the cross. God chooses vulnerability.

We resist vulnerability—and rightly so. Most of us can tolerate only so much risk and loss in our lives. But loss avoidance does not the good life make. (This is why I dislike the modern blessing "Be safe!" If safety were my top concern, I would stay in bed.) To live truly is to know loss. Pastor Serene Jones says this: "To be human is to live only a hairbreadth away from the unbearable."[17]

Being church means walking along that hairbreadth line. It's an exercise in gracious vulnerability. We extend our arms, open to God and to others. Jesus did something like that on the cross.

Thus the church of the Crucified One can never become the church of the invulnerable. Our origin is on Golgotha and our destiny is with the "Lamb that was slain" (Revelation 5:12 KJV). The dotted earthly line between the two is the way of the cross. That's the narrow way. We will not be able to walk with the crucified Christ through Babel's construction zone. Our hearts always long for Babel's impregnable walls and high tower, but Jesus leads us away from that city, scattering us under the unbounded sky—trouble in ten thousand languages.

---

17. Serene Jones, *Trauma and Grace: Theology in a Ruptured World* (Louisville, KY: Westminster John Knox, 2009), 18.

Even Pentecost, the moment when God so generously empowered his church, was not the reverse of what God did at Babel. The Spirit came down. (Wind! Tongues! Flame!) But the capacity to understand each other still depended on God. No Spirit, no comprehension. If anything, Pentecost was the deepening of God's Babel deconstruction project. It was the deepening of our need for God and our dependence on God's Spirit for the church's life and mission and verve.

This is as it should be. The authentic church will be the church that looks over the abyss into the depths, the church that faces its own mortality, the church that sometimes *dies*. Even in dying, the church is a sign of our absolute need for God. This is learning to depend on God, and gratefully acknowledging "our dependence upon God and upon other human beings is a mark of wisdom and a key to living well and dying."[18]

Lord Jesus, receive our story

When Stephen, the first Christian martyr, was dragged outside the city and stoned, his last words were prayer. Just before he forgave his murderers, Stephen said, "Lord Jesus, receive my spirit" (Acts 7:59).

More than the death of a people or a building, the death of a congregation is really the death of a story. Yet our hope is in the One whom Stephen saw standing at the right hand of God (Acts 7:56), the One whose story never ends. Stephen told that story long form in Acts 7, and in his death he became a part of the story of God's faithfulness. Stephen released his spirit—and his story—to God.

Perhaps as congregations we can adapt Stephen's words and pray, "Lord Jesus, receive our story." Jesus' story does not end just because our particular chapter does. Death has no dominion over him. This is the Jesus we belong to. His story is resurrection.

---

18. Verhey, *The Christian Art of Dying*, 153.

CHAPTER 9

Befriend: On Not Being Useful

I have called you friends.
—John 15:15

I befriended a man in our little community who was semi homeless. During one period in our relationship, he developed something of a ritual. Once a week, he would drop by the church with a small frozen lasagna (his favorite food), which he would heat up and enjoy in our basement kitchen. Sometimes I'd sit with him and just chat; other times I'd help him out with larger issues in his life. At one point in our ongoing conversation, he turned to me and said, "You know, you're the most useful pastor I've ever met." I suppose I should have taken it as the compliment he intended, but *useful* wasn't exactly what I was aiming for. I just wanted to be friendly.

It's all too easy to want to be useful in our rural communities and congregations. After all, one of the dominant narratives of our time is the great neediness of rural places. As some would have it, they're backwaters of poverty and resentment, communities on the edge falling apart like rusty pickup trucks. And so we think that if we just roll up our sleeves and get to work, we can get things running again. It's an especially easy temptation for ministers to fall into, because ministry is perhaps the preeminent useless profession. We don't produce a value-added thing that can be tallied up, our efficiency measured on a spreadsheet. The most important work that we carry out doesn't have any outward use.

Some pastors relieve their need to be useful by taking on more concrete side duties. In my first year of ministry, I got antsy and asked a church family if they needed some help in their orchard. I suggested that I could probably chat up some of the fruit pickers about the gospel while I was at it. The family was skeptical. Pickers don't have much time to talk, and I would only slow them down. But I didn't come to my senses until another member of the congregation caught wind of my half-baked plan and chided me. If that was the way things were going to go, she said, they wanted equal time from me at her clinic. So much for that idea. I had just wanted to be useful.

But more than needing us to be useful, I'm convinced rural places need us to be friends.

Rural places don't always have friends. They may have admirers or those who pity them, but rural communities and congregations are too often seen as junior partners to the city, as places needing help.

Historically, this is how things have mostly gone. Theodore Roosevelt's National Country Life Commission sought to address migration to urban centers by making life in rural communities attractive, not just because that's where the nation's food came from but because the countryside was also seen as the source of our moral fiber. As writer Kevin Lowe documents in his history of American agrarian movements, *Baptized with the Soil*, the commission mobilized vast resources, both governmental and faith based.[1] Although the Country Life Commission succeeded in raising government awareness of the challenges of rural communities and made concrete progress in the form of rural electrification, improved roads, and land-grant universities with their county extension offices, the broader movement was hobbled by its mildly

1. See Kevin Lowe, *Baptized with the Soil: Christian Agrarians and the Crusade for Rural America* (New York: Oxford University Press, 2016), 6.

paternalistic structure: concerned city people making helpful suggestions on how country people could improve their lot.

What this approach ultimately lacked was a sense that rural people and places are peers of the city. It lacked a sense of friendship—which just happens to be what rural people and places most need. It's out of a sense of friendship that the church relates to rural people, communities, and land in ways that are authentic, ways that express the abiding love of God. It's a friendship that's ultimately rooted in friendship with God.

The Jesus way of friendship

There was a time when Jesus was eating with his disciples and he told them he would no longer call them servants, but would instead call them friends (John 15:15). It was the night he was betrayed, and of all the things that Jesus could have chosen to talk about, friendship might seem the least important. But with the cross looming and his palms tingling where the nails would cleave, Jesus had a burning desire to talk about friendship. He wanted them to understand that their relationship to him wasn't based on what they could do for each other. It wasn't a servant-master relationship. It was friendship.

Jesus probably turned the disciples' world upside down when he called them friends—just as he did when he took a towel and washed their feet or when he put them on notice that the "first shall be last" (Matthew 19:30 KJV). In the disciples' day, many people looked at friendship in instrumental terms. Instrumental friendship asks, what can I get out of this relationship? It's quid pro quo: you scratch my back, I'll scratch yours. This sort of friendship was a privilege of adult, male, free citizens and was aimed at enhancing their power and self-sufficiency.[2] It was about alliances between patrons and clients. It was about being useful.

But Jesus overturned any notion of being useful. He had no interest in being useful to those around him, least of all to the disciples. Jesus refused to be defined by others' expectations and

2. David Matzko McCarthy, *Sex and Love in the Home: A Theology of the Household* (Eugene, OR: Wipf and Stock, 2001), 171.

refused to be used by them. He threw cold water on the disciples' need to try to form alliances with him. When the mother of James and John attempted to play Bathsheba and guarantee her sons a seat at the table of power, Jesus promised instead that they could share in his suffering (Mark 10:37).

Jesus tapped into an ancient, biblical vision of friendship. He modeled and taught the kind of relationship we see in the great friendships from the Scriptures: Naomi and Ruth, David and Jonathan, Deborah and Barak. Jesus would have known the words of the sage Sirach recorded in the Apocrypha: "Faithful friends are a sturdy shelter" (Sirach 6:14). The kind of relationship Jesus imagined was not a power relationship—not even a useful one. It was based on love (John 15:12-13). It was about joy (15:11).

Jesus surrounded himself with friends: the twelve and the seventy/seventy-two and many others in a broad, outer circle of relationships. They were people who sacrificially committed their lives to being with him (Luke 18:28-30). Jesus was joyful at their successes (Luke 10:21). He poured his heart out to them and revealed his deepest anxieties (Matthew 26:38). This friendship was possible because of Jesus' sacrificial love for them, a love that led him even to die for them (John 15:13).

The friendship Jesus lived out is more like what the apostles called koinonia: communion (1 Corinthians 10:16-17). It's what the early church cultivated around the Lord's table and in each other's living rooms (Acts 2:42, 46). It's the friendship that begins in God, extends through the church, and opens out into the world. And it's utterly *useless*: that is, it has no further end beyond being together in Christ.

Practicing this sort of friendship in rural communities requires some reorientation on our part. All too often, our sense of mission leads us to build alliances, to look for like minds who can help us fill board positions and work the food pantry. This can be a good thing. But we must be cautious not to allow an instrumental view of relationships to edge out communion, which is the basic commitment of friendship with God and one another.

The danger is that rural communities and congregations can become our projects. Writer D. L. Mayfield found herself doing just that in her work among African refugee communities in Portland, Oregon. Mayfield describes how the Holy Spirit gave her a rude awakening. She discovered that her truest role in working with immigrants was "to swallow my own impulse to save and to focus on the long game. To be a friend, the truest form of advocacy there is."[3]

Befriend people: On not forming a committee

We met a young mother when we knocked on her door at random, neighborhood-evangelist style, to introduce ourselves. Let's call her Juanita. She had an apartment full of kids and one on the way. Pretty soon, we found ourselves dropping by to chat and play with the kids. They would drop by too, often right at lunchtime. Or dinnertime. It wasn't so much that they didn't have enough to eat. It was more that coming to our place was like going out. It took some of the load off.

Juanita and family didn't attend our church. They were somewhat connected with another local congregation. One evening after a joint event at that other church, a well-meaning woman approached me. "I hear you know Juanita," she said.

"Yes."

"Well, you know about all her problems then," the woman said. "I want to form a committee to help sort things out for her. I think you and your wife should be on it." It came out in short order that Juanita would not be on her own life-management committee. Of course not.

Now, I would like to report that I waggled my finger and told this lady to respect Juanita enough to let her make her own decisions. But I have to be honest and admit that I skirted the whole issue and gave a weak shrug. "Okay," I said.

The committee never came to pass—or at least, the church lady never followed up with me, having perhaps decided I wasn't life

3. D. L. Mayfield, *Assimilate or Go Home: Notes from a Failed Missionary* (New York: HarperOne, 2016), 91.

coach material after all. But Juanita and family kept dropping by. We got to know her story in dribs and drabs while my wife played with the new baby on the floor or set the table or while I corralled the kids and ran them outside for a game of tag as the bread baked. We got to know Juanita's mother. We met Juanita's brother and sister, both enrolled in colleges on the coast. We met her husband, who was rarely around because he traveled to find work. It was all a very natural sort of progression—befriending Juanita and her family.

Of course, calling our relationship "friendship" is a bit tricky, because it wasn't exactly the friendship of peers. We observed certain boundaries. But she wasn't our project. The aim of our relationship was the relationship itself. Juanita wasn't our fixer-upper. She was just Juanita. Sometimes we helped the family out, but it wasn't about managing their lives. We weren't the least bit *useful.*

I've done my share of fixing and managing (or attempted fixing and managing). There was the elderly gentleman from Mexico spending the winter with his son and family. His daughter-in-law asked us to come over and talk to him about some communication issues they were having.

So my wife and I ambushed the man. We showed up bright and early, armed with a Bible and a smile. The pastor is here to see you. What chill words. He ducked into the basement, swigged some fluorescent mouthwash, greased his hair back, and reappeared in the living room. We learned something that morning: flash pastoral visits don't lay the best foundation for dealing with complicated family dynamics.

There was the family we tried to help one winter with some new mattresses and an old steel bunk bed frame someone was getting rid of. When the cold metal thawed in the warm house, wasps came out and stung the kids in the night. Small detail: the folks who donated the frame had stored it outside all summer.

Believe me, I've done plenty of botched fixing.

But we didn't try to fix Juanita—or at least, not fix her much. We mostly just played.

Here's what happens when we befriend people: we become humans to one another. We stop being projects. In friendship, the other is not consumed, just as the bush was not consumed when God burned bright all through it and Moses had to take off his shoes. God said, *I am who I am*. God meant: Take me as I am. This is what you get.

In friendship, we are who we are. Together. We get who we get. We learn to "really be people's friends without wanting anything," says Daniel Janzen, who serves a congregation in rural Carrot River, Saskatchewan.

There's a reason Jesus told his students to love their neighbors as themselves. Love turns them into neighbors. Love is what makes neighboring possible. It's the vulnerability of love, the beginner-ness of love that lets us inch our way into relationship with another, even though we don't understand what that relationship will mean or how it will change us. Neighbors are those who care enough to draw near in love. To become a neighbor is to live out something of the way that God has drawn near to us, which is why Jesus pairs love of God with love of neighbor as the two greatest commandments. On these "hang all the law and the prophets" (Matthew 22:40).

This sort of love matters everywhere, but especially in rural places, because it's this love that pours forth in friendship, and it's friendship that gives us the courage to accept rural places as they are. Friendship allows us to accept that everything might not turn out all right, that rural people and churches almost assuredly won't live up to our expectations. It's neighboring friendship that allows us to stay put despite disappointments and our yen to define rural communities and people either by what they lack or by what they might become. Love saves us from turning people and communities into projects.

Befriend community: The need of only one thing

Here's a rule of thumb: love and be loved enough that there are tears shed when you leave.

We cried when we left the first community we served in Washington State. My vision was so smeared with tears that I could barely see the road. Our little sons were quiet and still in the back seat. We had befriended the community. And the people had befriended us. Now the turnoff sign was fading in the rearview mirror. We weren't going back.

At its heart, befriending rural communities is all about coming to the basic realization that the destiny of the rural church is tied to the destiny of the rural community. Wherever we're going in rural places, we're going there together. In the church, this means we begin to act as a friend of the community, not just as an actor within the community. As the community goes, so goes the church. The thriving of one is the thriving of the other.

The apostle Paul called the Galatian churches to this outwardly oriented vision. He wrote, "Whenever we have an opportunity, let us work for the good of all, and especially for those of the family of faith" (Galatians 6:10). At the very least, this means seeing our ministry as a ministry to the whole community—for the good of all. Rural towns and fields are our parish, whether they know it or not. Working for the good of all means seeing people not as mere targets for evangelization but as neighbors worthy of our concern, care, and friendship.

This might seem a triviality, a given, but congregations all too often weigh people according to their utility to the church, either as those who might join (or not) or as those who might have some gift to offer (or not). It's a conquest mentality. Who can we capture? Participation in the community is about gaining market share, about reeling 'em in. The tools of the conquest mentality are savvy marketing and shiny events. Other congregations are competitors.

Or we take on a stance of resistance, seeing the church as over and against the community. Our tools are critique and protest. We fixate on the broken places. We cast ourselves as gadflies and prophets, which can be vital roles in rural communities, but which, on their own, are inadequate.

I'm convinced we need to move to a third stance: not conquest or resistance, but *solidarity*. Just as God has given himself in Jesus in solidarity with us, and just as Christ gives himself again and again to the church, so we give ourselves to the community. The church exists for the life of the world, lived out in this particular place.

This is a concept that lies at the heart of who we are as the people of God. As writer Paul Wadell puts it, "Worship, particularly the Eucharist, ought to be a sign of solidarity and unity not only among Christians but also with all of humanity."[4] Christian worship sets our orientation to *out*. Lacking that outward focus, we would not be the church, not be the body of Christ, not be the called-out, called-together ones who gather in Jesus' name. We would be a tribe, and the world has plenty of tribes already.

What's required of the church in rural communities is solidarity. Solidarity goes beyond having a warm feeling about a place. It's not just that we happen to like our neighbors. In fact, we may not like them all that much. As Pope John Paul II wrote, solidarity is a "determination to commit oneself to the common good."[5] Solidarity is following Nehemiah's lead in building up the community (Nehemiah 2:18).

What makes this a particularly powerful stance in rural places is that the "common good" is often right before our eyes. The run-down park is not managed by an inscrutable bureaucracy. Your neighbors sit on the city council, and the mayor knows your name. The common good is not an abstract concept.

One place we see this is in the intensity of community engagement that happens in rural places. If you've got half a head on your shoulders, you'll be asked to serve on boards and committees of every stripe. One pastor I interviewed served as an EMT, the chair of the school board, and a ski instructor at the local high school, all while pastoring two congregations and raising a family. His story is not unusual.

Solidarity is what Jeremiah was getting at when he wrote his letter urging the people to "seek the peace . . . of the city" that was not their own (Jeremiah 29:7 NIV). It's living and working

4. Paul Wadell, *Becoming Friends: Worship, Justice, and the Practice of Christian Friendship* (Grand Rapids: Brazos, 2002), 157.

5. John Paul II, *Sollicitudo rei socialis* [Encyclical Letter on Social Concern], section 38, December 30, 1987, http://w2.vatican.va/content/john-paul-ii/en/encyclicals/documents/hf_jp-ii_enc_30121987_sollicitudo-rei-socialis.html.

for the good of all. Solidarity doesn't lead to any tangible benefit for the church, except possibly the value of a good name. But that's not why we practice solidarity. Solidarity is a moral stance, a way of living out love for neighbor. We befriend our community in concrete and practical ways. Solidarity is a key practice in the world's smallest places, which have slipped out of solidarity with the power structures of our age.

Solidarity is about relationship. Filling slots on the local parks and recreation board is secondary. Solidarity is not another word for usefulness. It's communion, which is why solidarity finds its source and expression at the communion table. What we're doing is witnessing to God's enduring love: God's solidarity with us. It will be expressed in abiding, in serving, in holding the community in prayer. But solidarity is more than the sum of these things.

And it's hard to get right. Declaring that we're "living in solidarity" can give the impression that we're kicking our life up a notch. We're neighbors with a double plus, not just any old people living on the block. We're living in *solidarity*.

The problem, if it can be called that, is that solidarity is chosen, and this choosing opens us up to the risk of a false sort of solidarity—a solidarity rooted in privilege, mouthed through lovely teeth, whole and white. Because if solidarity can be chosen, so too at any moment can it be *unchosen*. We moved in. We can move right back out. It's the reality of the missionary, who can tap a few numbers into the screen, flash the blue passport, and be in Disney World tomorrow. The neighbors can't.

I once started up a conversation with a young man seated next to me on an airplane. He was engaged and compassionate, and something about the flight had jostled my philosophical bone. After the standard "So, what do you do?" set piece, in which I described my rural ministry, I asked in a fit of overly earnest, unironic self-reflectivity, "Does living in solidarity with a poor, rural community mean that you have to drink poisoned water?" Talk about melodramatic.

You see, we lived in potato country, and potatoes are a hungry, hungry crop—though apparently even spuds aren't hungry enough, because the fertilizer bonanza applied to the land hadn't all been absorbed. Leftover nitrates had leached down through the ashy soil and loose gravel and made mischief in our aquifer. In our minds, the choice was fairly simple, if a bit alarmist: either drink poisoned water (it'll turn your babies blue!) or install a fancy reverse-osmosis filtration system. We sprang for the filter and called it good. Many of our neighbors could not make the same choice.

Yet the problem isn't so much that we can make choices. The problem is that others *can't*, and in our desire to live in virtuous solidarity, we end up discounting the power inherent in our choice. We undermine our own impulse to solidarity by living *over* neighbors in all the subtle ways that make such a difference: the flexibility of our schedules, our easy confidence around law enforcement, the invisible web of contacts that can be called upon for help, the kale in the garden.

Like D. L. Mayfield and her husband in Portland, we move into the rural community, or the challenging town, or the low-income housing complex, yet somehow manage "to view it all as a bit of a lark, an 'experiment' in downward mobility."[6] It's not possible—or even desirable—to feign poverty, lack of education, or rurality. We are who we have become. Solidarity doesn't mean becoming something we aren't, though most of us don't understand or believe this. We glom on to Paul's words as our justification, adopting the local identity in order to "win" some to the gospel (1 Corinthians 9:20-21). Like missionaries who too quickly adopt local dress, our solidarity, while well intentioned, comes off as a sham in the eyes of the locals.

Any living worthy of the *solidarity* tag requires abundant humility, a horse-pill dose of Philippians 2:3: "Regard others as better than yourselves." The truest solidarity with rural communities flows not from our capacity to affect a kind of rural persona, but from the humble traits and actions that make friendship possible and rich—mainly, abiding, listening, vulnerability, caring, and sharing life as equals. That's it.

6. Mayfield, *Assimilate or Go Home*, 132.

Consider this story: There was a time when Jesus went to visit his friends Mary and Martha. Martha zipped about the kitchen. She hustled. She bustled. She got all aproned up and useful and did things for Jesus. Meanwhile, Mary sat at Jesus' feet and listened to him. When Martha got miffed at Mary's utter lack of attention to the urgent tasks at hand, Jesus said: "Martha, Martha, you are worried and distracted by many things; there is need of only one thing. Mary has chosen the better part, which will not be taken away from her" (Luke 10:41-43).

So it goes in rural community. We're the Martha church shimmying our Martha brooms, all aproned up and useful and doing things for Jesus. So much to do, so little time.

But there's something else, a better part that will not be taken away. I'm convinced there is need of only one thing in rural communities, and it's friendship.

Befriend the land: They're not making any more of it

My landscaping motto is simple: mow less, mo' food. I don't plant anything that doesn't yield food, although my wife goes in for a few flowerpots. We built a raised bed in our front yard and seeded it with rows of kale. We put up a fence in the back and trained blackberry brambles over it. We tore out our lawn near the apple trees to plant strawberries. We got laying hens.

All this food means that our grocery bill is low and our capacity to can, freeze, and share is high. But it's also a way that we care for God's green earth. Everything fits together. The soil yields garden produce. The veggie scraps are composted with leaves and chicken manure. The compost is spread over the garden to renew the soil's fertility. It's our little backyard nutrient cycle, our way of befriending this patch of land.

The people of God are the people on the land. God gave the land to Abraham, his friend forever (2 Chronicles 20:7). God instructed all humanity to tend and guard the land (Genesis 2:15), and God gave particular instruction to his chosen people on how they must give the land rest from intensive agriculture (Leviticus 25:2), must allow the land to be a breadbasket sanctuary for people on the edge (Leviticus 23:22), and must provide for the Levites from the produce of the land (Deuteronomy 14:27). Even in warfare, the land of others was to be respected. Do not cut down fruit trees—your fight is not with them (Deuteronomy 20:19). The earth, after all, is the Lord's (Psalm 24:1). It's God's country. The very definition of the Promised Land is "a land that the Lord your God looks after" (Deuteronomy 11:12). The land praises God—the "mountains and all hills, fruit trees and all cedars!" (Psalm 148:9). At the end of time, the land will rejoice in the fullness of God's kingdom (Psalm 96:11-13). We really can't exaggerate the centrality of the land to the biblical narrative. Writes theologian Walter Brueggemann, "The Bible is the story of God's people with God's land."[7]

When friendship with God and others broke down, so too the relationship with the land suffered. Idolatry and injustice were land problems (1 Kings 21; Isaiah 5:8). It's no accident that when God removed the people from the Promised Land for a seventy-year stint, it was seen as a kind of pent-up justice, what 2 Chronicles calls the "sabbath" of the land (2 Chronicles 36:21).

The reason for this was simple. Care for the land implied care for others—especially for future generations who would inherit and care for the land and for those on the margins of society who also occupied the literal margins of the land. "The land is mine," says the Lord; "with me you are but aliens and tenants" (Leviticus 25:23).

Borrowing a page from the biblical story, I'm convinced that friendship with rural people and places must include friendship with the rural land. We're called to befriend the land. This is the stuff of the agrarian vision, which we touched on briefly in chapter 1. Agrarianism sees care for the earth and all living things as exquisitely bound up with care for community. In this commitment, the agrarian vision taps into a deep biblical core.

Over the last century or so, many Protestant denominations and parachurch organizations dedicated tremendous resources to

7. Walter Brueggemann, *The Land: Place as Gift, Promise, and Challenge in Biblical Faith* (Philadelphia: Fortress, 1977), 13.

agrarian issues and awareness, particularly among rural churches.[8] The Catholic Church took up the agrarian mantle by founding the National Catholic Rural Life Conference, an agrarian outfit dedicated to preserving rural communities and family farms.[9]

Yet despite the decidedly agrarian cast of much Christian work in the twentieth century, much contemporary agrarianism comes off as a sort of rediscovery. Many authors plot a story of biblical proportions, one in which a preindustrial rural Eden was colonized by the forces of Big Ag, fell, and now stands on the edge, balanced between the complete degradation of the earth and salvation through a renewed agrarian vision. While the concerns of contemporary agrarianism are authentic and vital, much agrarian writing is produced by urban writers with an idealized, almost wistful vision of rural communities and farming. It's often disconnected from the experiences of rural people and farmers.

Thus we who care for the land and desire to commend such care to others—particularly in rural communities—often find ourselves caught between folks who walk away at the mention of herbicide and those who think the farmer's best friend is a spray tank. The conversation takes on conflictual hues and becomes a proxy for larger political and philosophical arguments. At its worst, the exchange looks like urbanites scolding longtime farmers before hopping back into their Priuses and heading for the city.

Yet I sense that many involved in food production are not completely at ease with the status quo. Awareness of the issues at stake, and a willingness to consider other options, has been growing for some time now. It was concern for the topsoil that prompted farmers across the Midwest to convert to no-till techniques. It's a desire to pass on clean water and productive cropland to the next generation, as well as a growing market (mostly in the cities and suburbs) for organic and local foods, that has encouraged farmers

---

8. Kevin Lowe, *Baptized with the Soil: Christian Agrarians and the Crusade for Rural America* (New York: Oxford University Press, 2016).

9. See David Bovée, *The Church and the Land: The National Catholic Rural Life Conference and American Society, 1923–2007* (Washington, DC: The Catholic University of America Press, 2010). In 2013, the organization's name was changed to Catholic Rural Life.

to explore alternative production techniques, sometimes including the use of horses.[10] We have not always lived as friends of the land, and many of us are more ready than ever to do something about it.

Remember that potato field near our house, the one I mentioned to the young man on the airplane? In the spring, after the earth had received a mighty antinematodal dousing, the farmer (or more likely, the contract spray company) put up along the edge of the field signs marked with a skull and crossbones and a menacing warning along the lines of "You will die if you walk in this dirt." (My memory is a tad sketchy on the exact wording). No one questioned that the potatoes would be okay to eat.

The whole situation strikes me as emblematic of how we treat the land, a microcosm of the ways that care for land and neighbor intersect—or don't. Our small boys played beside that field. We breathed its poisoned dust. Even so, our exposure was minimal compared to our friends who lived in trailer homes in the middle of orchards. That sea of apple blossoms is a glorious sight in spring, but stuff wet towels under the windows and keep the kids indoors when you hear the wicked buzz of the spray plane overhead.

Something has to change. We have to return to friendship with the land. It's a simple idea: Defuse the narratives of crisis and guilt, with their modes of critique and shame, by instead speaking positively of friendship with the land. Treat the earth as you would a friend. Care for it. Respect it. Reshuffle the relationship so that it begins in solidarity—a commitment to the common good of the land—which is also the common good of rural peoples and communities.

Nowhere is this link between the good of the people and the good of the land more obvious than when that friendship breaks down. We see that breakdown in places like Treece, Kansas, with the egregious depredation of heavy-metal pollution that destroyed the community,[11] or in concentrated animal feeding operations

---

10. Dan Charles, "By Returning to Farming's Roots, He Found His Dream," National Public Radio, December 31, 2016, http://www.npr.org/sections/thesalt/2016/12/31/505729436/by-returning-to-farmings-roots-he-found-his-american-dream.

11. See chapter 3.

(CAFOs). In the CAFO system, animals such as hogs or cattle are raised in small spaces. Their manure builds up to noxious levels, often directly harming nearby agricultural land and waterways and also harming neighboring families and communities, not least because of the stench and the damage to roads and wells. Often, local communities have little power to protest new mass confinement operations, which are backed by corporate funds and connections. One Illinois resident, working with others near the rural community of Bernadotte Township to challenge a new CAFO facility, commented in a news article, "The rural citizen is getting run roughshod."[12] He was expressing the simple truth that we're all bound together. When we fail to extend friendship to the land, so too do we fail to extend friendship to those who live on the land.

There's not any one thing that we do or don't do to live in friendship with the land. It's a matrix of life-orienting commitments and practices that treat the land not instrumentally, not as meaningless crop-production substrate, but as a peer to be respected and cared for. Friendship with the land, just as friendship with God and one another, is something we do with our whole selves and lives. It's a posture of caring, something all of us—not just farmers—are called to in Genesis when God set humanity in the garden to "tend and guard" the land (Genesis 2:15 AMPC). It is God's original *vocatio* upon our loves and lives lived out on the dust of the earth.

Friendship with the land will mean becoming people who cart in their own table service in order to avoid Styrofoam, people who have a plastic bag drier by their sink, people whose chickens are pecking through their compost and who are glad to see a good stand of hairy vetch in the garden (and who know what vetch is, and why it's hairy). It will mean becoming people who are willing to walk with and listen to and understand the concerns of farmers trying to make a living on the land in an age of low commodity prices and with the 1980s farm crisis still a fresh memory. It will

---

12. David Jackson and Gary Marx, "This Is Not Farming: Plan for a Hog Confinement Facility Sparks Revolt in Fulton County," *Peoria (IL) Journal Star*, January 1, 2017, B7.

start with engagement with the land itself. Touch it. Smell it. Love it. Work it. Recognize the whole fraught process, the shaggy mathematics that have to work out for dirt to yield food.

Above all, friendship with the land will take a return to the biblical notion that the land is always God's—never ours—and that to truly love people as Jesus has commanded, we must love the land that sustains them.

What land do we befriend? A friend of ours speaks of a longing for land that creeps up into his throat all poetic-like sometimes. He drives out into the country and perches on the back of his pickup, gazing over fields that belong to others. He doesn't own land beyond a house and yard in town. He asks, what is my relationship with the land?

It's not so different for any of us. Those who have been entrusted with much land have a responsibility to love much. It doesn't matter how much or which land we love, so long as we love some patch of it, some little square—even if it's just a planter box jammed with corn and tomato vines and hot chilies on the south end of the trailer. Love the one you're with, the ground beneath your feet. Professor and farmer Patrick Fleming, riffing on Wendell Berry, writes that we cannot "love the land without loving a particular piece of it."[13] Find your particular piece and start loving.

Friendship with the land helps us live with contradiction and complexity. We can't be content to tell a simple story that pits the Big Ag Goliath against plucky organic David. There's more to caring for the land than the choice of conventional or organic methods. That organic sweet corn is lovely, but getting it into your hand required nitrogen from pelletized chicken manure trucked from an industrial chicken farm one hundred miles away. It required tossing ten worm-bitten ears to find the perfect one. It required intensive tillage—and the mycelium wreckage that accompanies breaking the soil structure—to keep the weeds down. Things aren't always clear cut. Friendship allows us to live in the tension.

---

13. Patrick Fleming, "The Family Farm," *Humanum*, September 13, 2016, http://humanumreview.com/articles/farming-and-the-family.

And friendship allows us to remain in relationship with those who hold views different from our own about how the land should be used. What I've discovered is that there is a diversity of approaches to the land among rural people. Many see land as a commodity to be exploited. Naturally so—their livelihoods depend on it. GMO seeds and synthetic herbicides haven't been foisted upon farmers by wicked multinationals. They've been welcomed and accepted by folks who want to put the kids through college. We have to be willing to allow rural people to be rural people and not insist that they take on some role as agrarian guardians of the earth. Friendship means meeting people where they're at. Challenge and change can only flow out of ongoing relationship.

And yet there are voices dissenting from within rural communities, sometimes from surprising quarters. The rural community in Nebraska that I mentioned in chapter 1, the town that turned down the offer from a large meat-packing plant to set up shop in their area, was concerned—among other things—about the plant's impact on the earth. One resident is quoted as saying, "We've got to protect the land. They're not making any more of it."[14]

In the end, friendship with the land reminds us that our care for the land is rooted in our overall vision of life with God and one another. The land is sacred because it is given and sustained by God and because it gives life and sustains human community. All of it—land, people, and community—meets on the same common ground: friendship with God.

Befriended by God

The ancient church father Gregory of Nyssa wrote that "becoming God's friend [is] the only thing truly worthwhile."[15] All friendship is ultimately rooted in friendship with God, what Jesus speaks of as the abiding of a branch in the true vine (John 15:4).

14. Scott McFetridge, "Tiny Nebraska Town Says No to 1,100 Jobs, Citing Way of Life," Associated Press, May 2, 2016, http://bigstory.ap.org/article/dd5cc190b42b4375830a97d163dbb5fd/tiny-nebraska-town-says-no-1100-jobs-citing-way-life.

15. Gregory of Nyssa, *The Life of Moses*, trans. Abraham Malherbe and Everett Ferguson, Classics of Western Spirituality (Mahwah, NJ: Paulist Press, 1978), 137.

Friendship with God isn't something we choose. God chooses us. We are befriended by God. And this matters, because when we talk about befriending rural people and places, there's a risk that we will focus on our initiative to befriend.

But true friendship comes from a choosing that is greater and more sovereign than our own: God's original choosing of us. God befriended us first. We didn't do much. Now here we are, graced by birth or calling, by work or marriage or happy accident, with the possibility of befriending rural people and places. It's a little mysterious and providential. Only one piece of it was up to us. And it all started with Jesus' words: "I have called you friends."

CHAPTER 10

Dream: Zion on the Migrash

I saw the holy city, the new Jerusalem, coming down out of heaven from God.
—Revelation 21:2

Once, when I was on a teaching trip to a congregation located in a starkly rural community in the Andes of Peru, I stood at the back of the church while another pastor interpreted the Scriptures. It was a typical evening, filled with song and testimony, teaching and prayer, people milling in and out beneath dangling lightbulbs. And there was a pile of butchered wooly llama pieces stacked on the floor at the back of the church, covered in a scanty blanket. Kids were goofing around back there. A little girl had chosen the bloody blanket to take a nap on.

One of the Peruvian pastors caught me observing the tableau—*Still Life with Little Girl and Llama Parts*. "You're probably wondering what sort of place you've ended up in," he said.

I suppose I *was* wondering, though it's nothing I haven't wondered about every rural place I've served. Yet the question for me has never just been, *Where have I ended up?* The real question is always, *Do I love this place and these people?*

In the Scriptures, love of place and people is embodied in the dream of Zion, a vision of city and country walking together into the future in neighborliness. Zion points us beyond any sort of privileging of rural or urban and reminds us that neither can go it alone. We need each other.

Nowhere is this more clear than in the concluding vision of Scripture: Zion coming down out of heaven, the foursquare city with twelve foundations (Revelation 21–22). Zion is the perfect city of God. It's Jerusalem, but it's more than Jerusalem. Biblical scholar Ellen Davis calls Zion an "icon" of Jerusalem[1]—what Jerusalem will look like when God dwells in her perfectly. Zion is also an image of the church, and in this way Zion is more than any one city. Rather, Zion is what it looks like whenever God dwells with God's people.

We catch glimpses of Zion throughout the Old Testament. Zion is the city where God places his name (1 Kings 11:36) and dwells (Zechariah 8:3), the city God defends against all comers (Isaiah 31:5), the city of God (Psalm 48:1), the holy city (Nehemiah 11:1), the city where old and young flourish (Jeremiah 31:13). "May they prosper who love you," sings the psalmist (Psalm 122:6). That's Zion.

The biblical vision of Zion is partly rooted in the ancient law of Israel, with its instruction on how the Levitical cities were to be plotted out. In Numbers 35, God spoke to Moses and commanded the Israelites to set aside special cities for the Levites to live in. As the tribe charged with the priestly ministry, the Levites did not inherit territory within the Promised Land, but instead were sprinkled among the other tribes and granted their own towns and cities. These cities were to be surrounded by a green belt, a swath of open land called *migrash* in Hebrew. According to Leviticus 25:34, migrash was not to be impinged upon or sold. Migrash could not be converted into city or used for any purpose other than nourishing the well-being of the city it surrounded. It was not to be plowed or sown, but had a parklike character—a green space

---

1. Ellen Davis, *Scripture, Culture, and Agriculture: An Agrarian Reading of the Bible*, 2nd ed. (New York: Cambridge University Press, 2009), 163.

for animals and people. Migrash existed in relation to the city, and the city in relation to migrash. Each was intended for the good of the other. Migrash was sacred open country, a kind of holy rural surrounding the Levitical cities. Migrash was God's country.

Later rabbis, including the influential teacher Maimonides, would interpret the command to establish migrash as applying not only to cities intended for the Levites but to all Israelite cities.[2] Some Jewish teachers credit the biblical vision of migrash with having an even broader influence, inspiring the nineteenth- and early twentieth-century "garden city movement."[3] Indeed, British writer Ebenezer Howard's seminal book *Garden Cities of To-morrow* imagines urban centers ringed with open green space, cities interpenetrated by agricultural land. Writes Howard, "Town and country *must be married*, and out of this joyous union will spring a new hope, a new life, a new civilization."[4]

Howard struggled to bring his verdant, utopian dream to life, though not for lack of interest. His book went into a second print run, and two model cities were attempted in England, as well as several communities in Sweden, Japan, and the United States. In addition to being inspired by the biblical migrash, Ebenezer Howard's vision drew currency from the ideal of the English country town, which privileged agriculture and closeness to nature. While the garden city movement as such has mostly fallen by the wayside, the general principle of incorporating green space in city planning has gone mainstream.[5]

Yet migrash is not limited to any cityscape philosophy. Migrash plays a role in the prophetic vision of the Scriptures. In the ecclesioculture we've developed in this book, migrash helps us map

---

2. Earl Schwartz and Barry Cytron, *Who Renews Creation?*, 2nd ed. (New York: National Youth Commission, United Synagogue of Conservative Judaism, 1995), 20.

3. Jon Greenberg, "Lessons for Regional Planning: The Biblical Migrash Principle Provides a Response to Urban Sprawl," MyJewishLearning, June 30, 2008, http://www.myjewishlearning.com/article/lessons-for-regional-planning/2/.

4. Ebenezer Howard, *Garden Cities of To-morrow* (London: Swan Sonnenschein, 1902), 18 (italics in original).

5. See Jane Jacobs, *The Death and Life of Great American Cities* (New York: Vintage Books, 1992), 17–19.

out a way that city and country can journey together toward an identity that is bigger than rural or urban alone. Zion and migrash exist together, exist for the good of the other. Zion and migrash help us dream of God's future for rural and urban.

Back to the future: Zion on the migrash

When the prophet Ezekiel caught sight of God's heavenly Zion, he saw the city of Jerusalem refounded. The temple was at its heart, with life-giving water pouring from beneath the temple's threshold and plunging toward the Dead Sea. Trees with healing foliage that bore fruit in every month of the year lined the river (Ezekiel 47:12).

But Ezekiel didn't just see God's future city. His was also a vision of migrash restored around the city (48:17). The prophet saw Zion on the migrash (48:15), the city of God rebuilt on God's country. Ezekiel's city is a place of justice with honest weights (45:10) and proper offerings (45:13-16), a place where the festivals to God and the sabbaths are kept (45:18–46:24). God dwells in that city, and it's been renamed: "The Lord is There" (48:35). It's a vision for Jerusalem and the land restored, but it's bigger than that. It's a vision for how God's people everywhere can dwell. And in the prophet's vision, the city of God is wedded to God's country.

Interestingly enough, when Ezra and Nehemiah arrived on the scene years later, they don't seem to have attempted to build this city. While they returned to Israel with an imperial Persian mandate to reconstruct Jerusalem and the temple, Ezra and Nehemiah didn't turn to Ezekiel for their blueprints. Rather, they understood Ezekiel not to be conveying a vision of a literal city that could be translated into bricks and mortar, but rather something different, something grander and mightier, a vision that wasn't limited to any one city. Perhaps Ezra and Nehemiah instinctively knew that Ezekiel's prophecy was a vision for God's people living on the land with God at the center.

Like Ezekiel, John the Revelator from his high mountain perch (Revelation 21:10) envisions a restored Zion, the culmination of salvation history. John sees a cubical city broad enough to encompass nearly the whole of the Roman Empire.[6] It's the city of God for the people of God, and strikingly, the migrash has not disappeared. God's country is still there. It's just taken on a new form.

As in Ezekiel's vision, the water of life still flows from the city, though the healing tree is now singular and straddling the water (Revelation 22:2). But something interesting has happened. The tree is no longer outside the walls of the city. In the book of Revelation, the tree is within the city. The garden is downtown. Zion no longer stands centered on the migrash. In John's retrofitted vision, the migrash has come inside. It's the migrash *in* Zion. The holy rural has been brought into the heart of the holy city.

At the same time, Zion's garden heart is an echo of Eden. If the story of Scripture begins in a garden, then it ends in a garden city. The garden is not destroyed or in conflict with the city of Zion. The two coexist. The city shelters the garden. The garden enlivens the city.

It would be easy to look at the vision of Revelation and take it as a plan for how city and country might coalesce in new ways. Work to bring the migrash into Zion, the rural into the heart of the city. Till community gardens.[7] Promote community supported agriculture. Protect farmland at the "rural-urban interface."[8] Seed lettuce on the rooftops, and let tomatoes tangle up the balconies.[9] In the spirit of Ebenezer Howard, reclaim stumbling Detroit for farming, the Motor City for a garden city.[10] Certainly, migrash

---

6. J. Nelson Kraybill, *Apocalypse and Allegiance: Worship, Politics, and Devotion in the Book of Revelation* (Grand Rapids: Brazos, 2010), 176.

7. Laura Lawson speaks of urban gardens as a "bridge to virtues attributed to country living and the agrarian lifestyle" in *City Bountiful: A Century of Community Gardening in America* (Berkeley, CA: University of California Press, 2005), 289.

8. Douglas Jackson-Smith and Jeff Sharp, "Farming in the Urban Shadow: Supporting Agriculture at the Rural-Urban Interface," *Rural Realities* 2, no. 4 (2008), http://www.ruralsociology.org/assets/docs/rural-realities/rural-realities-2-4.pdf.

9. Elizabeth Arakelian, "Skies of Lettuce: Rooftop Greenhouses Sprout in Big Cities," NBC New York, April 18, 2016, http://www.nbcnewyork.com/news/national-international/Gotham-Greens-Rooftop-Greenhouse-Cities-Earth-Week-374768021.html.

10. Stephanie Held, "Ten Detroit Urban Farms Rooting Goodness into the City," *Daily Detroit* (MI), July 6, 2015, http://www.dailydetroit.com/2015/07/06/10-detroit-urban-farms-rooting-goodness-into-the-city/.

in Zion speaks to these realities. The truly human life requires contact with green space, with growing things, with gardens and trees and the unbounded wild. We won't live well until we get a little dirt under our fingernails. The city needs the country.

Migrash in Zion also speaks to the reality that the country needs the city. Rural life only becomes rich and full when joined to the life of the city, with the city's diversity and innovation, its anonymity and mobility, its ferment.[11] Just as city dwellers must beware the country music stereotype of rural, so we who live in rural places cannot succumb to the temptation to write off cities as dumpster fires of hedonism and violence, rap albums come to life. That's Babylon, and Babylon is not the measure of the city.

But ultimately, as Ezra and Nehemiah knew, the relationship between Zion and migrash is about far more than urban planning. It's about God and God's people dwelling together on the land—what Walter Brueggemann refers to as Israel's yearning for "a place with Yahweh."[12] This is a vision of the church. Ezekiel and John, prophets old and new, show us what it looks like to live with God and one another, city and country people together. It's a vision we need now more than ever, for even in our suburbanizing age, urban and rural still hold power to define us—often more than we might like to admit.

Relocated to zip code Zion

Take the 2016 U.S. presidential election. Polls revealed a nation split along the ragged line between rural and urban.[13] Donald Trump earned a small percentage of the vote in the nation's largest cities, and Hillary Clinton did poorly in the hinterlands. It's a trend that has sharpened since the 2012 election, in what the *New York Times* named as "a growing alienation between the two groups,

---

11. Harvey Cox, *The Secular City: Secularization and Urbanization in Theological Perspective* (1965; repr. New York: Macmillan, 1971), 33.

12. Walter Brueggemann, *The Land: Place as Gift, Promise, and Challenge in Biblical Faith* (Philadelphia: Fortress, 1977), 5.

13. Aaron Zitner and Paul Overberg, "Rural Vote Fuels Trump; Clinton Loses Urban Grip," *Wall Street Journal*, November 9, 2016, http://www.wsj.com/articles/rural-vote-helps-donald-trump-as-hillary-clinton-holds-cities-1478664251.

and a sense—perhaps accurate—that their fates are not connected."[14] Increasingly, rural and urban have come to occupy what has been widely called "the two Americas."[15] There are commonalities and relationships, to be sure. It's not just a city-or-country thing. But two distinct ways of life, alternate value systems, and divergent economic interests were indeed brought to light in the 2016 election—and at least some of it was a result of where people lived.

Faced with this reality, the church needs to reclaim the vision of Zion on the migrash and learn the art of relocating. I don't mean relocating physically. On the contrary: one of the most vital gifts we give our communities is being present. We show up, and we stay put. But God does not dream of a people divided into city and country. God dreams beyond these binaries of a people gathered from "all tribes and peoples and languages" (Revelation 7:9)—and addresses. It's city slickers and hillbillies together. God envisions the migrash in Zion, the city of God with God's country at its heart.

Thus we need to learn to relocate ourselves in relation to God's dream, to define ourselves not only by where we are but also by where we're headed, and to begin to imagine our destiny intertwined, city and country together.

As the church, we haven't always understood the implications of God's vision. Our eschatology has pointed us in the wrong direction. Eschatology is our theology of the end and the purposes of time. When Isaiah says the lion will lie down with the calf (Isaiah 11:6), that's eschatology. When Paul says that Christ will conquer death and God will be all in all (1 Corinthians 15:28), that's eschatology. When John says that God's people will "hunger no more, and thirst no more; the sun will not strike them, nor any scorching heat" (Revelation 7:16), that's his eschatological vision

14. Emily Badger, Quoctrung Bui, and Adam Pierce, "The Election Highlighted a Growing Rural-Urban Split," *New York Times*, November 11, 2016, http://www.nytimes.com/2016/11/12/upshot/this-election-highlighted-a-growing-rural-urban-split.html.

15. Tim Wallace, "The Two Americas of 2016," *New York Times*, November 16, 2016, https://www.nytimes.com/interactive/2016/11/16/us/politics/the-two-americas-of-2016.html.

of the future. Eschatology is where history's going. It's God's goal for the world. Eschatology is our understanding of the future God is working toward.

There are secular eschatologies as well—beliefs we hold about the direction and meaning of time. Among them are convictions that technology will fix our most pressing problems, that we're becoming more humane, that life is generally getting better. Claims like these may or may not prove true, but each of them points toward a vision we hold of the future—our eschatology.

Most of us have an eschatology. It's what comes to mind for us when we imagine God's plans for the future. It may be implicit, a vision we would have a hard time articulating, but it's our eschatology nonetheless. And for many of us, our eschatology is urban. We believe that time, the cosmos, and human reality end in a city—albeit a heavenly one with streets of gold. After all, the concluding chapters of the book of Revelation describe "the holy city, the new Jerusalem, coming down out of heaven from God" (Revelation 21:2).

I met a man who confessed to me that he was disappointed by the book of Revelation's promise of heaven. The way he understood it, heaven was a city. And the problem with this heavenly city was that you couldn't get out into the great outdoors. "Some elk hunting would be nice," he said. "What's heaven without elk hunting?" That was his eschatology. The way he read Revelation, when God brought history to its perfect conclusion, it would look like a cubed city. So long forests and fields and wilderness. So long elk.

Yet even beyond the fear of losing wide-open spaces, there are profound implications of accepting an urban eschatology. Theological and social convictions often cleave along rural and urban lines, with urban congregations taking more liberal views while rural churches defend traditional beliefs. It's a generalization, yet one that is surprisingly predictive.

Over the last few years in my own area conference, individuals and congregations have struggled to discern faithful practice around sexuality. We've often found ourselves speaking to each other over the rural-urban divide. It wasn't just disagreement over biblical interpretation; sometimes it seemed that mutual incomprehension and geography played a big role (though certainly not the only one). Some people in urban churches seemed surprised that members of rural congregations were resistant to same-sex marriage. Underlying much of the back and forth was an urban eschatology: many in urban churches understood themselves as the vanguard of the church, representatives of a more liberal order brimming into the cities. They had seen the future, and it was a city like theirs. What's more, some saw rural congregations not only as taking positions in disagreement with their own, but as actively holding back progress toward God's future city.

Urban eschatology is the theological equivalent of what some social scientists believed a century ago: that rural was a category increasingly shed as civilization progressed to an enlightened urbanity. And just as eschatology imagines where we're headed, it also grounds and guides our actions in the present. So when we believe, even implicitly, that God's dream for humanity is embodied in a city, then we act in ways that privilege the city and the viewpoints that arise in the city.

But God's dream is more complicated than that. God is not calling us to the city. Our future hope is not to become urban. God's dream is of urban and rural people drawn together in him, Zion and migrash journeying together, a people relocated so that they find their life and identity in nothing less than God himself. It won't be their nation or occupation or address that makes them who they are. It will be the fact that they stand in relation to God and to the Lamb (Revelation 21:22), relocated to Zion.

There are two Christian practices that—if we pay attention to them—help relocate us to zip code Zion: the Lord's Prayer and the Lord's table.

Our family drove cross-country after leaving Washington. Somewhere in the mountains of Colorado, as we sat for breakfast in a little motel, someone asked us, "Where are you from?" It was a question we had been asked dozens of times before, and our answers were always straightforward. But this time was different. Where exactly *were* we from? Just then, it felt like nowhere.

We had no permanent address, no jobs, no house. We were in between, relocating.

"We're leaving Washington," I said. "And we're headed to Peru."

What if it's a little like that for all of us? Where are you from? Morton, Boston, Warden, Cuzco, Moundridge. But we're headed to Zion.

Jesus' model prayer says something about where we're headed. Jesus prays, "Our Father who art in heaven." Our Father is not limited to the temple in Jerusalem nor housed in some imperial capital. The Father is in heaven, and the Father's *in-heaven-ness* relocates us beyond our place to God's place. We're moving toward God.

The early church experienced the relocating power of this prayer. From their gathering place in Jerusalem, the disciples at first imagined God's earthly kingdom pinned to the geography of Israel. "Lord," they asked, "is this the time when you will restore the kingdom to Israel?" (Acts 1:6).

But Jesus had a wobblier set of boundaries in mind, a kingdom that extends "to the ends of the earth" (Acts 1:8). And so these disciples, centered in the practice of prayer (Acts 2:42)—including, undoubtedly, the Lord's Prayer—found themselves being flung out into the world. So long and shalom, Jerusalem. Howdy, Antioch and Philippi, Corinth and Athens and Rome. They were a people relocated—literally. Even Peter, the sturdy fisherman from rural Galilee, ended up in Rome.

More importantly, they were a people whose identity had been relocated away from the tricksome dotted lines of *urbs* and *rus* and national allegiance to a new "citizenship . . . in heaven" (Philippians 3:20). Theirs was not the dream of Babel, with its false security of staying put (Genesis 11:4). They may have been from many places, but they were marching toward Zion, toward their Father who art in heaven.

So too does celebrating at the Lord's table relocate us. When we break bread and share the cup that Christ has given us as his body and blood, we enact what theologian William Cavanaugh speaks of as the "geography of the Eucharist"; we join "the narrative of the pilgrim City of God."[16] The broken bread of the Lord's table relocates us in the body of Christ, and that body is global and eternal. We occupy the Eucharist.

I've experienced the relocating power of the Lord's table. On election night 2016, a smattering of us from local congregations gathered to celebrate communion. The idea of election night communion didn't originate with us, but in the fierce intensity of the season, we were looking for something to hang on to, something to ground us. We adapted a liturgy and prepped music and readings. There we were, a handful of pastors, wondering if it might just be us who gathered that night to break bread and share the cup. We hoped that maybe a few others would straggle in. Who knew? We might get twenty people. We didn't even bother with microphones.

I sat in the front row, praying my way through my notes. I could hear people trickling in behind me, and I was surprised when I twisted around to look. The sanctuary was filling. People were showing up, hungry for something solid, something potent. We longed for some sign that whatever happened that night, our lives were defined not by presidents and elections but by our allegiance to Christ. We broke bread and shared the cup and were sent out into the chill night as God's people, relocated by the Lord's table.

The nitty-gritty rule of love

Relocating ourselves to Zion says something about who we are: we're a church that seeks to discover our identity and allegiance not in our address but in Christ.

But there's more to it. You see, while our destiny is Zion, our forwarding address is earth. Our feet still have to be planted on the ground in whatever neighborhood we find ourselves. The church may know where it's going, but we still need to be where we are. This is going to require a shift in our thinking. It's ecclesioculture: a loving vision of cultivating churches of all sorts in places of all sorts and dreaming with them toward God's future.

---

16. William Cavanaugh, "The World in a Wafer: A Geography of the Eucharist as Resistance to Globalization," *Modern Theology* 15 (1999), 182.

Ecclesioculture is the sort of thing Paul did when he wrote his famous letter to the über-urban church in Rome. It was a church that he didn't know and hadn't founded. Paul had to win their respect. He spoke humbly, self-effacingly, referring to "my gospel" (Romans 2:16; 16:25). He looked for common relationships (16:1ff.). He urged flexibility for a variety of ways of living out their common faith (Romans 14). He spoke of the need for each other (12:4ff). He thanked God for them (1:8). He solicited their prayers on his behalf (15:30). He blessed them (15:13).

But Paul didn't just love the church in Rome as he found it; he also called the church toward God's dream. Paul spoke of the creation "longing" for the day when it will join in the "freedom of the glory of the children of God" (Romans 8:19-21). Paul began where the church was at, but he didn't stop there. His ecclesioculture called him to dream with the church about the future.

Love compels us to dream. We love the rural church where it's at, but so too do we listen for God's call for the future of the church. Like Joseph of old, we're dreamers (Genesis 37:19). We see Zion on the migrash, migrash embedded in Zion, and we dream of city and country embracing that reality. We dream of a humanity that's greater than us and them—in all the ways that us and them are estranged—and that has become the broad *us* of the people of God held together in Christ.

I don't know which is harder: dreaming the future church or embracing the present one. But I'm convinced that love is what allows us to live in the tension. We inhabit our neighborhoods fully and truly, tending the special promise of the rural church, while remembering that we are always journeying toward an identity that is neither rural nor urban but found in Zion with migrash at its heart.

I haven't always managed this kind of love for the rural church.

There was a time during my first year in ministry when I walked my conference minister around the outside of the church building. It was a brilliant summer afternoon, the sky wide and scuffed with clouds. In the field next door, the sun was painting the wheat stubble in yellow ochre. The wind tousled the grass.

"Take a look at that," I said, pointing to the church. There was a large cross made of metal pipe fastened to the wall just below the roof. Long ago, someone had attempted to fancy up the pipe cross with a coat of metallic gold spray paint. The gold had mostly disappeared, peeled back by age and exposure. Now it was just a leaden gray. "Don't you think we could do better?" I asked.

My conference minister contemplated the cross from where we stood in the lee of the building. "Oh, I don't know," he said. "Isn't it a lot like the people of this church? Solid. Strong. Good."

And it was.

He met my scruffy ecclesiology with his gaze of love.

For all our careful words and fine models, I'm convinced it comes down to this: loving rural people and places, communities and congregations. We respect their unique contours. We treat them with kindness. We love them. For whatever competence we may bring, none of it will matter if we aren't able to abide by the nitty-gritty rule of love. Love, and all the rest will follow.

Our destiny is Zion, city and country walking together into the future in neighborliness. Remember Ezekiel's words. The name of the city of God is *The Lord is There.* The Lord is in that city. The Lord is in the sacred open country too, those rural places—the beloved earth.

It's all God's country.

Amen and Amen.

Acknowledgments

I wish to thank:

My wife, for picking up the pieces so that I could write.

My sons, for being patient while I wrote.

Herald Press, especially Amy Gingerich, for taking a chance on me and inviting me to write this book.

My editor, Valerie Weaver-Zercher, who gave sharp and kind advice to see this project through.

Pastors who made space in their busy schedules for me to interview them.

The staff of the Moundridge Public Library, who went the extra mile getting me books I needed for my research through Interlibrary Loan.

The congregations I have served: Warden Mennonite Church in Washington State, West Zion Mennonite Church in Moundridge, Kansas, and our friends in the mountains of Peru. ¡Añay waykeypanaykuna!

Soli Deo gloria.

The Author

Brad Roth serves as pastor at West Zion Mennonite Church in Moundridge, Kansas. He grew up baling hay, tending sheep, and shearing Christmas trees on a farm in Illinois. He is a graduate of Augustana College, Harvard Divinity School, and Anabaptist Mennonite Biblical Seminary. Brad has a heart for serving God and God's people in rural communities. He's passionate about sharing faith in word and deed and living out God's love in the community. He and his wife, Lici, enjoy bicycling, tending a garden, keeping chickens, and playing with their two sons. He writes about encountering God in the everyday at DoxologyProject.com.